Praise for Kai

"It is the best of its kind tha
Autobiography of a Yogi"

Adrian Gilbert - Author of 'Blood of Avalon' and 'The Holy Kingdom'

"Superbly written, deeply emotional and empowering, this trilogy is a delightful gift and a powerful testament of wisdom, self-belief, courage, determination and uncommon grace. Joshi's vivid and honest account of her troubled and brave childhood in India, adolescence in London and her remarkable journeys through holy sites and *ashrams* is breathtaking and will keep you engrossed. Her lack of bitterness at the traumatic experiences she encountered as a child and how she overcame her life traumas of self-knowledge and actualisation is truly inspiring and healing, and will surely help others to overcome theirs."

MonaLisa Chukwuma - Author of 'Define Yourself - and Become the Architect of your Future'

"Smita is a bridge and guide for anyone who is on their journey back to the inner light source consciousness within us all. She opens the depth of her own diverse experience to mine the jewels, the pearls of wisdom that is an offering to the modern world from the roots."

Shiva Rea - Master Yoga Teacher and Author of 'Tending the Heart Fire'

"The path to greater self-awareness and understanding that brings us happiness can be rocky and, at times, even treacherous. Smita has been there and got the T-shirt and came back to share the gems of wisdom so that you don't have to do it the hard way. In the *Karma & Diamonds* trilogy, Smita shows how the happiness and fulfilment that we seek are often closer to home than we think. Her account is as entertaining as it is frank. Prepare to ride a roller coaster with her."

Tom Evans - Author of 'New Magic for a New Era'

"A page turner with a difference. Smita Joshi has given us an absorbing, heart-warming and inspirational account of how it's indeed possible, with vision and self-belief, to rise above the challenges of life and succeed with gusto.

Karma & Diamonds is a gripping trilogy about the struggles of a courageous woman conquering the challenges life throws at her. A whirlwind storyline packed with travel, action and emotion, it is often funny but will drive most of us to tears as we identify with the characters and witness many tragic events Smita gets confronted with. Yet, her journey is inspiring and optimistic."

Arvind Devalia - Author of the Amazon bestseller 'Get the Life you Love'

"Without ever preaching, Smita inspires and enlightens the reader to connect to their own inner Self and live life fulfilled. She shows how it's possible to collaborate with the inner Self, even in the most dire of circumstances, to create powerful, wholesome outcomes. Read it as just an engrossing story or allow its deeper messages to alter you forever. One thing is for sure, you will not escape being touched and blown away by this unique story."

Chris Day - Author of 'Turning your Knowledge into Income'

"In this series of books, Smita Joshi has gifted us with an opportunity to follow the struggles of a young British Indian girl as she navigates family tragedy and upheaval, deep traditional expectations and massive inter-cultural differences - whilst at the same time fighting a never-ending battle to trace her own unique path into womanhood, financial success and spiritual freedom.

It is a gem of a tale to inspire all those seeking to transcend limitation, both inner and outer, and all those seeking to become the ultimate source of their own truth and power."

Robert Thé - Anthropologist

"I loved the *Karma & Diamonds* trilogy. This is a heart-warming and true-to-life account of the life and spiritual journey of a brave and determined young British Indian woman.

Book One, *Moon Child*, chronicles Smita's life from a trauma in early childhood to the difficult move from India to England in her early teens, and on into young adulthood, where she realises that to find any peace she has to take a huge leap into the unknown.

Book Two, *Web of Karma*, follows Smita as a young woman on a spiritual journey who also has to develop and grow within a cut-throat and male-dominated business arena. She has to learn how to synchronise her inner spiritual life with the outer mundane one. In this book, Smita faces her demons not only from this life, but from past existences too. At the end of all this, she then finds herself with a life-threatening illness to deal with.

Book Three, *Diamond Revealed*, shows Smita's steady spiritual growth and physical recovery as she becomes more in tune with what she calls her 'Inner Diamond'. Just when she thought her life was predictable, love comes her way. She now has to learn to navigate this new aspect to life, while continuing to integrate the mundane with the spiritual. Old doubts spring up, and Smita has to dive deep in order to feel her way forward.

All throughout these three books, Smita is deeply connected to her own on board 'Guru', and is always seeking a deeper meaning to her life and existence. While a serious, and at times heart-wrenching book, it also has a wonderful thread of humour woven through. The author has been courageously honest in her accounting, which leaves the reader with a strong connection not only to the story but to this amazing woman too. The character building and scene setting are excellently written, and draw the reader right into the pages, where they walk over the hot coals right along with the author, and feel her tribulations and joys in a personal way. The examples she gives of her life experiences, and the teaching she receives, are clear and easy to understand, and will provide help and guidance to seekers the world over. Here is an enjoyable and informative journal of how a person can move from a life full of struggles to find fulfilment and happiness."

Harmony Kent - Author of 'Elemental Earth' and 'The Glade'

"Smita has done a wonderful job of telling the universal story of each of our heroic journey home to our true Selves. Across continents and lifetimes, she encourages us to trust our inner voice, so we can heal, find more peace and happiness, and to show up as who we truly are."

Nick Williams - Author of 'The Work We Were Born to Do' and 'Pivotal Moments'

Amazon Reviews
for
Karma & Diamonds - Book 1, 'Moon Child'

"Dramatic, moving, inspirational and enlightening - I really enjoyed it."

"Most amazing read ... pulls at your heartstrings, very well written and moves fast. One of my favourites now..."

"Written with an intimacy that takes you into the story, once you start reading you cannot stop, eloquent, colourful and intense ..."

"I was captivated by this remarkable story of this spiritual journey. At times I felt it was me and my parallel path."

"Interesting for someone like me who finds it difficult to find the time to read ... with a book like this I found myself making time as it was just riveting."

"There have been so many a-haa moments in Smita's story which I can so resemble and relate to. I'm amazed and shocked both at the same time ... I feel like I have just read my own story."

"A reflection of my life is staring me right in the face! I think this book has come at the right time for me and I thank you,

Smita, for writing it. I will now look forward to reading your second book which I am sure will be as gripping as your first."

"This is a brave, sensitive, heartfelt account of the early life struggle of a gifted spiritual woman. The author gives a wonderful readable account of her journey from a troubled childhood in India to becoming a successful confident woman in the UK. For those who reflect on the mysteries of life and spirituality, this book is a must-read."

"Smita Joshi is a wonderful writer. This book is full of insights and is a great and moving read which identifies how life experiences are of lasting consequence. I could not put it down and cannot wait to read book 2."

"One's journey to self-awareness, acceptance and healing can be traumatic for many of us, with some never reaching the end of the journey. I enjoyed this book tremendously because it struck a chord in me: bitterness about personal traumas can be overcome through self-knowledge and a belief in our inner-voice. The story is compelling and gripping – a must for anyone who is interested in how people can overcome traumas in a world of shifting personal and cultural values."

"Was wrapped up in this book, which explored the powerful dynamics that challenged Smita as she aspired to search for her truth. An interesting read which exposes insightful philosophical messages."

Amazon Reviews
for
Karma & Diamonds - Book 2, 'Web of Karma'

"It's thought-provoking and inspiring and like the first book I could not put it down ... Another page-turner, you won't be disappointed if you buy this book. I can't wait for the third book."

"Reading through the pages it felt like an onion with layers being peeled away, very deep and inspirational...very thought-provoking and soul searching. As an Asian man born and bred in the UK, there is a lot to relate to in the book which I was very pleasantly surprised to discover and it should be on everyone's reading shelf. Seriously looking forward to the third helping."

"Following a recent diagnosis of a terminal illness and wanting to seek solace, after retiring from a 42-year career, I found this book truly inspiring. ... Smita's journey takes us through some amazing events that can only be described as miracles as Smita follows her gut instincts. The final chapters answered a lot of my questions, that I as a practising Hindu had been searching for in a lot of religious books. As soon as I read a paragraph and a question arose in my mind, I found it was answered by Pujia Swamiji. This book has landed in my lap at 'the right time and at the right place'. Is it a miracle or is it my time to heal myself?"

"As a Westerner, I was sceptical about past lives and thought I knew how *karma* worked. But this story has really given me a deeper understanding of the complex nature of our past and of our deeper nature. The author's relationship to her Higher-Self is an eye-opener for me. I couldn't put this book down. Read this if you want a great story with purpose that will inspire you to discover yourself."

"It was just as amazing as I'd hoped and would highly recommend reading this incredible and inspiring story."

"I was very privileged to be the very FIRST person to read *Web of Karma,* Smita Joshi's second enticing book from the trilogy *Karma & Diamonds.* I was so gripped and taken aback by *Moon Child* that I couldn't wait to read her second book. The only problem was she hadn't published it at the time. Disappointment struck and so I pulled a few strings and asked Smita if she would let me read her rough unedited copy of *Web of Karma.* I was smiling like a Cheshire cat when she kindly agreed to this. ... It's an amazing read and like the first book I couldn't put this book down. ... It really is an eye-opener of a book but at the same time an easy read that anyone can happily sink into with a classic hot Indian Masala cuppa."

"Absolutely loved this book too! ... So much content about Smita's ever unfolding spiritual journey. Very inspiring read leaving the reader buzzing with curiosity and intrigue."

A gripping journey of Self-discovery
across continents and lifetimes

Karma & Diamonds

Book 3 -
DIAMOND REVEALED

Smita Joshi

Published by
Filament Publishing Ltd
16, Croydon Road, Waddon, Croydon,
Surrey, CR0 4PA, United Kingdom
Telephone +44 (0)20 8688 2598
Fax +44 (0)20 7183 7186
info@filamentpublishing.com
www.filamentpublishing.com

The right of Smita Joshi to be identified as the author of
this work has been asserted by her in accordance with the
Designs and Copyright Act 1988.

ISBN 978-1-911425-84-7

Printed by 4edge Ltd

This book is a work of non-fiction based on the life,
experiences and recollections of the author. In some
cases, names of people, identifying characteristics and
occupations, places, dates, and sequences or the detail of
events have been changed to protect the privacy of others.
Some characters are composite of several others.

For my Dad

&

With the deepest love and gratitude to
my beloved
Mum,
Grandmother
and
Mahadevi, the Mother Eternal

Acknowledgements

I have so many people to acknowledge for their love and encouragement in bringing about my project and I am grateful to each one of them.

I offer my heartfelt gratitude to:

The three brilliant docors who saved my life.

Tom Evans, for being an inspirational and exceptional mentor.

Harmony Kent, for excellent editing of the three books.

Pieter Weltevrede, the artist extraordinaire, for allowing me to share his divinely inspired art on my book covers and website (www.karma-and-diamonds.com).

Robert Thé, for his skilful insights with the early version of the book as well as for his practical encouragement throughout.

Arpit Kaushik, whose earliest feedback encouraged me to keep going.

Lucie Feighan, for her priceless insight and friendship over the years.

Arvind Devalia, for being an awesome stand for my completing this book.

Mark Booth, for helping me to shape this book into its current form.

I'm deeply grateful for the work of Landmark Education and the massive difference that it has made in my life, and to the world in general. I especially thank the phenomenal leaders (current and previous) at Landmark Education - David Ure, Nick Klyne, Johnny Tenn, Nick Andrews, Jonathan Stanley among others - for the mind-blowing inspiration that they've been in my transformation.

Elizabeth Klyne, deep gratitude to you for showing up as the angel who pointed me to the one doctor in the world who could help save my life.

Love and big thank you to Randyl Rupar and Judith Kahlealani Lynne for sharing their incredible knowledge and healing capacities; Trish Regan for opening up her beautiful home for meaningful meetings; and Douglas Webster for teaching me to be at one with the ocean.

My Love Man, Edwin, whose patient commitment and unwavering devotion pulled me through my darkest moments of writing, when I would rather have given up. I love and adore you - more than I could put into words in any trilogy.

Table of Contents

Author's Introduction

This is the book that I wish someone had written for me when I really needed it. The *Karma & Diamonds* trilogy is a compelling and uplifting set of stories about dealing with modern life, stories you want to pick up and be touched and inspired by again and again.

It's a handbook for living the contemporary life while being connected to something deeper within.

The ancient sages of India have described *Atman*, the higher Self, in great detail in the sacred texts. However, accessing it and connecting to it is a whole other matter. Why is it important? How can you access it? How does it look and feel? What difference will it make to be more aware of its presence? What difference will being connected to it make in your life? How can it improve the quality of your everyday life?

I have written this trilogy for those of you who, like me, are seeking to harness your inner radiance and power—whether it be for being more peaceful, feeling more alive and vibrant, or living the best life you possibly dare to.

"Be courageous.

You will be reminded,
by someone who really knows you,
of who you truly are.

Then, it will be easier for you
to accept that truth for yourself."

1

Right Place, Right Time

Overwhelmed, I gripped the phone so tightly my knuckles had turned white. Elizabeth sounded worried.

"Are you alright? What happened? Did you suddenly fall? It sounds serious."

"I ... I'm in pain!" I managed to say, unable to continue talking. "I have to go, I'll call you back." I cut the conversation short.

I'd not spoken to my friend in more than a year, and just lately I'd been getting strong urges to call her. Unable to fathom why she was suddenly so prominent in my thoughts, I gave her a call. Only minutes into the conversation, I found myself in agony. The excruciating pain crippled me, and I could only shriek and scream incoherently.

It took every little bit of my vigilance and focus to deal with these awful sensations. I did the best I could to manage the sharp, shooting tremors. I took the painkillers that Dr 'Hammerhead' had given me, but they would take half an hour or so to kick in. In the meantime, my nervous system, pounded by the torment of the cramps and spasms, was exhausted and I passed out.

When I finally came to, I felt disoriented and completely at a loss. Just then, the glint of candlelight from my meditation room—my place of refuge—caught my eye. That was it. That was where I needed to be. That was what I needed to do.

This room had become the power spot of my house. Not a large space, by any means, but something about its position set it apart.

My shrine, set on a low, oblong *sheesham* wood table, was decorated simply, with a carved wooden statue of Lord Ganesh at the centre back, and four different types of large crystals in each of the corners. Much larger geodes of amethyst and citrine energised two diagonal corners of the room, while a tall brass statue of Lord Buddha, meditating, sat in another corner, looking down at a huge, heavy piece of beautiful rose quartz at his feet.

Pictures of Lord Shiva, in his form as the ascetic *yogi* and another as the warrior destroyer, adorned the pale lilac wall above the shrine. A large, colourful picture of Lakshmi Devi sat centre stage, beneath the two of the mighty Shiva. The deep aubergine back wall and the sheer burgundy and gold *sari* curtains complemented each other. These colours highlighted the multiple rainbows that fell on the walls when the sun pierced and refracted through the cluster of dangling hexagonal crystals hanging at the window.

Whenever I hit a brick wall in life, or wanted to create something brand new for the future, I disappeared into this room for hours on end. I found that whatever I asked for in there came into being sooner or later. It was as if it were a portal into other realms.

When I tapped into my Inner Diamond, the best solutions would find their way into my awareness and the resources would show up right in front of me. The answers were already there, but they were on the other side of the veil of consciousness. I needed to look beyond my knowing and fearful mind and allow a different wisdom to come forth.

Many years ago, I had been intuitively shown a formula, my secret method, that I would use when I wanted to pull towards me something new, like where best to live, a house, neighbours, car, job, and even a partner. I created almost all of my business opportunities this way and used it even when I wanted to transform a relationship with someone. It was also my cosmic travel brochure, so to speak, that I would open to discover where I could travel for my next big adventure.

In fact, it worked so well and with so little effort, that I used it for the most everyday of things, even for finding small items, like that perfect dress for a party. I could find the next book to read with information that would prove perfectly useful. Or, to the exasperation of my friends, the perfect parking spot in the centre of London, even in the busiest periods. The beauty of this system was that it worked effortlessly every single time and had me be in exactly the right place at the right time.

Different to everyday praying, it was a process for creating what I needed to show up next in my life. It was about casting intention. The skill lay in being crystal clear about the intention of what I wanted to create and then being able to articulate it in a way that left little or no room for misunderstanding.

Most interesting to me was that the things I had asked for, and which came into being, were always those I had wanted without any shadow of a doubt. They would be those things that I had wanted mind, body and soul. My desire and intention were aligned, palpating with my commitment.

Desperate from pain, fatigue, and worry, I sat down in the serene atmosphere of my meditation room and started to write, asking to be shown exactly what it was I needed to know to heal myself. I had learnt years ago that if I wanted to bring something into existence and didn't know how to do it, I should ask it of the benevolent universe. It was exponentially more creative that than my ego, which was constrained by all kinds of limiting thoughts, opinions, beliefs and past conditioning.

The one condition being that the intention had to be articulated in a crisp, concise and impeccable way such that even a three-year-old could understand it. There could be no room for vagueness, ambiguity or fuzziness. It had to be crystal clear.

The paradox, however, was that the description or articulation could not be so tight as to be a shopping list. If it was, I might get it or it could take my whole lifetime to arrive or not at all. It had to be expressed and stated so that I asked for the *essence* of whatever it was I wanted to create, not the thing itself. I could, for example, ask for the partner to show up where we would be perfect for each other. I could ask for the qualities that I wanted in this person and in our relationship. Asking for David Beckham or a 6ft 1in, handsome, sexy, blond man from Belgravia with a net worth of a billion pounds wasn't a good idea—unless I was certain to be in supreme luck!

Conversely, though clarity was a feature of casting intention in this way, in order for it to come into my life, I had to keep my vision open to the actual form it could show up in. This wasn't a prescription, and where, when and how the request would arrive were none of my business.

My job was to create with inspiration and let go of the outcome, while holding the knowledge that success was inevitable.

On a large A4 sheet of paper, I wrote a note to my higher Self, which one of my teachers, Chris Griscom, called 'the megaphone of the soul'.

My full name, postal address and contact details were at the very top of the page, followed by the day, month and year. It had to be clear that it was I who was making this request to the universe to bring a new reality into my life: not my mother, not my neighbour, but me.

"My beloved higher Self," I wrote, "by divine will, with ease and joy, in a manner that is effortless, I ask that you grace me with the following:

"Let me know and see clearly where I must go to find the expertise that I need right now to help me to heal my pain and endometriosis as soon as possible.

"Let me find myself in front of the most effective, competent and skilful doctors, surgeons, nutritionists and any other people that I need to get 100% healthy.

"Let me find the money necessary to be able to afford to take action, once I know what I need to do.

"Bring into my awareness exactly what else I need to know, that I do not know right now, to triumph over my endometriosis, pain, and damage to my body, mind and spirit.

"I welcome all divine assistance that is willingly available to me to make this process magical and miraculous.

"All of what I ask, I ask to be achieved with complete integrity and without harming anyone."

As I ended the note, I felt the openness in my heart flood with love for this divine connectedness, and I expressed in my note the deep and profound gratitude that overwhelmed me.

Now it was a certainty for me, a knowing, that all would be well.

As per the protocol of the ritual, I then placed the piece of paper in a steel bowl (it made me chuckle to call it my 'cosmic postbox'), which was carefully placed on top of several thick ceramic trivets I had bought on my travels in America. I offered it up into the sacred fire to the other side of the veil of consciousness.

Ritual, I found, made sacred what would otherwise be a dull, mundane act. It allowed me to thread my soul into the needle of daily activity.

When I woke up the next morning, it was time to get ready for a heavy day's work which, in this case, involved a flight to Paris for meetings with board members and senior executives of one of the largest companies in Europe, where I was at a critical stage of negotiating a multimillion dollar deal.

When I got home that night, even though it was late, I called Elizabeth to complete the conversation of the day before. Concerned, she quizzed me about my condition. I told her about how it had come about, what Dr Hammerhead had said at my bedside that day and also about the subsequent responses from the two other specialists.

"I just don't know who else to go to. It seems all these doctors are much of a muchness but I know that something can be done. I just find it hard to accept what they're telling me about not being able to operate. The only thing is, my pain is getting worse. Now it comes on, without warning, as it did last night, twice or three times a day. It's too much for my system to bear."

"Well, of course it is," Elizabeth said. "Look, there's a really good specialist I know. He is used to dealing with these types of issues. I'm sure he'll be able to help. And if he can't help you himself, I'm sure he'll know some of the best experts in the field."

Even before Elizabeth had finished speaking, I felt a huge sense of relief.

"Here's his number. Call him first thing tomorrow morning. His name is Dr Adam Joseph. Call him, make an appointment to see him as soon as possible, and let me know what he says."

Something told me that this was the reason I had needed to call her.

Hope flooded back into me and I felt my power return. I somehow knew, beyond a shadow of a doubt, that magic was about to weave through my life, and that life was about to start anew.

2

Hope Meets Grace

I arrived at Dr Joseph's clinic in Paddington, having persuaded his secretary to fit me in for the earliest appointment possible. A skinny, lean man of average height in his mid-fifties came to greet me himself in the reception area. He made me feel instantly at ease with his warm and affable manner. I told him everything that I felt he needed to know and handed him the photographs of my interior that Dr Hammerhead had taken during my laparoscopic examination. I could not help being impressed that, unlike the so-called experts I had met before him, he responded with mental and emotional reflexes that were impeccable.

"The first thing I want to do is for you to get a complete scan. Harry Cameron, my colleague, is one of the best ultrasound specialists in the field and he works just downstairs, so you don't have to go far. I'm going to ask him to see you straightaway as an emergency," Dr Joseph said.

Harry Cameron himself came upstairs to meet me. After a short introduction by Dr Joseph, he led me to the area where he worked. Some way down the stairs, we heard Dr Joseph running out of his room and into the corridor, shouting, "Don't forget to look at the kidneys!"

Within minutes, I was already being scanned and an accurate picture being formed of what was really the cause of my ever-growing distress.

Harry Cameron was thorough and sensitive in his approach, a complete contrast to my previous experiences. These two had made more progress in the space of an hour in getting to the bottom of my condition than I had been able to get out of half a dozen doctors in the space of two years. I waited upstairs in reception with a sense of hope. One would have expected me to be feeling anxiety or worry, but I was genuinely excited. I knew that I had come to the right medical experts finally, after searching for a long and agonising two years. I was excited that, even if the news was bad, with the best help possible I had it in me to conquer whatever was thrown at me.

As I waited for Harry Cameron to deliver his report to Dr Joseph, I felt my heart fill with a warm gratitude to my higher Self forever being by my side, for bringing Elizabeth to my mind, and urging me to call her.

Twenty minutes later, the receptionist led me back into Dr Joseph's room. He looked grave and greeted me with a look of deep concern.

He asked me to sit down and told me what the photos taken during my surgery and my new scan showed. "I'm sorry to tell you that what we've found is that you have the severest level of endometriosis—grade 4. This is very serious. Indeed, it could be life-threatening. From the pictures taken during your laparoscopy, it looks like some of your organs are stuck to the intestines. The scan also shows that there are a number of cysts in both your ovaries. You need to be operated on with the utmost urgency, but I can't operate on you myself as your condition has advanced far beyond grade 3 endometriosis. What you need is the expertise of someone who specialises in such advanced and complex endometrial conditions. However, I do work with a senior surgeon who's an absolute expert in dealing with the more severe cases. So, I'm going to refer you to him. His name is Callum Mackintosh."

I felt comfortable with Dr Joseph, and said, "Oh! I was hoping that you would be able to help me yourself. It's just that I've had such bad experiences with so-called experts."

"Oh, no, no. Callum Mackintosh is really one of a handful of surgeons worldwide who has the skill and experience of working with the most complex of such conditions. He's excellent, and I'll be happy to work with him. Don't worry, I'll make sure I'm present with him during the operation." Dr Joseph's words took away some of my anxiety.

Despite his top credentials, Dr Joseph was humble enough to know his limitations and refer me to someone whom he considered even better than himself when it came to my condition. Unlike the previous doctors, within a space of just one hour, he had done and said all the right things to inspire my trust.

I thought I had heard the worst but Dr Joseph continued with his prognosis. "I'm afraid your left kidney looks especially enlarged and I would also like to refer you to a consultant urologist, David West."

Shocked, I said, "My kidney? What's that got to do with things?"

"Well, it's not uncommon in these types of situations for the kidney to become implicated. It looks like your left ovary has been enlarged for quite some time and appears to have trapped the left ureter, which carries water from the kidney to the bladder. This means that the left kidney's not been functioning properly and it may be damaged, but the extent of its function is something David will be able to look into."

My heart sank. This was not good news. Heart, liver, and kidneys were vital to a healthy life. However, right at that moment, I was so relieved to have found an expert who knew what he was talking about. That he was well connected to the best medical experts in the area in which I was suffering was a bonus.

"Look, rest assured that you're now in good hands and I will do my utmost to make sure that you are looked after," Dr Joseph said. I could see he meant it.

It was a bad day, but it was a good day.

Over the course of the next two weeks, tests and more scans showed that my left kidney had indeed lost all but three percent of its function. The outlook was grim. It was unlikely that it would ever recover to its normal capacity.

It was a stroke of good luck that Dr Joseph had created a team of not one, but two experts and himself to tackle my severe condition.

Callum Mackintosh looked like he could be in his mid to late fifties. His rise to eminence in the medical elite of Britain granted him the distinct air of self-assuredness that came with superior knowledge, exquisite skill, and excellence in his field. Unlike Dr Hammerhead, he would show himself to be one of those genuinely competent and accomplished people that did not need to hide behind the facade of arrogance.

A man of few words, he didn't mince his words. He got straight to the point during my first consultation with him, and said, "Your condition is extreme. It's a good thing that you found me when you did. If left unattended, this could develop into cancer and even more pain."

I fell into stunned silence.

He continued, "Yours is indeed one of the worst cases of endometriosis that I've seen, because there are many adhesions; that is, organs that are stuck to each other, due to retrograde menstrual flow, the blood that's flowing back into the pelvis. There's also an aggressive growth of endometrium outside of the womb."

My jaw dropped. Was he talking about me? He went on, "There's also an unusual number of cysts, in each of your two ovaries. I should think that they will have caused you considerable pain."

You could say that again.

"But consider yourself lucky that there aren't any cysts in the fallopian tubes. Because that would be troublesome if you wanted to conceive.

So Dr Hammerhead hadn't exaggerated after all when he said that it was all "f*#@ed up down there".

"Look, that may be as it may, but I'm confident that I'll be able to free those organs, take out a large part of the excess endometrium, and remove the cysts," he said. "And if all goes well, by the time I'm done with you, there's no reason why you shouldn't be able to have children, too." He chuckled, embarrassed, realising the unintended innuendo that was counter to his sombre professional style.

I was in shock, but calm. "Will you have to cut me open? How long will it take to heal? Will I be left with scars?"

"The extent of your condition is so severe that it's highly improbable that I'll be able to get all the organs lasered free in one laparoscopic or keyhole surgery. It'll be a major operation of at least four hours. I'm afraid it's very likely that it will be necessary to have a second operation, possibly in about six months, and possibly a third one soon after that. I'll be sure about that when I've done the first," he said, breaking yet more devastating news to me.

I was emotional, close to tears. "How has this condition grown so aggressively in my body without my realising it? Where has it come from and more importantly, have I caused it in some way that maybe I haven't been conscious of?"

"Endometriosis is a little understood disease. We haven't figured out what causes it and the probability points to it being genetic. So don't go blaming yourself. And it's called the 'silent disease' because it develops in the background without any indications that it's there. So you really must not go blaming yourself for it," Dr Mackintosh said, assuring me.

I still couldn't help wondering if I had, quite literally, been 'stomaching it'—if this was the result of internalising my frustrations, anger, and sadness; of suppressing my vulnerability and sensitivity. Was this the price that I had paid for standing up for and pursuing what I believed to be the holy grail of my life: freedom to be my own person, to be true to myself?

"Why don't you go home and think about what you'd like to do. Let me know tomorrow if I should go ahead and book the operating theatre. This is a matter of urgency, so I'm prepared to find a slot for the surgery to take place within two weeks from now."

Now that the truth about what was making me sick had been fully established, I expected to feel relief but instead, it was more like the earth had caved under my feet and collapsed on top of me, a deluge of bad luck, much too heavy to bear and all I had the strength for was to let it engulf me.

I put aside my emotions, mustered every ounce of courage and positivity to come out alive, and found myself saying, "I don't need to think about anything. Let's do it." I would have to tap into every possible resource at my disposal to come out on top. The doctor had made it clear that I carried a life-threatening condition. Being true to myself meant facing it and dealing with it powerfully, by being all I could be.

That evening, I went home and sat in the room where I meditated. I had lived for almost two years with extreme pain and in the knowledge that my days were numbered. "Two years, at most," Dr Hammerhead had threatened. Of those two years, he had wasted eighteen months putting me on medications that had simply not worked.

Dr Mackintosh had earlier taken great pain to insist that my condition was one that was little understood by science, but I still could not help feeling that it was somehow the impact of the rotten *karma* of guilt and self-hatred that I had strung up for having disrespected my parents and grandparents, for having gone against the grain of my culture, and for having been so strong-willed in following my own path.

Today, however, a glimmer of hope had appeared in what had been long, dark, *dark* period, alone in the wilderness.

I knelt on the hard wooden floor in front of my home shrine in my meditation room, and lit up a *ghee* butter lamp and incense that illumined the twilight of this summer evening. With my eyes closed, I thought of my higher Self, full of gratitude for this exceptional turn of events. From the depths of my core, I was thankful to the gods and goddesses who lived in the cavern of my heart for the amazing grace of having Elizabeth care enough to direct me to someone who could help, and for this team of very special doctors showing up in my life, perhaps just in time to save my life.

The gratitude, like a healing force, gave way to confusion and then grief, and the blend overwhelmed me. At times like these, I found that writing, free flow, in my journal, helped me to work through the unarticulated tangles of my thoughts and emotions.

Notebook in hand, I started writing. The pen moved frantically as I jotted down the jumble in my mind. "Wasn't it just a few days ago that I was hounded by the thought that I might die soon? Then, in the last few days, my new doctors gave me a glimmer of hope and I felt ecstatic to have found them. Hope of a new beginning made me feel light. And today, I committed to surgically dealing with my disease. I felt relieved, but now that it's all sinking in, I realise I'm an iceberg of frozen emotions."

I stopped and took a sharp intake of breath. "While I've been busy taking action to get to the root of my issue, I've forgotten about how I actually feel. What's right there is shock—I'm in deep, deep shock. How could this be? How could I be in such a desperate situation? I just don't understand!"

Then I noticed that the ink beneath my pen dispersed in a drop of moisture. I wiped it with the back of my hand, looking up at the ceiling to see where the droplet had come from, only to realise that it was a tear. Mine.

I continued in illegible handwriting while more tears blurred my sentences even further. "And what if something were to go wrong during my operation?" I could not control my weeping.

Dr Callum Mackintosh had told me they would do as much as possible using laser technology, through one or two small one centimetre incisions. "However," he had said, "if there is too much bleeding or if the area I need to work on is out of my reach through the keyhole, then I might well have to cut you open and do an open surgery."

I carried on scribbling, and wrote, "What if he had to do this? I could end up with a huge gash in my stomach to heal. And how long would it take to recover? I can't afford to stay off work for more than just a few weeks!" Panic and worry consumed me. My nerves were frazzled.

"The endometrium tissue is all over your intestines," he had warned. "There is the possibility that, if during the surgery any part of the intestinal tract gets perforated, we might have to fit you with a colostomy bag." He had said it with such matter-of-factness that, during our conversation, I didn't have time to think of the far-reaching consequences of walking around for the rest of my life with a stoma bag, carrying my waste products on my hip. But now, behind closed doors, in the safety of my sacred space, I panicked. The risks and reality of my forthcoming surgeries were exploding into stark, heavy realisations. More salty droplets seeped onto my page, the writing beneath totally blurred, just like the events of my life. What a horrible mess I was.

I reached out for the tissues. Shock, panic, and helplessness had taken a firm hold. For perhaps only the second time since my childhood, I felt like a victim of my life.

My pen raced ahead of my thoughts. "How will I control what the doctors are going to do when I am under anaesthetic? What if I wake up, only to find that during my operation, they had to do something drastic that will alter the course of my life forever? Is it better, after all, to suffer the pain, however agonising, and let myself die a slow, natural death? Isn't that preferable to waking up from my operation only to find that I've lost normal functioning?"

I felt trapped and devastated. Still feeling the venomous effects of the awful medication that Dr Hammerhead had put me on. I felt confused and unwell. My will, too, had taken a battering, giving way to the mind monkeys to rampage and run riot.

I wrote, "What's happening to me? Why now? How could I have not seen this coming? Is this my punishment for having gone against my family's wishes?"

I felt a bitter taste in my mouth, while the salt in my tears irritated my face.

More questions continued to flood in through my pen. "In my compulsion to be free to be myself, have I hurt more people, my dear elders, than I intended? Has their anger and pain rebounded on me? Am I now somehow cursed? Is that possible?"

The sobs were desperate. The last thing I had intended was to harm anyone on my account.

More fear crept up, now darker and more fierce as I questioned my existence. "Is this the result of some atrocious past life *karma*? What awful things could I have done to deserve this? Could it be that I am actually a nasty person, deluded in believing that I'm fundamentally good? Perhaps my life, this time round, has been built on a pile of horrendous things I did in previous lifetimes?"

Criss-crossing thoughts fired through my head like bullets in a war zone. "Who can I turn to? Is there anyone in my life that's strong but compassionate enough to be able to understand me right now? To support me, without judging, through this illness? Anyone that can let me be as vulnerable as I feel in this moment?"

"What I would not give for someone to give me a hug and say to me right now, 'You'll come through this. I'm here for you'!" I scribbled, salt drops gushing from my eyes, sniffling, yearning to be held and comforted.

I had more wonderful friends than a girl has a right to have, but which one of them could deal with something this intense? Supporting a person with a debilitating illness is no small feat.

I felt so utterly alone. I kept wiping away the droplets flushing my eyes and kept my hand moving with the outpouring of thawing feelings.

"It's all your fault," my mind monkeys chided, condemning me. *"You're just trouble. It was just a matter of time before you had what was coming to you!"*

"No, no, no," I burst out, unleashing another downpour of tears.

The mischievous monkeys continued, unrelenting, *"You should have been kinder to your parents. Your grandparents said that no good would come out of your leaving the family. Consider this your comeuppance. It's no less than you deserve."*

"Shut up! Shut *up!*" I screamed through the tears. "You weren't much help to me, were you?" My heart felt like it was about to explode. "This is all too much!"

The last thing I was capable of right now was calming the mental monkeys. But of one thing I was clear: I had to stop blaming myself.

I sobbed, crumbling, and feeling more lonely than ever before. A huge surge of depressed thoughts, fear, and all kinds of unexpressed emotions welled up within me, threatening to erupt like a volcano. I tried to suppress them and get a grip on myself but, this time, their force was overwhelming and I could no longer hold myself back. I wept and wept and wept, like there was no tomorrow, wailing, engulfed by the misery of my situation, unable to control myself.

As the force of trapped unacknowledged emotion spewed forth, I started to shudder and choke, at times unable to catch my breath. All the while, I had the thought, *Stop it! Stop it!* But could not.

There was no one I could call on for help. My spirit sank. How on earth would I get through something as serious as this?

"You are not alone!" I heard the familiar, soft whisper of my higher Self, ringing out in my inner ear. *"You are being helped and guided. You have been taken to the right doctors. They will help you. Turn even more within and trust that you are not alone."*

"If you're going to heal yourself fully and once and for all, you will have to stop hiding from yourself. It'll take baring your soul." These words appearing on the page were not now coming from my fear and anxiety. *"It'll mean confronting your darkest fears, and moving through the most agonising pain. You'll have to look for unresolved issues lurking in the nooks and crannies of your being."* I had that familiar sense of my higher Self emerging with its guidance through my pen.

The insight struck me that the surgery was just a fix, that the deeper healing was down to me. It was time to drop a few more veils of illusion that I lived behind unknowingly.

"That prospect feels like climbing Mount Everest with my bare feet," I scribed on the page.

"Be courageous. You will be reminded, by someone who really knows you, of who you truly are. Then, it will be easier for you to accept that truth for yourself," the Diamond had me write through the deluge of tears.

That sounded like a prophesy, and I had no idea what my Inner Diamond meant by it. Yet.

"You will see it in due course."

This was a conundrum that I did not have the energy to resolve right now.

On feeling the vibration of my Inner Diamond in this emotional wilderness, my weeping, as though going through the eye of the needle, turned from bleak desolation to the solace of gratitude once more. Despite this, I still could not bring myself to stop crying, the stuttering having turned into hiccups, making my belly ache with the raw pain of my humanity.

My mind went numb from all these thawing emotions, and I must have continued to weep for hours until I could weep no more, my eyes so sore that they could stay open no longer. Then, drained and exhausted,

I fell into a sleep, there on the small rug on the wooden floor, barely covering myself with the blanket I used during meditation.

When I woke up the next morning, I began to see, once again, a glimmer of light in the darkness of my situation. With hindsight, I now understood that a while back, no sooner had I asked my higher Self with all my heart to help me to heal my pain, Elizabeth had popped up in my mind, leading me to find, like a needle in a haystack, Dr Adam Joseph, who in turn led me to the very best doctors in the world, available right here in London.

In the flow of this grace, I also learnt that as part of my salary package, my company's health insurance would be able to cover me for all the treatment that I would need over the coming months.

In between my three operations, each four hours long, I had no alternative but to continue working in my demanding international job. Thanks to Dr Callum

Mackintosh, however, whose masterful handiwork was so exemplary, I was able to recuperate fully in less than six weeks from each operation.

My ability to pay my mortgage and bills was more important to me than ever, because if I had lost my house, though I could have had a roof over my head with my parents, it would not have been a feasible option. Their health was fragile, and seeing me in such a vulnerable condition would only have added to their troubles. Besides, at the age of seven, I had vowed that I would never be a burden to them or anyone else.

Why had I suffered for so long? Why had I not asked my Inner Diamond for help much sooner? As soon as I'd asked, my higher Self had found a way of getting me in front of a team of three of London's most eminent and celebrated specialists who could help me with my condition.

More consciously connected than ever before, I resolutely committed to co-creating life with my higher Self's brilliance, with its unerring wisdom as my guide.

I sensed that life was only just beginning.

The best was yet to come.

3

Angel-Bird

It happened late one evening in May, after sunset, when the sky had turned pitch black, exactly one week following my second surgery. After lighting a stick from a pack of frangipani incense that my dad had given to me, I sat down in my usual spot on the floor of my meditation room. The fragrance of the burning frangipani signalled to my mind and body that it was sacred time, the time to let go.

Shortly after returning home from the hospital, I'd begun to meditate more, at least once a day, sometimes twice. It became a normal part of my convalescence. As much as it helped me to nourish my spirit, it was a quiet time to consciously direct energy and tap into my body's healing capacities. It also helped me to anchor into my 'new' body, now lighter and freer, relieved of old pain and disease that had long been a silent part of me.

The room was pitch black, even though the curtains were not drawn, it being a New Moon, and the usual silver glow absent. In the thick silence of the still, peaceful evening, I found it less difficult to detach from my otherwise unruly, often fear-based, automatic mental chatter. My breathing spontaneously became calmer and deeper, aligning with the silence. Without forcing my mind, breath, or inner vision to go this way or that, merely by allowing the moment to be okay just as it was, I slid into deeper consciousness. I kept dropping, falling, as if in a void of deep space, without a net beneath. A bit like bungee jumping but without the bungee. I called this 'surfing the void'. It helped me to let go of my needing to control life, and just trust. Far from being scary, it often exhilarated and energised me. The silence grew deeper and richer, empty yet strangely fertile.

Behind the back of my physical eyes, the inner sight of my third eye became active, just as real as the outer. Out of the darkness emerged a tiny speck of light. It grew bigger and brighter, expanding, and then it receded back and formed a screen-like white curtain in the background of utter darkness, as in the cinemas.

Right in the centre of my awareness, another tiny speck of flickering, fluorescent light arose, projected on the white curtain. It flashed more luminous by the moment, grabbing my focus. Glistening greens, burnished blues and incandescent indigos dazzled in front of my inner eye. As the dancing colours became more steady, I could make out an outline of a form, but I couldn't see completely what it was. My inner vision came more into focus as it adjusted to what was being projected on the curtain, and I could see that it was some sort of a creature. Its translucent image became more life-like in my deeper mind's eye. It absorbed all of my attention, until it grew bigger and brighter, filling my entire focus, a ball of pure brilliance. It looked at first like a huge, glowing, brightly coloured peacock. As it expanded in my view, I realised that it could only be a half bird because though it had wings, from the waist up its form was human. And it appeared to be sitting in the very centre of my room!

What was this I was seeing? How strange. Was I imagining this or was it really sitting there in front of me? Spooked, I opened my eyes to see if it really was in the room. And there it was. Large, slender, and regal, dressed in the finery of silky feather-like garments.

I was much too astounded and distrusting of what I saw. Could this 'thing' really be sitting right in front of me, across the width of my room? I closed my eyes again to see if it had gone away in my inner vision, but there it was too, sitting with elegant poise, lying on its side, its head held up resting on its right hand. Whatever it was, it lay draped contentedly across the wooden boards of this room, like a content Buddha after he had just discovered nirvana. The glowing being carried itself up to sitting with an air of majesty, and faced me.

I opened my eyes once again, and it was still there—right there in the centre of my room. I closed my eyes and the being did not move. My spooked fear and panic dissipated in its presence and, instead, I felt a spontaneous delight awaken in me. From it emanated a warm, glowing, loving energy as it watched me with kindly amusement. Something about its energy overwhelmed me, pressing into my heart, discharging deep-seated fears and triggering tears of relief and joy, which slid down my face.

As if hearing my question telepathically, it replied, "*I am Michael*," revealing a magnificent velvet voice. "*I am here with you.*"

Once my nerves settled down, I realised that I was in the presence of an angel. It was granting me what, in India, we call a *darshan*, a view or vision of a divine being. I mentally bowed my head to the beautiful being in front of me. In its glow, I too became transparent and luminous, as if my Inner Diamond had come to the fore, flashing bright. The cells of my brain felt warm, aglow with sparkles, ignited by the angel's light.

Then the angel took the burning frangipani incense stick and waved it in the air, squiggling what looked like letters of the alphabet. Transfixed, I watched. He, Michael, spelt the words *Hawaii* in thin air, and then indicated the word with his index finger. My mind suspended, I couldn't think, only observe, merely witness. He stayed with me for a few moments more, then he vanished into the same thin air that he had come out of.

My brain and nervous system were alight, saturated, in overload with a heightened sensory perception to which I was not accustomed. At the same time, my heart was full with an indescribable joy, appreciation, and gratitude for this unusual and remarkable experience.

As the distinct contrast of my experience came into focus, I realised that the angel-bird Michael had graced me with his vision through the portal of my third eye, a view into a world existing in parallel to the one we know. To me, it felt as real as the one in which I walked, talked, touched, ate, and moved around in every day. It seemed somewhat like living in two countries with contrasting features. In the world seen through the third eye, I was not always able to see details in the same crisp way as I would see it in the physical world, sharp and immediate. Rather, I saw what was in front of me in its totality, as if in a 3D experience, more multidimensional, where sound, speech, colour, contrast, and so on, were as much *felt* through the senses as seen and heard in a truly holistic, holographic experience.

Time had stood still in this experience, and when I got up from the 'meditation' my senses were overwhelmed. Even though it was still only ten o'clock in the evening, I headed up to bed. Sleep claimed me as soon as my head hit the pillow.

That night, I drifted off into a restful slumber of a quality that I wasn't accustomed to. I had a dream so vivid and lucid, so clear, that I remember it to this day as though it had just happened.

In the dream, a beautiful woman walked towards me as I sat at the edge of a still lake lit up by the bright warm rays of a late afternoon sun. Birds tweeted in the background, punctuating the silent stillness suffusing the grassy green banks of the lake. She walked with the graceful gait of a goddess, elegant and assured in her every step. Her face oozed a natural beauty, her bronze complexion radiated a gentle golden glow, and her long dark brown tresses tumbled beneath the curves of a slim, shapely waist. She stepped closer towards me and I could make out her rich green gossamer *sari*, woven intricately with embroidered gold borders. Flower buds of tiny crystals scattered throughout her long, exquisite garment. The closer she got, the warmer, more animated, her presence felt. With a smile, she came and sat beside me on the green grass, exuding a calm vibrance that made me feel more awake and aware than in an actual waking state. I heard the thought, *Meet the Goddess in Green.*

She just sat next to me for a while, silent, as we both gazed into the transparent lake. Then, in the mirror of the lake's surface, a reflection emerged. A large, tall, six-sided quartz crystal, the likes of which I had never seen, became vividly visible, as wide as two or three eight-year-olds bound together and as tall. I had never seen such an enormous crystal, and its beauty took my breath away. The Goddess in Green took my hand and pointed with her left. As she did so, a pod of dolphins emerged from the depths of the lake and started swimming anti-clockwise around the quartz column. They went round a few times, then went wider into the lake and played, jumping out of the water, twirling, spinning, and revolving five or six twirls before diving back down into the lake and starting all over again.

"Go and heal yourself," she proclaimed, looking into my eyes. *"Go to the dolphins. Free your playful spirit once again. Go to the temple with the grand crystal and start life anew."*

She stroked my cheek with the back of her ethereal finger, taking in my face. I could hold her gaze only momentarily before moving back into my normal sleep reality.

"Free your
playful spirit
once again."

4

Synchronicity

The next afternoon, I was due to meet with my old friend Gina, who had returned from six months of travelling around the world with her husband. We had arranged the meeting the previous week, almost as soon as she had landed. We wanted to get together before the demands of everyday work life hijacked her.

Gina had continued to be my dear friend and mentor since my teens. We had stayed in touch over the years, sometimes seeing more of each other than at other times, depending on our work and travel schedules, or on how much time was devoted to developing a relationship with the respective man in our life at the time.

We met up in the specialist coffee shop at Ealing Broadway in West London.

"You're radiant, Gina!" I remarked at seeing how alive and healthy she looked.

"Thanks, Smeets," she replied. "It's been an incredible six months. We've had an amazing journey." The waiter interrupted us to take our order. "I'd like a cappuccino and a piece of cheesecake, please. What would you like, Smita? Cappuccino also?" I nodded. Gina knew I avoided loaded calories wherever I could. "Now, what were we talking about?"

As the waiter left us, I asked Gina about her various experiences during her travels and whether it had given the rest and inspiration she had been craving. She told me the stories from her travels and places she had been to. Then, she started to tell me about the last part of her trip and I listened, stunned into silence at the synchronicity of what she was telling me.

"Our last stop," Gina said, "was in the Hawaiian islands. It was really the highlight of our trip. There, we met a man who was incredibly in tune with the dolphins of that region—how they behave, their whereabouts off the coast of the Big Island of Hawaii, and so on."

As Gina talked, my heart beat faster, my attention fully switched on.

"He took us out with some others on a boat, a few miles off the coast, and taught us how to swim with dolphins. In the wild, mind, not trained in a resort and injected with medicines. It was just exquisite, snorkelling with dolphins in the wild! They're such intelligent creatures and so much fun!"

"Wow! How amazing is that." I said, goosebumps all over my arms. Though I had heard that they were special creatures, I had no idea that it might possible to swim with dolphins. I wanted to just keep listening to Gina.

"Yes, we were lucky enough to do that several times and then we went to another of the Hawaiian Islands, Kauai," Gina continued, "And there, we went to this Hindu Monastery with its own temple."

"Really? A Hindu Monastery and temple of Kauai? How unexpected."

She nodded with a huge grin on her face."I know. Isn't it?"

"How did you come to know about it?" I asked.

"Well, one of the women who came with us on the boat to swim with dolphins was from Kauai. Leah had lived in Kauai for more than ten years and told us about so many of the hidden gems on the island that she said we must take the time to visit," she said.

"I thought of you and wished you could've joined us there. There was this massive quartz crystal column, at the centre of the temple. They said it was a Shiva *lingam*. I remembered from going to temples in India with my mum all those years ago that it was the main symbol of the Hindu god Shiva. The place itself was magnificent. You would love it there!" She stopped to take a sip of her coffee.

"Doesn't Shiva represent transformation?" she asked. "I always think of him as an ascetic *yogi*, deep in meditation, lost in the cosmic dance or dance of life. I remember my mum's *Guruji* telling us that Shiva is depicted with the third eye, which when open, keeps the universe spinning and when it closes, the universe is destroyed, only for something new to come into creation by the divine Shakti, his consort. He, the destroyer, and she, the primordial creative force, come together in a sacred union that makes a whole." Gina's eyes grew distant as she remembered.

I smiled. "Gosh! You've learnt well!"

"Isn't the third eye also known as the inner teacher or *antar guru* in Sanskrit?" she asked, going off-track from recounting her travels.

Then the dots connected between what Gina was sharing about her travel experiences, and what I saw in my meditation and dream of the previous night. My eyes must have lit up and face broken into a wide beam because Gina stopped talking and said, "What are you looking so pleased about? Have you just spotted the man of your dreams or something?" She looked around. A hundred thoughts whizzed through my head. It dawned on me that if only I go out of my own way, my Inner Diamond would inevitably steer me so that my life worked gracefully.

I shook my head, still in disbelief at this series of coincidences, this gratifying twist of events.

"*What?* Are you going to tell me or do I have to resort to torture tactics?" Gina said, now more curious.

"You won't believe me if I tell you! You'll say I'm making it up," I replied, not knowing how to gather my tale quickly enough to come out of my mouth sanely.

She gave me time.

"So," I started. "I had my second surgery two weeks ago and I'm just beginning to get back into normal life. The doctors have categorically told me not to go back to work before six weeks. They said it's important that I

63

avoid all kinds of stress for that time. I can travel by air after three weeks, but only if it's to go somewhere for rest and healing."

"That's a good idea. Getting away would do you the world of good. Believe me. I know what I'm talking about." She beamed a cheeky grin, her teeth ever whiter on a tanned face.

I joshed, "You jammy dodger!" Then continued to explain, "When I came to see you, I was perplexed by this vivid but bizarre dream I had last night. And just before I went to bed, during my meditation, something else happened that was unusual and out-of-the-ordinary," I said, still feeling the effects of that meditative state.

"Really? What did you see? What was the dream?" she asked, curious.

Wired with excitement and oblivious to the din from the giggling schoolgirls who had just entered the café, I told her about the dream. The waiter brought over our second round of coffees. I told her about the angel-bird squiggling the word *Hawaii* in the air with the lit incense stick and the Goddess in Green showing me the enormous, tall quartz crystal in the lake's reflection. I shared with Gina about her telling me to go to the dolphins and to the temple with that crystal.

"Of course, it seems obvious now. But when I woke up this morning, the dream and what I saw in my meditation were two separate occurrences. Both were cryptic puzzles that were bugging me. And I hadn't thought about going away so soon after my surgery. But listening to you, it's obvious. I should go swimming with dolphins: *free your playful spirit once again,* the Goddess in Green said. *Go to the temple with the grand crystal and start life anew,* she said. And the link to both is Hawaii." I looked at Gina, pleased as punch, my eyes about to pop out of my head. "I mean, there are a million temples in the world. How would I know which one has a crystal in it? And how would I know that it's the one that I saw in my dream? I'd never even heard that it was possible to swim with dolphins, and in Hawaii for that matter, except for the ones in tourist resorts, let alone go on a trip where you might actually be able to do it. What are the odds that here you are, the very next day after my dream, telling me that you've just come back from Hawaii, having done those things and been to the very temple with a massive quartz crystal column."

"That *is* pretty amazing." Gina looked impressed. "You've really been fine-tuning your ability to tap into that other intelligence, haven't you? Good for you, girl. Well, that's settled then. You have to go to Hawaii."

" ... the more you've been resisting
a particular issue,
the harder it's likely to erupt."

5

The Big Island

As I boarded my flight three weeks to the day after my second surgery, my skin tingled with anticipation. This was going to be a magical, mystical journey. I was going on my own and had never been to Hawaii before, nor had I any friends there. Gina had, however, given me one contact. It was that of the dolphin man who had taken her and her husband out on the Pacific Ocean to swim with dolphins. His name was Dan. She had said that Dan knew a lot of people on the Big Island and he might well be able to introduce me to some of the locals.

Other than visiting the Shiva temple in Kauai and swimming with dolphins off the coast of the Big Island, I had made no plans whatsoever for my trip ahead. This was to be my biggest lesson yet in listening to my Inner Diamond and trusting it, my innate Self. It had told me that each next step would become evident as I went along and that *it* would be my astral satellite navigation system on this journey. The only prior arrangements I had made before I left London were booking a room at a hotel in Keauhou, Kona, west of the Big Island, as well as in Kauai and renting cars on the two Islands.

As the airplane taxied along the runway at London's Heathrow Airport, I could sense that my life, too, was also about to take off in some unknown but positive way.

"Miss Joshi, the car we were going to give you still hasn't been returned by the previous driver so we're going to give you a free upgrade," the assistant from the car hire company at Hawaii's Kona Airport told me. I had hired a small saloon car but was given the keys to a swanky Sebring convertible. When I arrived at my hotel, as a result of some mix-up with their bookings, they too gave me a room two categories above the one I had paid for—a suite with a sizeable balcony, or *lanai*, that directly faced the sea.

Little had I known at the time of booking that this hotel would have a well-preserved ancient Hawaiian temple, a sacred *heiau*, on its beautiful grounds. It seemed, that just like in India, you were never more than a stone's throw away from the next temple. The trip had begun well and the generous free car upgrade and staying at a hotel with an ancient temple on its grounds were gifts that were an indication of more to come.

My fourth floor hotel room overlooked a shore of black lava rock. Being high up and with no adjoining balconies, I kept the door to the balcony open, 24/7, for the next twelve days. It ushered in a constant cool breeze in otherwise hot temperatures that, to a Londoner mostly cooped up indoors, felt heaven sent. The rippling, rhythmic sound of the ocean waves rolling onto shore was music to my ears as I stood for ages, watching the vast ocean that lay directly in front of my room and soaking in the sunshine of the tropical climate. The sea beneath my balcony was home to a turtle of unusual proportions that was more than twice my age. It floated around below, ebbing and flowing with the gentle waves, seeking his next meal or merely hanging out, swimming with time.

The next day, after a long, leisurely rest, I called Dan. He invited me to meet him at his home and gave me the directions to his hilltop residence. I set out late morning to meet him. As I drove along Mamalahoa Highway en route to Dan's house in Captain Cook, I caught sight of a roadside café called the Coffee Shack. It was literally a wooden shack with about ten cars squeezed directly in front of it and people queuing up to get inside the café. "Go there tomorrow," I sensed this prompting from my Inner Diamond.

The Hawaiian climate was to die for. Hot and sunny with a light cool breeze that gave an unmistakable feeling of being in the tropics. Men walked around in Bermuda shorts and brightly coloured, gaudy Hawaiian shirts that I thought were only worn in TV programmes like *Hawaii Five-O*. Women, regardless of their shape and size, wore little more than bikini tops covered by small T-shirts and short skirts. Everyone was dressed ready to take a dip at a moment's notice in the ocean or in one of the bays. I was in heaven! Or Paradise, in local speak.

There was a distinct feel in the air on the Big Island. It was palpably primal, vibrant, alive. The whole of the Big Island of Hawaii was a pulsating, live volcano. Remnants of volcanic explosions of old, solidified black rock framed its shores, that reminded us of its former fuming glory, that it was once red-hot molten liquid lava gushing down the mountainside to unite with the fluid ocean.

The atmosphere was entirely different to that of London or the UK in general. It was even distinct from the most powerful spots in India or America or Bali or anywhere that I had been. Hawaii was a paradox. You could be driving along the road, with glorious views of the ocean below, thinking you were in a well-developed country. Then, just one turn off the main road and you could find yourself quite by surprise on a dusty old dirt track that could well be in a rural Balinese village.

When I turned off the main road towards Dan's house, I found myself on such a road, an unpaved dirt track along a steep hill, amidst a small plantation with trees that bore mangoes, coconuts, bananas, pineapples and other luscious fruits. The higher up along the hill I got, the more rough was the terrain, making me wish I had a four-wheel drive.

Finally, as I reached the top of the hill, I saw Dan waiting for me outside his bungalow. A tall, well-built, middle-aged expat American with a receding mop of burnished hair, he came over and gave me a warm welcome and hug.

"Thanks for making it up here," he said. "Come, let's sit on the *lanai*." He led the way through what looked like a fairly simple accommodation with basic creature comforts consisting of wicker and cane furniture, a light wooden dining table, a well-used wicker rocking armchair and some other bits and bobs. Dan offered me a mug of Kona coffee, and explained that it was a produce of the local area, a thing of great pride for the residents of Hawaii.

We came out on the balcony that showed off a picture-perfect view of this part of the Big Island, overlooking the stunning hillside below, facing an imposing ocean. I gasped with delight, my breath suspended for a moment while I gathered myself.

"That's Kealakekua Bay," Dan said, pleased at the impact the view had on me.

And what a view it was. Overlooking a picturesque hillside dotted with pretty houses, the hills rolled down towards the bay, a near perfect arc that framed an expanse of the bluest cerulean I had ever seen, a piece of the Pacific Ocean that stretched out far and wide into the horizon, where it met with its mirror image of the clearest azure sky. There, a cloudless blue sky and a breathtaking blue ocean merged and blended seamlessly into a single illusion, making it gloriously impossible to see where the ocean ended and the sky began.

I had never seen such a majestic panorama. This, to me, truly was paradise on Earth.

"So, this is why I bought this place, for the magnificent view," Dan said. I'd forgotten all about him.

"Magnificent, it truly is." My remark felt inadequate.

"And you have access to this every single day? It wouldn't be hard to get used to *this*."

I agreed to go with Dan later that afternoon to the Kealakekua Bay where spinner dolphins were often sighted. We took our snorkelling gear, as Dan said that it was a good idea to get acclimatised to being in the water before we went out into the ocean, over the coming days, to swim with dolphins. He said that there was a protocol in how to swim with dolphins. It was important to be at ease when you were around them and understand how to behave in their presence so that they felt comfortable in approaching you.

On the way there, I asked him about the island and why its energy felt so primal.

"Geologically," Dan said, "it's a hot spot, a huge magma chamber in the middle of the Pacific Ocean that's directly connected to the spinning core at the centre of the planet, which acts as an antenna. So on this island, the energy and vibrations that this 'antenna' picks up from the universe are felt more closely and directly." I listened with interest.

"Isn't Hawaii linked with the old land of Lemuria?" I asked.

"It's a place full of contradictions. It is commonly understood as being geologically a new place. Yet there is a belief that runs through old legends and the people of these islands that claim Hawaii to be the ancient land of Lemuria," he replied.

"There's an earthy, primal vibrancy to this island but it seems to me that an ancient air also pervades the place," I said.

"The power of the volcano is not to be underestimated. And that includes the Kealakekua Bay and the ocean around the island. The locals say that it pushes to the surface within people all those issues that are hiding, just below the surface of their awareness or hanging out in the blind spots of their consciousness," Dan said.

"You mean, the Big Island's energy has people spontaneously getting in touch with their unresolved fears, anger, or similar issues?" I asked.

"Absolutely. The volcano's palpating energy brings these things to the surface, and the more you've been resisting a particular issue, the harder it's likely to erupt."

I joked, "So, what you're saying is, resistance is futile!"

"Yes! That's it. Equally, for those of us who are ready to take our consciousness to the next level, there are unexpected surprises that can prove to be life-altering," he said.

We drove down the Napoopoo Road from Captain Cook and parked in the ample car park reserved for the bay. With few entrances into the water at Kealakekua Bay, we entered by walking over a long, unfriendly footpath from the area known as Two Steps, minding the black lava rock that surrounded it. The water was crystal clear and beautifully warm, twenty-eight or so degrees centigrade, just ideal for snorkelling and diving. A stunning, well-preserved coral reef flourished, attracting a wealth of exotic fish that enhanced the underwater scenic beauty of the bay.

I prided myself on being like a fish in the sea, comfortable and at ease in the ocean. As an advanced scuba diver, I was accustomed to encountering sharks and other sea creatures so I did not expect to be daunted by coming across a few friendly dolphins. But today, in the waters of the enthralling Kealakekua Bay, I found myself breaking into a panic within moments of getting into the water. I was neither submerged and buoyant in the water, nor able to rest my feet on a sandy beach. Beneath were jagged reef coral and rocks and, very quickly, we were in deep water with nothing to do but keep afloat. The further we went out of the bay, the more agitated and insecure I became. Thank goodness there were no dolphins here today, because I was much too scared to be anywhere near them. For some reason, unexpected and unfathomable to me, without the safety net of my scuba air tank, I found myself unable to venture further even on the surface of the water. Fear gripped me. Actually, I was terrified. Was this what Dan had meant about the volcano's energies bringing to the surface hidden fears or unresolved issues?

Meanwhile, Dan lay on his back with his face to the sunny, cloudless blue sky, floating in blissful repose.

When he noticed that I was struggling and in a panic, he got to work on teaching me to float on the surface of the ocean. I had to lie on my back without splashing or moving my arms or legs, just to relax and float. But I could not do it. Instead, I splashed around, my arms and legs vigorously busy, and floundered hopelessly.

"How could you possibly not move your arms and legs, or at least hands and feet?" I yelled out to Dan, panicking. "Surely, I'm bound to swallow water through my nose or snorkel."

Dan swam closer to me, and like a wise *guru* spare with words, counselled, "Trust the ocean to support you."

My immediate reflex was to resist his advice.

Yeah, right. My thoughts turned cynical. How simplistic could you get? I'd find myself at the bottom of the ocean before you could finish saying 'trust the ocean to support you!'

Meanwhile, I carried on splashing around and trying very hard to float effortlessly.

"Trust the ocean to support you!" Dan shouted again, over the noise of the waves.

What on earth did he mean, 'trust the ocean'? How can you trust the ocean? It'll swipe you away in an instant and make you breakfast for a grateful shark! I paddled even harder and stayed on my front.

"Trust the ocean to support you!" Dan shouted for the third time, now more emphatic with each word, as though talking to a foreigner in his own land.

Suddenly, the words of my wise friend, Gina, came crashing into my ear, along with another large ocean wave, "Smita, you feel you have to push the sun to come up. You know, it knows how to do that all by itself."

Then something in me switched, as if from left brain to the right and like a flaming hot brick from my hand, my resistance dropped. In that instant, a kind of magic happened. I stopped waving my arms about and furiously paddling my panic-stricken finned feet. I let go of trying *very, very* hard. I let go of trying to control my rational mind, of trying to control the ocean, and simply started flowing with it. And *voila!* I had found that sweet spot of trusting: myself, the ocean, and its flow.

I put the snorkel in my mouth, positioning it so that the spout faced upwards and not sideways by my ear. Then, turning onto my back, I became more aware of the ocean beneath and around my body. I stopped resisting and allowed my body to get in tune with its motion. I fell in with the rhythm of the ocean's constant movement. Allowing my mind and body to be calm, I watched the sky above me as the waves cradled and rocked me, bobbing up and down on the ocean like a light, unsinkable cork.

I was floating!

The feeling of floating on my back on waves of the salty water, communing with the glorious, vast sky above, was one of the most liberating and joyful things that I had ever done and I was in my element.

I was getting better at recognising when resistance was running the show, and that was part of the trick. Resistance, however, did not always look or feel the same, manifesting in different ways in different situations. With the laser beam of awareness and with self-honesty, I could not escape these negative aspects of my own ego. Only then did I have the choice to let it go.

My ability to trust in myself had deepened. Though it ebbed and flowed with the rhythm of life, like me on the waves of the ocean, it may not necessarily remove the challenges it could throw up but made it possible to rise to them with greater ease and grace.

A whole new world had been shown to me. Dan had said something simple and yet taught me something deeply profound. His words had been an epiphany to me. I, an expert in the art of trying very, very hard at everything, at life, was being asked at the metaphysical level to trust the ocean of life to fully support me. It was as if my higher Self had been speaking to me through the megaphone of Dan's mouth. I was being asked to rely less on my metaphorical scuba air tank and to have greater trust in the breath of life, to float through life with more ease, to find play and joy, and not by ceaseless effort and striving.

"How could I not have learnt to float like that before? It's simply blissful," I asked Dan as he drove me back to my hotel. "I absolutely loved that experience. It was so liberating. And fun."

"Well, sometimes we're not ready to let go of our deep-seated survival habits. And they've become so engrained as a part of how we get through life that we don't even realise that they're there," he said.

"That's so true. I knew I liked to drive things, but had no idea that I was such a control freak. It's become so like second nature to me that I don't know myself apart from it. I mean, until today, I could not have given you examples of where on a daily basis I'm controlling and forcing outcomes."

"Right, because you've integrated that skill to the extent that it's automatic," he said.

"Yes, and it's much worse because I like to think that I'm always working on myself so I'm more open than others to see my hidden flaws and limitations and change them," I said, seeing clearly how much a victim of my own habitual mind I had been. What ought to have been my strength had become a hindrance, an impediment to my own happiness and fulfilment.

I now realised that the life-threatening disease I was in the process of healing was possibly a reflection of how I had distrusted not just myself but life.

My higher Self was teaching me to trust in life and feel safe by letting go, paradoxically, of *having* to be in control.

"I loved and valued my intellect, but it could often hold me back from stepping into experiencing the magical and the sacred.

I had learnt to put my intellect aside, suspend disbelief so to speak, so that I could experience something beyond the limitations of my rational and cynical mind."

6

Chakra Cobwebs

Dan said that we would be able to go to swim with dolphins a few days later, with friends of his who operated a boat service for these types of trips. In the meantime, he offered to introduce me to some of the other folk on the island.

"If you're not too tired, tomorrow evening we'll all meet at Tracey and Ralph's. Tracey leads a meditation once a week and, normally, there's a fair turnout. It'll be good for you to meet some people on the island." I had no other plans and was only too happy to go along. Besides, who knew what serendipity lay ahead?

The early evening sun gave a gorgeous glow of oranges and pinks bursting through the light scattering of clouds. While I drove to Tracey's, who also lived in Captain Cook, near Dan, a rain shower left a spectacular band of colour on the horizon ahead. I had to stop the car so I could soak up the life-sized vibrant rainbow that arched over the road, right there in front of me. Not a day went by while I was there when I did not see at least one rainbow. The quality of light on these islands produced exquisite colours that amplified the sense of anticipation and magic that drenched the Hawaiian air.

The warm summer shower unleashed a fresh fragrance of hot damp earth, which took me back to my childhood in Porbandar, India. My young friends and I used to frolic and have the most fun splashing about in the first monsoon showers, after the acrid heat of the never-ending Indian summer.

I parked my car a few houses away from Tracey's and made my way to her front door. Ralph, Tracey's husband, answered. He was another expat American of medium height and average build.

"Come in, come in. We've been expecting you." He gave a warm welcome with a vigorous handshake and ushered me into the lounge through the light and airy hallway. Tracey walked in with a tray of water, healthy drinks and crunchy nibbles. As soon as she saw me, she put the tray down, came over, and greeted me with a hug. She introduced me, one by one, to the dozen or so people already gathered.

People met here once a week to network, catch up with friends, and generally to support each other with their respective work and projects. Being on a small island, belonging and feeling a part of the community was all the more important. As the evening went on, Tracey asked a woman called Jo to sing. Jo told us that she used her voice to open and clear blockages in the *chakras*, the wheel-like nerve ganglia that the ancient Indian mystics said are present at certain points along our spine. "Why don't you give a demonstration of how you use your voice, Jo, to activate the *chakras*?"

"Oh! Okay. I wasn't planning on doing that today, but okay," Jo said. "Let's see. Shall I begin by saying a little about the *chakras*, in case people aren't familiar with them?"

"Great, why don't you do that," Tracey nodded.

"Okay. So, many of you are familiar with the working of the energetic body. You may already know that *chakras* are centres within our subtle, energy bodies, let's call them spinning wheels of light, because they are part of our electromagnetic field. They resonate with our physical body, thoughts, emotions, and habits, and hold onto the patterns that we tend to live our lives to and that determine, for good or bad, how our lives unfold. You know, karmic patterns that we might feel trapped or stuck in." Jo looked at me as she spoke. I nodded, wanting to know more.

She continued, "Each *chakra* has a specific function and if that *chakra* is impaired in some way, it can block it from spinning freely. So, if you repeatedly have a hard time expressing how you feel about a difficult situation or something that's important to you, over time it could block the throat, the area of self-expression. What I do is use my voice in a particular way. I use sound to clear the cobwebs that might be clogging up a person's *chakras* so that they can spin. This allows the life-giving force, *prana* or *chi*, to flow freely, increasing a sense of balance and well-being on the physical level. On a metaphysical level, you find a deeper connection within, a greater sense of who you are, your essential Self."

Jo, a petite woman of ample proportions, gave us a sample rendition of her unique voice. She unleashed a loud, long note that had the wooden floor planks release a tremor or two. Her high-pitched, high-decibel voice reverberated in my body and sent shock waves through my nervous system, which didn't know what had hit it. Jo's vocal rendition blasted out any remaining jet lag in my body and had me startle up wide awake and alert, as if I had just knocked back three strong Italian espressos in a row. Partly, it was because what came out of Jo's mouth was pleasant but different, *alien* even. Partly, because it was so powerful that I instantly felt its loud, high-pitched resonance, perhaps enough to break a slightly defective crystal goblet, penetrate through the pores of my skin and into the cells beneath. For such a tiny woman, Jo's voice was tremendous. A sophisticated instrument. She made a cacophony of harmonious sounds, much like a soprano moving up the musical scale, but there was something unique about how she used these vocals. The siren-like sounds she made were alien to me but, nonetheless, they caused a tingling sensation in the base of my spine, the area of the sacrum, around the navel, and to the solar plexus. It was as if Jo's voice was a tornado that had gathered speed and swirled through these points in my body, coming out the other side, sucking up anything in its way, and clearing these wheels of light, which I had no idea had been 'blocked'.

Jo stopped her chant-like singing after a transformative three or so minutes, leaving me feeling lighter, energised and enthralled. I wanted to know more, experience more, of whatever Jo had to offer.

After the meditation, I thanked her for this wonderful, healing experience.

"Why don't you come with me to the volcano to experience the mystical Hawaii? I've done healing work at the Kilauea Crater and I can tell you, it's a powerful experience," Jo said. "As it happens, I'm free tomorrow, if you have the time."

The effects of Jo's talent were already at work on me and I needed no further convincing. "Let's do it."

"We'll have to leave early, mind, very early. So that we can make it there for sunrise."

The next morning, I picked her up at five thirty from the post office on the corner of where the highway met the road to the Pu'uhonua'o Honaunau National Park. This park was also known as the Place of Refuge. In the days when Hawaiians lived according to the law of their community, anyone who committed a crime could turn themselves into the Refuge. There they would be safe from prosecution because the Refuge offered every person the opportunity to repent and reform. Today, the Place of Refuge was open to people to enjoy its peaceful seaside beauty.

I arrived a little early but Jo was already waiting for me in the car park of the post office. She got into my car and we were on our way to the Volcanoes National Park, an hour and a half to two hours away, along the Mamalahoa Highway. The morning air was crisp and fresh, even a little cool for these tropics, preparing for a hot and humid day to come.

"I've made some rice pudding for you to offer to Pele at the crater rim," she told me. I wondered who Pele was, but didn't want to ask.

"I've also brought along some of my special homemade macadamia nut chocolate," she continued.

"That sounds delicious ... and dangerous! It's very kind of you, Jo." Her generosity moved me. People on this island seemed more open and friendly than any I had met in a long time.

"Oh, you're most welcome. It's a good idea to make an offering of something that you've made yourself as well as some fruits. The native Hawaiians revere and honour their Goddess Pele with offerings of this kind. We'll be doing a ceremony at the rim of the volcano's crater. The offerings are a token that express their gratitude for Pele's protection and blessings," Jo said. "The ceremony that I'll be conducting at the crater is to connect to Pele. We will ask her to call in your ancestors so you can also make an offering to them."

The making of offerings to deities and honouring ancestors was all too familiar to me. I believed that you could never express gratitude enough for those on whose shoulders you stood and for the lineage that gave you the privilege of this incarnation.

I changed my mind about asking. "So, tell me about Pele."

"She's a Hawaiian goddess. Legend has it that Pele was the fierce goddess of fire, lightening and volcanoes. Her home was believed to be the fire pit called Halema'uma'u crater, at the summit caldera of Kīlauea, where we're headed. It's one of the most active volcanoes on the planet, by the way."

"Very interesting," I said, listening intently.

The more I learnt about the Goddess Pele, the more similarities I discovered between her and the Hindu Goddess Kali, also depicted as fierce, with dark skin and long, jet black flowing hair, similar to Pele's. Kali was the feminine divine force of transformation but with the tender, compassionate heart of a devoted mother. Pele, too, stood for transformation of the base human emotions into its higher, divine nature.

We continued to chat until Jo asked me if I had any Bollywood music on my iPod and insisted on hearing some of my favourite tunes for the rest of the drive. We arrived at the crater rim at around seven o'clock and parked the car in the parking area closest to the crater. The sun was still rising, casting soft warmth through the dewy mountain mist that would need some more coaxing from the sun's rays to disperse into a hot, humid, sunny day.

"We're going to do a ceremony at the rim of the crater. I've found it has really powerful results," Jo said.

I had no idea what kind of ceremony she was planning on doing, or how, or what kind of powerful results there would be. Going by how much freer in my body I had felt after just three minutes of Jo's vocals from yesterday evening, I could not help having faith in her unique gift for healing, and I was as open and excited as I could be.

I'd expected to see the volcano spitting fire and lava, but was disappointed. We were on the side where the crater, an enormous bowl miles wide, was hot and ashen, with sulphur fumes escaping from occasional vents. There were, however, no flames or molten lava seeping anywhere. That said, it did have a distinct and special vibe.

Jo found a spot that she thought was appropriate to conduct the ceremony.

"I'm going to begin by singing directly into your body," Jo said. Not wanting to appear totally loopy to passers-by, I was relieved to find that she and I were completely alone here. "I initiate sound frequencies that recharge the electromagnetic field of the body and re-establish the flow of *chi*. The sounds that I vocalise will stimulate your body to create its own frequencies that help to bring it into alignment with your innate Self."

Frankly, I had no idea what she meant and if I hadn't already had a profound experience the previous evening from her vocals, I would have dismissed this whole expedition with sharp scepticism.

"The siren-like vocals weave the harmonics from the lower to the higher dimensions so that you can better harmonise and transform the energetic dissonance within your *chakras* into a harmonious flow," she continued.

I struggled to understand. "Are you saying something like you can step out of a mindset of suffering into that of harmony and ease?"

"That's very well put indeed."

Frankly, much of what she said sounded mumbo-jumbo to me, but my experience from the night before had intrigued me. I loved and valued my intellect, but it could often hold me back from stepping into experiencing the magical and the sacred. I had learnt to put my intellect aside, suspend disbelief so to speak, so that I could experience something beyond the limitations of my rational and cynical mind. This had been one of my most challenging yet valuable lessons and I no longer fought it. I kept letting go of the cynicism of that little judgemental, clever voice in my head and found myself buzzing with anticipation and excitement at what was about to come.

"Ah. So that's what was happening to me when you were doing your vocals at Tracey's yesterday evening," I said.

"Yes, I call it frequency shifting, where healing is one of the consequences," Jo said. "Then we will call in Pele and ask for her blessings and thank her for granting us healing in her volcano, this powerful, sacred land.

"Hale Makua, my teacher and a Hawaiian elder revered in these islands, taught us that we must walk with respect and humility," Jo said. To make offerings to the deity who was believed to be protecting this land was doing just that. Jo referred to an overlook at the Kilauea Crater as 'Makua's Office'.

"This spot that we're standing on has a lot of life force, or *mana*, and it's used for special ceremonies. It's also a place where people go to commune with their ancestors," Jo said.

She asked me to stand straight as she placed her right hand a few inches away from my root *chakra* at the base of my spine. Then, she vocalised a startling sound that was very different to the one she had demonstrated the previous evening. It was almost as high-pitched, but a little more shrill and more powerful, primal yet harmonious. It was a sound that came from the very depths of her being, her soul. I felt the light-sabre of Jo's vocal weapon piercing through my first *chakra* like a fierce laser beam.

She then moved up, singing one by one in the region of each of the seven *chakras*. Jo's powerful and varied tones blasted through each individual energy centre. I felt the nerves in the area of the first three become more sensitive, making me feel itchy around the spine behind my waist and down my lower back. I couldn't help fidgeting as I scratched the itchy areas. It was as if tiny filaments, like threads of a cobweb, were twanging and breaking away, one by one, clearing the *chakras* that they had been clogging up.

As she toned into my fifth *chakra* at the throat, the centre of self-expression, I felt a sense of shedding a heavy, cumbrous load that I was unaware of carrying. Suddenly, my throat burned with irritation that I could not assuage and I burst into a fit of loud, uncontrollable, continuous coughing. Jo didn't stop, and this irritated me more. I found it hard to breathe. I felt the sensation of being forced to inhale, of being gassed, with some noxious substance.

I wished she would stop that awful racket! Why didn't she stop? Couldn't she see that I was in danger of suffocating any moment? I tried to tell her to stop but the words became cinders in the fire raging in my throat. She continued in toning her siren singing for what felt to me like an eternity, until whatever was blocking my throat *chakra* had cleared, in its own time and of its own volition.

A surge of energy then went through me, up the soles of my feet, through my ankles. Up my shins, knees and thighs, into my pelvis and up my torso where my lungs opened to inhale an unnatural amount of air of this sacred spot. The air flooded my throat, neck, and head, where I sensed a spontaneous opening at my crown, now tingling as if crackling firelight had simultaneously travelled from the molten core of the volcano up my spine and into my head. This was something I had never felt before.

I was light as a feather!

In that moment, I became powerfully present to the privilege of *being alive* on this beautiful, intriguing planet, for being able to *feel* with such intensity. I felt a mixture of joy and deep humility for the magic of this palpable experience. The majesty of my surroundings, some of the most magnificent landscape with a mystical atmosphere, made it all the more easy to soak in gratitude.

Jo was silent, not wishing to puncture with words the unfoldment of my experience.

She led me towards an area closer to the crater rim, and invited me to take a seat on the ground. She chanted something in ancient Hawaiian to Goddess Pele, gesticulating with her hands as she placed small amounts of the rice pudding, fruits and her special homemade chocolate on a spot on the earth. Just as Jo had finished her chant to Pele, with impeccable timing, a bird flew low and directly over my head. I felt the gush of air caused by its deliberate glide a few inches above my head.

"Wow! Did you see that?" Jo said, excited. "That was the rare Nene bird! It's Hawaii's protected national bird. Take that as an indication that Pele has accepted our offerings and granted her blessings to the prayer we made at the beginning of the ceremony."

I, meanwhile, was in a state of an effervescent calm, contentedness and peace. After a few minutes, Jo, still marvelling, again said, "That Nene bird was playing the role of being a messenger of the Goddess Pele, delivering her blessings from the depth of the volcano, I'm sure of it."

Whatever the case, I felt full, absolutely full, with aliveness, calm and gratitude.

Perhaps for the first time in my life, I knew what it meant to be 'fulfilled'. I was fulfilled!

I felt blessed.

I thanked the Nene bird mentally and I bowed, kneeling on Pele's earth, and offered my gratitude to the Goddess and especially to my ancestors, known and unknown, for bringing me to this exceptional day. In this state of humility, it was only natural to ask them to forgive me for things I may have inadvertently done to disappoint or disrespect them.

In that humble, fulfilled moment, I became one, a part of the whole of everything.

"Turn off the torch.

Learn to be guided
by your own light."

7

Rendezvous

It was still only ten o'clock in the morning when Jo and I finished the ceremony at the Halema'uma'u Overlook. By now, we were well overdue for some morning refreshment, and stopped nearby in the village outside the National Park for coffee and a snack.

I was quiet, blissfully so. My mind, body, and emotions felt a new quality of fragile, subtle calm. Though I did not know how it worked, I let my system process the impact of Jo's commanding *chakra* clearing vocals. The time with her had been more powerful than I had thought possible, like a tornado whirling through aspects of me I didn't know were there.

"Now, don't go trying to analyse and figure out what's happening in you," Jo said, reading my mind as I began to think about how her vocals and my energetic *chakra* wheels might have interacted. "This work taps into your higher intelligence. So you just let that take care of you."

I chuckled, like a naughty child caught with her hand in the cookie jar, as I was reminded of my habit to push the sun to come up. I relaxed.

"I think it'll be good for you to spend some time in nature today," Jo said. "You know, it's still only ten thirty and we're close to the Thurston Lava Tube. Would you like to see it? Its energy is extraordinary. It'd be good for you to anchor after that amazing session we had this morning."

The work that Jo had done with me had certainly had quite an impact on me. I had never smoked or tried magic mushrooms or hallucinogenic substances but I felt the effect of something of that sort. My head was spaced out and my body felt a heavenly, feather-like lightness.

"Hmmm ... Grounded, I am not," I replied, euphoric. "You didn't put any hash in your macadamia nut chocolate, did you, Jo?" Although I joked, the truth was my head was light and I had sensations of floating in space. I wasn't anchored to anything or anyone. There was just space, space and more space in my being. I was light. The vibrations of Jo's exceptional vocals still echoed through my energetic body. "Let's do it," I said. "But I think I'd like to be alone for a while and let the work you've done sink in. Would that be okay with you?"

"Of course," Jo replied. "I completely understand. There's a beautiful forest area outside the lava tube and I have a book in my handbag that I would be happy to catch up with reading."

After our snack, we drove to the Thurston Lava Tube. The grounds around it were indeed beautiful. A wooden footbridge provided access to the lava tunnel. Just as I stepped onto the bridge, having left Jo to her reading, she came running after me. "I nearly forgot," she said, out of breath. "I packed this torch for you. Here, you'll need it inside the tunnel." How well she was taking care of me, and I had only met her the day before.

Carved through lush, tropical fern forest, the walk to the tunnel took about twenty minutes from where I left Jo. The closer I got to the tunnel's entrance, the more I picked up on an air of the ancient, infused with mystery.

Formed over many millennia, this lava tunnel was once a vital and active part of the Kilauea Volcano. It was hard to imagine now that where I was standing once had molten rock, as red-hot as the surface of the sun, flowing through it, faster than a horse could run. Today, lava travels from Pu'u O'o to the ocean in a labyrinth of lava tubes within the volcano. The Thurston Lava Tube, however, was a retired part of the lava network. As I stepped inside this prehistoric cave tunnel's entrance, once hidden by a thick covering of fern and stalactites, I sensed its serenity and calm wrap itself around me.

Electricity provided ample lighting around the entrance. Children, their imaginations ignited, stepped gingerly as they took in their parents' explanations of the significance of being inside this once vibrant cave. I went along, now and then placing my hand on the cool rock walls to see if my extrasensory perception might give me more insights to its story. The lights became dimmer and dimmer the further I went, until it was difficult to see more than a few steps ahead, and I eventually walked into the velvet air of jet blackness. I remembered Jo's thoughtfully loaned torch and turned it on. The light from the torch, however, proved too dim. The dense darkness of the narrowing tube of the tunnel simply absorbed it. The air was thicker too, and I wondered how far into the cavernous labyrinth it was possible to go. More than being afraid of the darkness, my imagination ran riot with the thought of what unsavoury creepy-crawlies might have claimed these tunnels as their territory. With nothing else to see inside, I decided to turn around and head back the way I had come, providing I could find the same way again, especially with the lack of light and directions.

I heard a clear prompt. *"Turn the torch off and keep going ahead."* Startled, I stopped. The voice was so clear that I looked around to see if there was a person nearby. In the darkness I could see no one, nor did I sense the presence of another person nearby. I turned around and went back the way I had come.

"Turn the torch off, turn around and keep going straight."

This time the voice was louder and more emphatic and I could distinguish hearing it in my inner ears. It was the voice of my Inner Diamond, more lucid than ever before.

"But there was a big sign outside, warning that it could get quite dark inside, and who knows what creepy-crawlies are hanging out in there? In any case, what's the point of going in where I'll see nothing at all?"

"Turn off the torch. Learn to be guided by your own light," the Inner Diamond said.

Hesitant, I tentatively stepped into the blackness of the lava tube, completely alone, not a soul in earshot. Jo's healing tones continued to reverberate through my being. My solar plexus, cleansed by the tonal purity woven in Jo's healing voice, spun open in the darkness to reveal a laser beam of awareness. The area at the centre of my chest, the heart centre, began throbbing, undulating filaments of heat radiating outward from its centre. I couldn't see a thing with my normal eyes, but my inner sight stirred into action.

"Go, step by step. Let Pele wrap her protective arms around you. Listen and be present," my higher Self whispered as I continued ahead in the pitch-black cave.

"Step more to the right," or *"stay to the left,"* the Diamond would guide from time to time.

My eyes adjusted somewhat to the monochrome blackness but I couldn't see beyond my fuzzy hand in front of my face. A minute or two later, I started to see in the dark, as if a bright spotlight was being flashed in front of me and it was my Inner Diamond that had become palpably present. As well as hearing its words, I now felt its presence beaming within me like a clear, brilliant, sharply focused light that made me fearless and serene as I walked deeper into the old lava cave. My solar plexus and heart centre kept growing, melding, a golden light pouring out of its centre, tiny at first and then expanding, becoming larger than my body, encasing it, then growing larger than the circumference of the tunnel walls around me. I lost feeling of my physical boundaries in the perception of this effulgent golden glow. The boundaries between my ego and the Inner Diamond, the higher Self, dissolved in the darkness.

"You see, you don't need a torch," the Self whispered, impressing its brilliance in my heart centre. *"Not when you are the light."*

I could not know how long this experience lasted, but I wanted to keep holding on to it, longer than I was yet capable of doing. Just as suddenly as the light and internal navigation had come, so it disappeared.

The power of that experience triggered an overwhelming release, tapping an involuntary flow of tears. The protective hard shell of my heart, heavy with countless layers of armour, stuffed with the excruciating pain and sadness of my past, melted in the emergence of luminosity of higher awareness, loosening the chains of disapproval, rejection, judgement, and my identity.

Just as the volcano in whose ancient veins I stood once coursed with and expelled fiery lava, so I was at the effect of its purifying power even now, hundreds of years later. I realised how hard and unforgiving I had been with myself, and how wrong I had made myself for causing heartache to my parents and grandparents for breaking away from the traditions that they valued above all else.

As a punishment, I had subconsciously decided to kill off my happiness. Here, in this eerie underground seclusion of an ancient lava cave, I felt safe to be myself.

It was, at long last, safe to be with my Self.

8

Lost and Found

I f I'd imagined my adventures would be over once I left the depths of the cave, I would have been sorely wrong. My Inner Diamond had other ideas.

When I came out of the darkness, the sunlight streamed on my face, bathing it in its golden glow. As I adjusted to my latest experience, I felt neither calm nor anxious but a sense of just being. I made a move to head back to Jo but a sixth sense had me stop. I looked around, not sure myself why I had stopped, and followed my instinct to turn towards the clearing in the wooded area next to the cave entrance. Immediately outside was a path to a primeval-looking lush green tropical forest of huge tree-sized ferns. They looked like they could have been the last descendants of the giant ferns from the days of the dinosaurs. As if time had stood still for aeons, I could almost see these dinosaurs living in the folds of this forest. If the mystical, mythical land of Lemuria ever existed, I fancied it must have been here.

The forest, with all its bountiful lushness, invited me, compelled me, to come in. I stepped off the built-up path and onto a diverging, little-trodden path into the woods. Its ground was overgrown with all kinds of verdure vegetation. While I had been in the lava tube, it must have rained, because the giant green leaves I was stepping on and that hung all around me were dripping droplets of cool water. I wondered what secrets the forest held in its ancient volcanic soil.

As I walked into the forest, I tried to remember the markings of an unusual tree that I passed and another nearby colourful bush and anything else that appeared memorable. Absorbed in the moment, it seemed as though I had walked only a few steps off the main walkway, but I soon realised I was already deep in the forest, and alone. I tried to retrace my steps but, having circled around on the spot a few times, trying to remember which way I had entered, I had lost my bearings. I walked this way and that, trying to find the tree with the special markings and the bush with the colourful foliage, but I had no idea which way to go to get back. There wasn't a soul in earshot.

I panicked. Oh my God! I'm lost!

In my panic, I tried to retrace my steps this way and that, but it was useless. I was well and truly lost, and my mobile phone had no signal.

There was no one I could ask for directions. Except my astral satellite navigation—the Inner Diamond. "I'm totally lost. Please help me to find my way back," I said out loud, desperate, sweat breaking out on my forehead. My heart pounded hard and loud, constricting my breath, and my chest tightened. Mental images of being the subject of a search party excursion came to my mind. How embarrassing would that be? I had to get out of here!

So much for that inner light of mine. Why did it allow me to come here? How stupid did I feel to be lost, in a woodland, of all things.

"You are not lost. You are always guided. Listen and be present," my higher Self said.

So, again, began the guidance from the formidable internal navigation system.

"Turn around and go ten steps straight ahead." I heard the prompting in my inner ears. I obeyed. *"Now, turn ninety degrees to your left."* I did just that. *"Now, stop and go forty-five degrees to the right. Walk five steps ahead."* And

so on went the precise direction of my Inner Diamond, crystal clear and absolutely uncluttered by fear or negativity. Within minutes, I found myself on the footpath outside the fern forest.

"Know that you can trust your Self to triumph, in any situation," said my Inner Diamond.

Jo's healing vocals had helped to clear away the cobwebs in my *chakras* and, as a result, I was able to hear my higher Self with succinct clarity. She had blown away the layers of dust in my inner vision and hearing so that I could connect more intimately to the innate intelligence of my higher Self and avail of it with greater ease to make more assured, fulfilling choices.

My Inner Diamond nudged me through my intuition to go off-track so that it could teach me something that I would never again forget: I could *count* on myself, my higher Self, not just in grave situations but also in the more everyday, mundane ones. *It* did not discriminate between the world of the Earth and extra-Earthly realms. It was pure, innate intelligence. It was woven into each and every aspect of life, on Earth and everywhere else. It was not the one that compartmentalised life in terms of material existence and spiritual.

It just is. The One. Everywhere. Ever present. Ever awake.

It was I who had just woken up to its multidimensional existence. It was I who had to learn to remove the labels and boxes in which I had placed it.

It was ever liberated.

It was now my turn to assimilate that the higher Self was an aspect of me. The time had come to free myself from my erroneous belief that it was 'out there', and that it and I were somehow separate.

For me, time stood still. Jo, meanwhile, had waited patiently, sensing that something special had happened to keep me gone.

As she saw me approach, she exclaimed, "Oh my goodness! Look at you! You're glowing! And you look so different! Wow! What happened?"

I just smiled. There was plenty of time to tell her about my adventure and, in any case, I was famished. She suggested we make our way for lunch at the Lava Rock Café in Volcano Village, which turned out to be a pseudo-Scandinavian wooden cabin with a cheerful and airy atmosphere.

"Y'all look like you've had a good morning on Volcano," the cheerful waitress said.

"You bet," I replied, equally cheerfully. "That's very perceptive of you."

"Oh, my dear, I've worked here for so long that I can tell when Volcano has touched a person. When that happens, you're never the same again," she said. Jo and I looked at each other, impressed.

"Interesting," Jo said. "Can you really tell?"

"Yeah, that *is* interesting," I said. "What have you seen with people that tells you that something special has happened for them at the Volcano? I mean, most people are just tourists, aren't they?"

"Well, yes, and they've no idea how powerful an energy Kilauea has," the waitress said. "Some people respond better to it than others. I can't say exactly what it is that I'm able to pick up on, except that there's a certain radiance that surrounds them. It's a kind of openness that hasn't yet caught up with their mind. I don't know how else to describe it. It's just something I pick up on." Jo and I listened, fascinated, and nodded.

"What's your name?" I asked.

"I'm Shelley," she replied, smiling.

Shelley, the clairvoyant waitress, took our order of a large vegetarian taco salad with fries for me and a chicken fajita for Jo, lilikoi (passion fruit) cheesecake to share, and cappuccinos. After the waitress left, I recounted to Jo my experiences in the lava tunnel and the fern forest.

"That's amazing," she said, "how quickly shifts take place when you're ripe and ready for them. And you've just arrived here. We must talk at the end of your trip."

Jo had to be back home by three o'clock that afternoon and it was now almost one o'clock. We had to leave urgently as the drive back would be at least two hours. I insisted on paying for Jo's lunch along with my own and gave the waitress my MasterCard. After I'd picked up my payment slip, we hurried out to my car.

An hour and a half into the drive back to Jo's house in Honaunau, I suddenly had the thought that though I had picked up my receipt at the Lava Rock Café, in the rush to get back, I may not have picked up my credit card. I pulled the car over to the side of the road and looked frantically in my handbag for my MasterCard. It wasn't there.

"I must have left it behind at the café," I said, panicked. "What shall I do now? I can't just leave it there and, besides, I need it. How could I be so airheaded? Let's call the café and see if they've got it."

When I got through to the café, whose telephone number was thankfully on the receipt, I asked to speak to Shelley, our waitress. She was still working her shift. "Oh, I'm so happy to hear from you. Yes, we have your card here. I'm so sorry, it was my mistake to hand you just the payment slip, without the card. By the time I realised, you had already left the car park. I was worried that you might get stuck somewhere without it."

"Phew. Thank goodness it's with you," I said, relieved that I didn't have to go through the rigmarole of cancelling the card and, even worse, being without it throughout my journey. I arranged to pick it up later in the day. "Would you mind waiting for me until I get there, please?"

Shelley confirmed that she would wait for me.

Once I'd dropped Jo off at her house, I filled up the car with petrol and drove all the way back to Volcano, along the same route that I had driven earlier in the day. That morning, I had wished I could spend more time at the crater rim, where Jo had conducted the ceremony with me, and I was very happy to have another chance to return to Volcano.

Traffic was light this time and I reached my destination at around quarter to five that afternoon. The café was still open when I got there and the staff greeted me warmly as they handed me my MasterCard. They offered me coffee and snacks for free, but I felt pulled to going back to the crater rim while the daylight held. The drive from the café to the car park nearest the rim was but a stone's throw. The car park had only five cars parked, with mine being the sixth.

As I reached the crater rim, I noticed that it looked different from when we were there early in the morning. Sunlight now lit up the low, flat crater which earlier had been shrouded in the early morning mist.

I went as far to the edge as I could comfortably sit and gazed at the massive bowl-like crater in front of me. Once again, with so few visitors in this part of the park, I had the privilege of having this awe-inspiring, majestic place all to myself. Soaking up the pin-drop silence, I sat still, falling into an open-eyed meditation, appreciating my awesome luck for being able to do this, alone, in this special part of our planet. My focus deepened and, other than the point at the centre of the crater on which my gaze rested, everything else faded into a blur in my peripheral vision.

Then, I saw something extraordinary. Right there, in the centre of the crater, a pyramid-like structure stood tall. It was glass-like and translucent. I remembered similar but smaller pyramids that I had seen some years earlier in Giza, Cairo. My vision had a hazy and ethereal quality to it, and I realised it was not of this world but from another dimension, not visible to our naked eye.

I continued to watch, mesmerised by the scene, not caring how I was able to see this translucent, ethereal pyramid. What was I seeing? Was it real or was I seeing through my third eye? Out of the front side of the pyramid, a door opened and something flew out. Whatever it was, it flew towards me. As it came closer, I could see its enormous wings, not one pair, but three, staggered one on top of the other. At first, I thought it was some sort of flying contraption, much like a sophisticated, motorised flying kite. But the closer it came, the clearer it became that it wasn't a contraption but a being, an enormous being with enormous wings.

The inner vision of my third eye had suddenly opened up to me, without ritual, without the effort of trying hard, and without notice—just as it had some weeks before in the middle of my meditation when I had been able to commune with the angel-bird Michael.

Now, the being disappeared out of view but, behind me, I heard three full flutterings of large wings. It had to be a massive bird. Naturally, I turned to look behind me in the direction of the sound, but saw nothing—it was more that I felt the presence of something or someone familiar.

"Welcome back!" the voice said from behind me—a voice that sounded remarkably familiar. It was no accident that I'd come back here once again today. The being's presence felt familiar too, along with its soft, velvet voice, which was that of the angel-bird Michael, the one that I had encountered in my vision.

"Now stand up, turn and face the sun," the familiar voice guided me and I did so.

I didn't know what to say, and could only observe, and keep being open to these extrasensory perceptions.

I joined my hands together in *namaste* to greet this vision of the now familiar Michael and smiled. I turned around altogether to face Michael, and the late afternoon sun cast its glow onto my face, bathing it in its warmth. I could see the being whose voice I had heard a moment ago. It was Michael, the same angel-bird as the one who had allowed me its vision at my home in London. Only now, his peacock feathers were no longer there, replaced by three sets of wings: the first pair silver, the second gold, and the third white.

Though I was simply observing, like a witness, my own ego mind was beginning to kick in with questions. What was this place? What about the pyramid I just saw?

Michael heard me and responded telepathically. *"This crater has an unusual energy. It amplifies the frequencies of the subtle realm that exists in parallel and just beyond Earth to co-exist."*

"What was that pyramid I just saw? That was strange. I don't believe in UFOs," I asked.

"What you were being shown was an ethereal temple. It's not something that is visible to the naked human eye, unless revealed through the third eye, here." He lifted his arm and pressed the pad of his ring finger onto the spot between my eyebrows, just beneath the centre of my forehead.

As he did so, the light of the sun pierced through and penetrated that very spot, flooding my head with an immense brightness, and sending my sensory system into an overload that I didn't know I was capable of withstanding.

Then, the angelic Michael moved his digit down to the centre of my chest, and the sun's angle shifted just then, throwing its warmth onto my heart centre, alighting it with a yellow-orange brilliance.

"You are ready for your wings, though symbolic they may appear, they are yours to keep, should you so wish," he said.

"Me? How do you mean? Am I about to die?" I asked.

He laughed, a loud, hearty laugh. *"Not at all! In fact, you are just coming alive. Awakening."*

It was good to see that angels too could indulge in satire and irony.

"Oh. I see." I felt pathetic.

"These wings, silver, gold, and white, are your initiation into the inner realms, its temples, and the Akashic Libraries."

"Really?" I asked, stupefied. "What will I do with them?"

"You will become more Self-aware and directed even more by higher intelligence," he explained.

"Will that impact my ability to live in the real world?" I asked. "I mean, I can't afford not to work or do the things I do now."

"The 'real' world, as you call it, will become much more interesting. Because you will have a greater sense of who you are. You will begin to access more of your capacities that right now are hidden from your view. They are out of your reach." Michael's presence and energy were now so close to me, its rays pierced into my skin as if through individual needles. I felt moved beyond myself.

"I see," I said, holding back tears of gratitude for his generous grace.

"You will be able to get answers to your deeper questions directly," he replied. *"You will be able to see the inner realms more clearly and commune with the divine beings as if they were here with you."*

Now my body was a-tremor as the incredible privilege of this encounter sank into my ego mind. I asked, unable to entirely let in what I was seeing, "Am I imagining this, or is this vision real? And are you going around making this offer to everyone on the island, or just me?"

Michael laughed again, endearing him more to me. *"It's perfectly natural to question and disbelieve. We are inviting you because, since you were a little child, you have been working ceaselessly on yourself, often through difficult situations. We are here for you, just you. You are now ready for the knowledge."*

He smiled at me. His presence oozed unconditional love, melting away my defences.

"This knowledge you are speaking of, what is it? What will it be useful for?" I asked in spite of myself, feeling silly like a child, wishing I could be more gracious in my acceptance of this grace. My ego wasn't buying into it as easily as my heart.

"Can you describe to me how a mango tastes? Can you describe to me the fragrance of a jasmine or a rose?" Michael asked. *"This knowledge will speak to you in many dimensions and in many different ways. Let's just say for now that it will help you in the next part of your awakening. Among other things, it will allow you to be at peace with yourself, see into the heart of things, feel richer contentment. You will find it inspiring to be of service to others."*

"You mean it's not just mundane knowledge, like just in a book, but knowledge or consciousness, of how to be human expressing its divine spirit?" I asked.

"There, you have it! We said you were ready to move into higher consciousness," the divine Michael said playfully, the light in his eyes twinkling.

"I believe I am," I replied, finally able to accept the invitation. Michael moved closer to me, enveloping me in a grace that poured into the darkness of my fractured heart, blossoming it fully open.

He pulled the silver wings from his back. Then I felt his gentle touch on the middle of my back, and a sensation of sail-like ethereal wings behind me. *"Silver,"* he said. Then he pulled the golden wings off his back and tapped me a little on mine and planted them there, saying, *"Gold."* And finally, he took the white pair of wings and gave me a final tap, this time on my upper back, and said, *"And white, too."*

I looked at him, not knowing if my bones were still holding up. In the warm light and love of this being's presence, my mind had finally surrendered my boundaries to his unconditional presence. *"You will be shown, gradually, how to use them. And use them well!"*

I was completely astounded. This experience and encounter had come unexpectedly out of the blue. Yet a question remained in my mind, now bigger than when I had left London.

Why had the angel Michael shown himself to me? He wasn't an everyday part of my frame of reference, though of course, growing up in Britain, I had come across the role of this angel and his significance in the Abrahamic faiths. So why show up for me?

" ... everything that I
needed to be whole,
truly was with within."

9

Dolphins

Dan dropped the big black sack with my snorkelling equipment, hired from Jack's Diving Locker in Kona, into the boot of his car. "Let's go," he said. He'd come to pick me up from my hotel so we could travel together to the marina where Captain Mike's boat was moored.

"You bet," I replied. "I've been itching for this day to arrive since I left London."

It was a typical Big Island summer morning, already hotting up at just seven o'clock, with the sun blazing with azure blue skies and not a single cloud in sight. Freshness filled the tropical air with subtle scents of the hotel's garden flowers and newly cut grass. I, too, was filled with anticipation and excitement. I had never seen wild dolphins, let alone swam with them, but since being on the island, I had heard many stories from people about the intelligence of these creatures. Many people believed that dolphins had mystical and healing powers. People spoke with reverence about these animals, implying there was something sacred about them. Despite being a seasoned scuba diver, I had never come across them before and decided to keep an open mind. In any case, I didn't need much of an excuse to be in the sea.

We arrived at the Honokohau Harbour and, after parking his car, Dan took me to check-in for the boat trip. The boat was a good size, big enough for perhaps twenty-five or so people. Dan introduced me to a congenial Captain Mike, who, along with his crew, was ushering guests onto the boat and busy loading up with supplies for the trip. Cling film-covered steel plates of cut, fresh pineapple and oranges, blueberry muffins, chocolate chip muffins, and mixes of Danish pastries, were brought on board, along with bottles of water.

Once everybody was on the boat, Captain Mike had everyone join in as he began with a Hawaiian ceremony that set a mystical tone to what we were about to experience. He said something in Hawaiian and then gave an explanation. It was an invocation and a prayer to appreciate that we were all part of the one universe, to connect with the spirit of the dolphins and that our encounters with them may be enriching for all concerned.

As we set off from the harbour, he explained the protocol for how to behave around the dolphins, what not to do to arouse their defence, and how to encourage them to be comfortable with you. Captain Mike's knowledge of these creatures was considerable and it was clear that he and his crew had an unusual connection with them.

I knew nothing whatsoever of the world of the dolphins and I couldn't wait to encounter them. The question that had been lingering in my mind was now foremost: why did the Goddess in Green specifically guide me to swim with dolphins?

I sat down with another lady from England, Alicia, on the deck of the boat, at the very tip of the boat's bow facing out towards the sea, hanging onto the steel railing while we dangled our legs, knees and all, down the boat's front. With the boat moving at good speed on this bright, hot and sunny morning, a heavenly breeze, warm and most welcome, caressed us top to toe. My long, dark tresses were flung back, blowing like ragtag locks while the sunlight bathed and glinted on the brilliant blue mirror of the Pacific.

Captain Mike seemed to be busy on the boat's radio and then, quite abruptly, he slowed the boat down and changed direction, presumably on instruction from whomever he had been talking with on his radio. The boat picked up speed again, moving further away from the charming Kona Coast. I wasn't quite sure what he was doing, but then he shouted out to tell us, "We're looking out for dolphin pods. They could be anywhere and show up any time. So please keep your eyes peeled for any movement that looks like it could be dolphins."

Everyone stopped talking, and went to the sides of the boat and looked out across the ocean for signs of dolphin life. Twenty or so minutes went by, but we saw nothing.

Now that I was here, travelling the open seas once more, I realised just how much my soul yearned being at sea. The yearning was familiar and deep, as if buried in the depths of my subconscious mind, perhaps from a past long ago. Though I hadn't been conscious of it, now I was here I felt as though I loved it so much that I could sell all my belongings just so I could be in the open sea air again, under the bare blue skies, on a boat or a ship. This felt all too familiar. The boat gave a sudden jolt as it collided with a big wave. The impact tossed the boat into the air and it landed with a heavy thud. As I strengthened my grip on to the steel railing at the bow, I had an unexpected flashback. I suddenly saw myself as *Capitaine* de Jourdain on a ship across the seas, perhaps around Asia or the Caribbean, navigating his ship through rough, challenging waters. It seemed my subconscious mind held memories that were imprinted deep in my soul and that occasionally escaped to the surface of my awareness as a desire or longing for something that otherwise felt anachronistic to my current life.

About half an hour after we had left the Kona Coast, Captain Mike hailed everyone's attention. "Look over there," he said, waving to his left. "There's a couple of dolphins at the surface." Everyone rushed to have a look, excitement building.

"Oooh! Look over there!" A woman let out a squeal. "Look, look! They're spinning!" Sure enough, a couple of dolphins had leapt out of the water and were airborne, twirling high and then higher, before nose-diving into the water again, disappearing completely out of our view.

A few minutes later, we spotted around six of them, not too far from our boat, gracefully dipping in and out of the water, delighting and thrilling us all. I was captivated. What mastery they displayed in the water and flying through the air, despite the substantial weight of their one hundred-and-twenty pounds or so. They allowed us to follow them with our gaze for a few minutes, and then they too went under and disappeared.

Spotted by one of the twelve-year-old boys, the next sighting happened about ten minutes later. Mike slowed and brought the boat to a standstill while the dolphins were in our view. They showed less exuberance than the last pod and gave us a display of dips and dives as they came up to the surface for air. After a while, they disappeared all at once under the ocean. We waited, expecting them to turn up again, but around ten minutes had passed and they were nowhere to be seen. Mike said they had probably gone on their way for good, and so he restarted the boat and sped off. We carried on scanning the ocean's surface for the next dolphin pod.

After what felt like an eternity, suddenly, as if out of nowhere, a pod of glistening grey dolphins appeared, perhaps thirty or forty of them, each one between six to six-and-a-half feet in length. They picked up their swimming speed and swam alongside the bow of our boat. Captain Mike kept the boat at a steady pace and the dolphins kept up with us, weaving in and out of the wake we created as we cut through the water. More dolphins joined in and competed for the supreme spot, ahead of the boat's bow.

Spontaneous squeals of delight rent the air as the dolphins boundlessly weaved in and out of the bow's wake, playfully leaping out of the water and spinning, maybe four, five, six, or seven times, before diving, snout down, into the ocean, only to start all over again. It was a game they played among themselves, a game of who could swim the fastest, fly the highest, and spin in the air the most number of times. And yet, all done in the spirit of vivacious joy.

This pod stayed with our boat for more than ten minutes. Captain Mike decided that it was time to slow the boat down and see if the pod would stay long enough for us to join them in the water. "Get your masks and fins on," he said. "It's time to go in." The crew gathered at the stern, and lowered two metal ladders that would give us entry into the water. People got into the water one by one.

I was ready, waiting my turn. Despite the heat and breeze, the hairs on my arms were erect with excitement. When scuba diving, I'd had plenty of practice jumping from a boat into the water, so I bypassed the ladder and leapt in, holding my mask in place with one hand.

Some of the children and teens, once in the water, were uncontrollable with excitement, creating too much splash, flapping with their fins, and making a lot of noise, chasing willy-nilly after this dolphin and that. I could see that the dolphins were quick to move away, only to be chased harder. I decided to swim around, looking under the surface to watch out for any dolphins nearby. Several came and went by much too fast, but remained close.

I swam around for a while, vigilant and hoping for any dolphins that might let me join them, but just being in the warm ocean, almost twenty-five to twenty-seven degrees Celsius, I was already on cloud nine. It was as though these waters had a special quality about them.

Then, one huge dolphin appeared from nowhere and glided through the water alongside me, almost taking my breath away. She looked sideways at me and swam past. I was struck by her energy. She seemed boundless and blissful, and the wide curved beam of her mouth gave her a joyous, smiling expression. Then she turned her head somewhat, glancing back at me, and dived ahead so that I could no longer see her. Her vibe was one of friendliness and fun. When she had moved past me, I couldn't help noticing a long dark scar just above her left pectoral fin and another, smaller, mark within two inches of the first. She came and went a couple of times more. She and I were getting to know each other. I thought of her as a 'she' because the words *'aanand saagar'* popped up for her in my mind, meaning 'ocean of bliss' in Sanskrit. I started thinking of her as *'Aanandi'*.

The same dolphin returned and again swam up to my right, alongside me. I slowed down my breathing and quickly steadied my movement as I didn't want to scare her away. Aanandi continued to swim alongside me, checking me out with her sideways glance. I could have sworn she was smiling at me, or perhaps it was that I couldn't help smiling at her as she checked me out, curious and purposeful. I held back from smiling too much, cautious that too much movement of my facial muscles might cause the waterproof seal of my snorkel mask to leak and steam up my mask. The last thing I wanted was to have to fiddle around with my mask in these precious moments. I looked at her, and realised she was looking directly into my eyes. My heart beat faster from the excitement of this interaction. It felt amazing to be so close to this magnificent dolphin.

I realised that I was now a way away from the others in the group. I could see some people perhaps as far as sixty feet away. The dolphin then speeded up her pace and pulled ahead of me. I watched her, thinking that she'd had enough of checking me out. But then she turned her head, looking at me, and slowed down a little. She was waiting for me to follow and catch her up. My senses perked up so that I was fully in the moment, present, and realised that this dolphin was inviting me to join her, away from the rest of the crowd.

I quickened my pace and followed her. After a while, she slowed down and once again joined alongside of me but, this time, she came so close as to almost touch me. I moved my hand to stroke her, but remembered that Captain Mike had specifically said that we were not to touch the dolphins as it would interfere with the bacteria on their skin and possibly harm them. I pulled back my hand but wished that I could stroke her long, dark scar and wondered how she came to have it. The glistening grey Aanandi glided ahead and dived down, circling beneath and behind me and to my left, then coming back full circle, floating alongside me to my right. I could barely contain my excitement. This creature was play personified, boundless with energy and joy. She came even closer to my horizontal body and deliberately, but gently, bumped into me. *She* wanted contact. *She* was inviting me to touch her. I extended my arm and placed it on her back. I stroked her firm, silky smooth exterior. Under my touch, I felt a tremor run through her back. She was loving this. And I was in ecstasy.

Then she picked up her pace and disappeared. I turned around and circled all the way round to see if I could find her again, but Aanandi was nowhere to be seen. I could see the rest of our group was at least thirty feet away but I made no effort to join them. I wanted to put into practice the technique of floating on the surface of the ocean that Dan had taught me some days ago.

Turning on my back, onto the deep blue of the Pacific, I adopted the yoga posture called 'the corpse', resting my arms and legs wide with face up to the sky.

I was floating again! Effortless, weightless, buoyant, with the vast, warm ocean contouring my every curve like a perfect glove, the ecstasy of being with the dolphin still coursing through my being.

This was so liberating.

I floated for a few minutes, then I heard the chirpy clicks, whistles, and squeals of dolphins. Not wanting to miss sighting them, quick as a flash, I turned over onto my belly and peered through my snorkel mask into the deep blue. And there she was again, Aanandi with the long, dark scar above her pectoral fin and another smaller one close by. This time, she had brought others from her pod with her, two adults and two tiny little ones. I was beside myself with delight. I had never seen baby dolphins, but I imagined that, like any other creature, these mothers were extremely protective of their young. I didn't want to alarm the new dolphins and their calves, so I once again tried to slow down my breathing into a calm, smooth rhythm and became almost still, floating face down, just watching to see what the pod would do next.

Aanandi, so svelte and graceful, dived deeper below me while her two friends swam a little ahead of me on either side, the two babies closely in tow. I, still keeping myself in watch, keen to win the trust of the two mothers, followed them on the surface as swiftly and smoothly as I could, enjoying the sun warming and tanning my skin ever darker.

Aanandi reappeared, this time with something floating from her rostrum. It was a leaf, a piece of seaweed, that she had gone off to pick up. She then let go of the leaf from her long, slender snout. One of the mothers glided over to pick it up in her beak and swam up, close to the surface. Then she dropped it, too, and the third dolphin went over to collect it. And so they played among themselves for a while, giving me a show of their play and friendship. The mothers allowed their little ones to join in after a while.

This was just exquisite.

Then something even more unexpected happened. One of the two mother dolphins recovered the leaf and she dived upwards, coming within an arm's length of me. She then held up the leaf between her teeth and waited for me to catch it, just as she sent it floating up to me.

This was beyond my wildest dreams.

The dolphins had been carrying out a ritual play among themselves, showing me how it was done and then invited me to play the game with them. I caught the leaf, dived down to demonstrate that I accepted their invitation, and let go of the leaf for the same mother dolphin to catch in her beak. The dolphins were so excited that I was participating in their play. Then it was Aanandi's turn to send the leaf in my direction, followed by the second mother dolphin.

This ritual play had a massive impact on me. Aanandi, who I gathered must have been the matriarch among this small pod, had somehow sought me out and allowed me the privilege of being accepted by her and her pod. She had seen something in me that had her trust me and take me in. Why had she chosen me?

Then, Aanandi glided ahead, leapt up into the air, dipped and dived back down again, and came back towards me. Her friends, the mothers, followed and did the same, one after the other. What happened next was so beautiful that I nearly forgot to breathe. When it was the turn of one of the mothers, she leapt out of the water and up into the air, but this time twirling and spinning, perhaps as many as six or seven times, before landing back, rostrum first, in the water. Her friend, the other mother, followed and gave a stunning spinning display too. As if this wasn't enough, the best was yet to come. Once the dolphins rejoined their calves, encouraged by their mothers, they too were eager to spin. So both the calves mustered up all their strength in their tiny little bodies and flung themselves into the air and managed a cute, half spin each.

After having a few goes, one of the babies dived upwards towards me and glided alongside me, full of beans, for a moment or two and then went back down again to join her mother.

I was in paradise, floating in sheer delight.

When the dolphins had enough of jumping, diving, twirling, and spinning, I found them circling, in a single file, beneath me. It was as though they, too, were mesmerised by the sunlight streaming into the ocean—a prism, refracting the golden rays to form a huge, fluid pyramid, casting a mystical haze under the transparent blue of the ocean's surface.

Aanandi swam in a circle, joined by the two mothers and calves. They went round directly beneath me in circles and sent up bubbles that looked like round and hexagonal glass crystals. The bubbles kept coming up towards me, travelling up the beams of light that flooded into the ocean. In this moment, there was just me with the dolphins, in what seemed to be another ritual game they were playing with me. Time stood still for me as these extraordinary beings danced around beneath me in a circle, sending up streams of crystal, glass-like bubbles in my direction, a mystical haze of sunlight filling the pyramid beneath the surface of the cobalt blue ocean.

I was utterly enthralled. Deeply touched and moved by this exceptional encounter, I was melting beyond repair.

These beings of delight, how generous they were. What could I possibly give them? It occurred to me that this pod had taken me into their circle and the bubbles were, in this ceremony swimming in circles, their gift to me. The ultimate that these dolphins could give me was their breath, all the more precious for these creatures submerged under water. They were giving me their very breath of life, their *prana shakti*, in a beautifully orchestrated ceremony, led by Aanandi, the matriarch.

I was moved to tears, my mask fogging up, at these profound interactions with these wild creatures. They had shown me the beauty in their ability to express their playfulness and joy. The Goddess in Green had told me in my dream to go and swim with dolphins and I now understood why. These beautiful beings had acted as mirrors for me. Simply by being true to their nature, they had shown me that, in dealing with life's challenges, I had shut down to my own innate nature. I had become too intense and serious and it was time to be true to my own inherent self.

They had demonstrated to me that it was possible to live with playfulness and with joy, even in a dangerous and wild world. This reminded me that it was perfectly okay to *feel* again, and not just the challenging emotions, but those lighter ones, too. It was okay to have fun again.

I felt an enormous respect for these elegant creatures, bringing up their young in the middle of a vast, wild, and unpredictable ocean, strewn with dangers every minute of every day. Compared to them, with all my comforts and luxuries, I felt clumsy in how I navigated through life.

Aanandi and her friends demonstrated that you didn't need much to be happy. You could be happy with very little, if you so chose. The rest was a bonus, not a necessity. It was I, only I, who was keeping myself from being happy.

Just like the dolphins circling round and round beneath me, playing with me in the prism of light, I too had come full circle, realising more than ever that, far from being a cliché, everything that I needed to be whole, truly was with within.

The secret was to dive into that ocean of *shakti*, the power source, and playfully create life, with ease and grace.

This was the power of the Mother Goddess at work, shown through these joyous dolphins that embodied ease and grace. All kinds of emotions ran through me. It felt as though somehow, the Mother Goddess had brought me on a journey to cleanse away the sticky remains of my past, here in this enchanted ocean. In the midst of Aanandi, the matriarch, and the two mother dolphins and their newborns, I was being graced a rebirth.

After a last glance at me, the pod swam away. It felt like a natural close to an extraordinary and fulfilling experience. I would never see these beautiful beings again, but would ever be grateful to them for what they had taught me, something that I would take away and integrate into my daily life.

Just as the dolphins left, Captain Mike waved and approached with the boat to pick me up. The others were already on board when I climbed in, animatedly recounting their personal experiences of seeing dolphins spinning and swimming after them.

I was bursting to share what had just happened and said, "That was just extraordinary! I actually played the leaf game ..." and stopped mid-sentence. It felt like too sacred an experience to tell others about until I had absorbed and integrated it within myself.

Captain Mike winked at me, smiling. He understood that something magical had just happened. He had enjoyed similar encounters himself with those exquisite beings, experiences that had him commit his life in service of having other people discover the special nature of these spirited Hawaiian Spinner Dolphins.

He turned to the group and said, "Those dolphins are wise creatures. They have a natural instinct for knowing when and whom to let someone into their inner circle."

10

Hidden Beach

At Kauai's Lihue Airport, I went to the rental office to pick up my rental car, essential for getting around the island. To my surprise, just as had happened on the Big Island, the agent cheerfully informed me, "Miss Joshi, you'll be pleased to know that we're giving you a higher category of car to the one that you've reserved." Reading the question on my face, he replied, "Free of charge." Ah, those sweet words that never failed to put a beam on my Gujarati face. Driving away in the top of the range luxury car, my heart was thankful for these beautiful blessings, now becoming the norm.

I was keen to take some offerings to the Hindu Monastery and Temple, where I planned to go the next morning. Mangoes, pineapples, and a beautiful flower garland or *lei* made with locally grown flowers. I also wanted to dip my feet as soon as possible in the sea, which to my disappointment, was impossible to do on the black lava rock shore immediately outside my hotel.

The hotel receptionist had told me to head south towards Koloa, where she said that I would find the fruits and garland I wanted to buy. Having driven about twenty minutes from my hotel, quite by surprise, I came into a breathtaking tree tunnel. The late afternoon sun poured through even the tiniest gap in the copse, its trees creating a magnificent canopy above. The streams of sunlight and the shade from tightly woven eucalyptus branches overhead melded to give an air of timeless enchantment that could have been as ancient as the island itself.

Like a gateway, the tunnel opened into the old sugar plantation town of Koloa, where among its quaint shopping parade was a small grocery shop with flower garlands that boasted and celebrated the tropical flowers cultivated on these islands. I picked a masterfully crafted garland of pink and lime green orchids, punctuated with fragrant jasmine, or *pikake*, that brought back vivid memories of my childhood in India, playing in my grandfather's passionately nurtured garden. The offering of this flower garland and fruits was my way, however humble, of expressing my gratitude for the healing and abundant blessings that enriched my life.

As I soaked up the welcome shade under the monkey pod trees in Koloa's shopping parade, I had my fix of Big Island's Kona coffee and a treat of Kauai's speciality, Lappert's ice cream. Whenever I travelled, I made it a point of acclimatising to the local environment by trying out, at least once, the specialities of the land. It was my way of embracing the local experience and, for my sweet tooth, having speciality ice cream and coffee on this bijou isle was about as close as it could get to being in paradise. The one thing that could top this was to be here but with the man who had stolen my heart. Alas, for that, I would have to wait a bit longer.

Curious to find out what else was in the area, I carried on driving further south along the road signposted towards Poipu. It wasn't too long before I realised that I must have missed a turning on the way as, just past a big hotel, I ended up on a wide and unpaved cane field road.

I was about to turn to go back when my instinct said to continue ahead, so I carried on. My belly came alive with little flutters, the kind which hinted I was about to discover something that would delight. At the T-junction, facing a mountain at the end of the unpaved road, I stopped and followed my hunch to turn right into a narrower dirt track with tyre markings that gave the impression it was a path that was in regular use. I went past a couple of turn-offs to my left, and after about a mile or so the dirt track became narrower and rock-strewn. Then, every few yards, it got rockier and narrower, becoming treacherous to drive along.

The further I went, the more my car became hemmed in by the rocky sides of the narrowing track until there were only inches between either side of the car and the tall, boulder verge. So far, I had not passed a soul. I could just about get my car though this single lane and, if a vehicle was to approach from the opposite side, we would both be in trouble. I drove carefully to avoid puncturing my tyres and wondered if I was pushing my car's capabilities on these stony, rocky, virtually off-road conditions. I could not see where this dirt track was leading to, and I had no idea how, if I got stuck here, I would get myself out of trouble.

I did not know where I was or where I was headed, or even why I was here.

Fear began to seep through now, and my heart beat faster and pumped harder by the minute. Beads of hot perspiration dampened my forehead. I stopped the car and tried to figure out how I might be able to turn around and head back to civilisation, but that was out of the question. The dirt track was at its narrowest with no gaps to manoeuvre other than go straight on. It would be impossible to turn the car around. Maybe I could reverse all the way back to the T-junction where I turned. I felt desperate but, having already driven a considerable way, which seemed like just a hop and a skip in this smooth, new car, I could not contemplate driving back in reverse. Now, I was worried. This road looked like it led to nowhere. What had I got myself into? It was almost five o'clock in the afternoon. How much longer did I have to get myself out of here before sunset? Muscles in my legs felt like they were melting and my knees turned lifeless. Panic set in. I got out of the car and looked around, hoping to see someone, anyone.

My head and intuition were now battling with one another. My head said to reverse all the way back, but my gut insisted there was something special at the end of this track, worth taking a risk for.

Amidst this battle, my mind weakened. *"What a stupid thing to do!"* said that critical little voice in my head that I had not yet succeeded in taming. *"You're pathetic!"*

"Thank you for sharing!" I said out loud. "I'll ask for your opinion when you've got something constructive to say."

That little voice of my fearful ego popped up from time to time and still had power over me. It brought up resistance, usually just when I was about to get a breakthrough with some big issue that I was hard at work on resolving. Nemesis to intuition, it would hammer my confidence and make me doubt my self, and sabotage my choices, especially my choice of partner.

Its jittery internal conversation confused me as to what to do and had my heart raging with panic. Should I risk reversing back, or risk keep going? In desperation, I put out a prayer to Lord Ganesh, the remover of obstacles, and asked—no, begged—for his help to get me out of this jam before the sun left the sky.

It was already too late to turn back and so my decision was made for me. I drove forward again and within minutes I came to an opening. It was just big enough to allow one car through. I peered through the gap and realised that it led to a clearing in an arched wooded area.

A couple of cars were parked in the clearing and I heaved a sigh of relief, strength returning to my shredded nerves. The thicket of shrubbery was dense and silent and I still did not know where I was or why I had felt compelled to drive here. I got out of the car, walked along a path that looked somewhat trodden, and within just a few paces, it led to a wide open scene.

I could not believe what I was seeing. Hidden from popular reach, it was a beach of pristine white sand with glorious views of a calm Pacific as far as the eye could see.

A bright, cloudless, late afternoon sky intensified a rich palette of oceanic blues stretching out into the horizon while gentle aqua salt waves rolled in a light breeze. I took off my sandals and walked barefoot along the soaked sand in the ebb and flow of the warm waves, thinking I had died and gone to heaven.

There was something rare about this secret spot and not just because it was picture-perfect stunning. The air was clean and energetically charged, oozing pure, *pranic* life force. In just a few minutes, my 'batteries' were recharged, mind, body, and spirit at peace, aligned with one another.

I walked along the beach, shallow waves washing my feet, and carried onto the very end where the soft sandy beach abruptly gave way to a lava rock shoreline that culminated into a canyon cliff. I hiked to the top of the cliff, from where I could see the ocean pitch and roll, and the waves competing high to topple and crash one over the other. Towards the cliff edge, I found a small, flat rock that looked like it would make a good seat from which to enjoy the view. I made myself comfortable there and took in the clean, charged air deep into my body. The emotional resistance driven up along my journey subsided, quelling my fearful little voice.

My eyes feasted on the beauty of the playful surf below and the proud mountain canyons behind me. Still astonished at my good fortune to have chanced upon this hidden shore, I acknowledged in my heart the gratitude to my Inner Diamond for guiding me here.

For a while, with an unrepressed smile on my face, I just stared at the magnificence of this piece of our planet and then, eventually, closed my eyes. I simply sat there on the rock, taking conscious breaths of the salty air, and listened to the chorus of waves crashing against the solid rock, millions of years in the making. As I listened more intently, I found myself surfing the sound of the waves. They began to divulge their rhythm and lyrics, the mystical *mantra* of AUM. I ebbed and flowed in deep meditation, entranced by the language of the ripple and roll of the crests below. Under cover of the now pink and orange streaked sky, amidst the thunderous crashing of waves, grew a rapturous stillness in my mind.

I soaked in every millisecond of every moment here, breath calm, smooth and long, slipping into that fragile spot of deep, silent emptiness, just being, with no place to reach.

After a while, the emptiness turned slowly into a hazy mist. I tried to hang on as long as I could to the blissful state of emptiness but it gave way to a movement in the haze, an undulating blur, a muted shimmer. At first, I dismissed it as being a trick of the light but the blur became bigger and moved towards me in my inner view. It came closer to me, taking form and shape, its hues now sharper, flashing tints of green and gold.

Then, the form became clear. It was a woman, shapely and beautiful, her skin glowing golden, as if some superior light powered her from within. Wrapped in sheer gossamer of greens with woven threads of delicate golds, her elegant being came closer and closer towards me until I could sense her energy. Her vibe felt familiar, as if I knew her. Now that she was even closer, almost directly in front of me, I could see that there was something strangely odd about her. Her gossamer *sari*, draped around her body and held up over her left shoulder, loosened its grip somewhat, revealing the blouse that covered her chest. She had three breasts.

It was the Goddess in Green with the three breasts who had appeared in my dream just after my operation. It was she who had told me in my dream to go to the temple with the special crystal and to swim with the dolphins.

Now the Goddess in Green was less than an arm's length from me, looking at me with the concern of a mother who had not seen her child in what seemed to her like aeons. I had never known such purity of feeling and could hardly bear to look upon her face, my strong will still at work, in case I might dissolve right there and then.

Her golden face lit up in a smile to melt the hardest of hearts and bring even the dead to life. She remained silent, scanning her hand in front of my third eye, and then heart centre, gracing me with her tender gaze. Her presence, pure love, pierced into my very being. Her hand swept over my solar plexus, alighting my inner senses and sending my awareness soaring. Once again, just as I had felt at the crater rim in the presence of the angel-bird Michael, the centre of my chest was compelled, despite the best efforts of my intellect to resist, to spin open like a lotus-petalled stargate that had a life all its own.

"You came to see me," she said, smiling. Like a little puppy dog, I just kept looking at her, tongue-tied in her awesome glow, feeling rather pathetic. I wanted to speak, but my intellect had disappeared, fear and resistance too, fell away.

In her magnetic presence, I could only 'think' with my heart.

"Of course, I did! How could I not respond to your call?" I answered, conversing telepathically, in the language of the soul, beyond words. "But why have you called me here?"

"It is time that you know who you are," the Goddess in Green replied. *"Just as you had to go through the traumas of your young years, so it is for you now to receive a transmission of your Mother's grace,"* she said, referring to herself.

So saying, she extended her arm and placed her hand on my right shoulder, and then her left hand on my left shoulder. Under her touch, it was as though my body was made of clay plaster. In the direct presence of her unconditional love, these layers of plaster that had protected my unhealed wounds, cracked willy-nilly, pieces of clay falling off my being until, piece by piece, all of the outer shell had cracked and crumbled to the earth.

"Devi Ma, am I imagining this? Are you really here? And if so, why do you grace me with your *darshan*, your blessings? I am just an ordinary, average girl, trapped in the maze of my own *karma*." I conveyed my pain, my heart feeling raw from the impact of this realisation.

"Yes, I am very much here, with you. Why you? Because your heart is true and I heard its call, again and again. I heard your soul's yearning to be free," she replied.

"So let me take your suffering. It is time," she impressed her words on me telepathically.

"The pain of being scorched with judgement, I see it. Let me take that from you. The agony of feeling rejected, surrender to me accepting you."

She waved off, like worn-out sheer chiffon scarves, layer upon layer of my old being as she communicated with me in that language beyond words, a language sensed. My deepest fear, my hardest resistance floated away, beyond choice and control.

My mind knew the difference between the reality seen through the eyes and that which I was now experiencing, through the inner eye. And yet, this was just as real, if not more so, as the everyday reality. Somehow, my inner reality became just as valid and true as the one I woke up to every morning and the two were no longer mutually exclusive.

Then she continued to speak, *"Feeling abandoned and that no one understood, sense me holding you now. Unbearable sorrow for your mother's pain, give it to me to heal. Grief of feeling you don't belong, of feeling alone, separate, let me take that too."*

I was now completely willing to surrender my old friends—sorrow and suffering.

Overwhelmed, a submerged well of hot tears gushed onto my face as the Goddess in Green held me in the grip of her gracious gaze, showing me what it was to be loved and unreservedly accepted.

She stepped forward, even closer to me, and wrapped her arms around me in a warm, loving embrace. In that moment, a spontaneous merging took place, unleashing a fresh flow of lifeblood in me. All that remained of me was that which was at my core, a brilliant, sparkling diamond, my very soul, all that I ever was and ever would be.

"It is time to see the light," my higher Self had told me earlier.

When I opened my eyes, the slowly waning sun painted the sky with strokes of intense golden oranges, peaches, and pinks. My face, still damp from the outpouring of purifying, salty tears, slowly dried. My heart, which had revolved open—a lotus catalysed into full bloom—felt more vulnerable than ever before. My ego and intellect, having had no choice, had melted, seduced in the power of this life-altering vision.

I did not know if the Goddess in Green had been my higher Self in disguise, or whether the Goddess existed in her own right. What I was certain about was that without the bridge that was my higher Self, none of these transformational experiences were possible.

I was light.

I was free.

That was all I needed to know.

11

Heavenly Temple

Early the next day, before driving to the Hindu Monastery and Temple, I popped into the Java Kai coffee shop in Kapaa for my morning coffee. I took a seat outside in the gentle heat of the not-long-risen sun.

"Morning coffee fix, huh?" an older man from the table next to mine asked. He must have been in his late fifties or even early sixties.

"Yes," I smiled. "Something like that." I loved that easy manner of Americans to start a conversation with perfect strangers, as if they had known them forever.

"That's a real pretty accent you have there. Where you from?" he asked, rather predictably. And rather predictably, from my British perspective, I had to constrain reacting to my own thought, *how can an accent be pretty?* That was like saying that the aroma of a freshly baked cake *tasted* fragrant.

"I'm from London," I said. "How about you?"

"New Jersey." He had grey hair mixed with remnants of blond from his more youthful days. He reached out to shake my hand. "I'm John. Pleasure to meet you."

We had a friendly banter for a few minutes while I drank my coffee. I then left to make my way to the temple, which opened at nine o'clock for a sacred ceremony followed by chanting and meditation. It opened to visitors for just three hours and I wanted to make sure I got there well before nine.

The flowery aroma of fragrant incense wafted over in my direction while I walked from the makeshift car park in front of the temple entrance. As in every temple, the very first statue to greet the visitor was that of Lord Ganesh, the deity whose blessings were essential for any endeavour to succeed. Above the stone statue of this formidable elephant-headed deity was a small but heavy metal bell. I rang the bell, while mentally chanting the relevant Sanskrit invocation, to declare a very specific intention: to invite pure and positive power into my heart while dispelling the negativity within me.

Next to his stone statue, a wooden container held a handful of incense sticks, thoughtfully provided by the temple for its visitors. Some had already been lit. Incense was offered to purify the ego and for its pleasing fragrance to draw the divine to us.

Always up for having my ego purified, I lit one and carefully placed it in the nearby sand bowl, an outdoor incense stick holder. At the feet of Lord Ganesh were several offerings of fresh fruit, presumably made by devoted visitors who had already arrived for this morning's proceedings. It had been worth the effort the day before to go Koloa to buy fruits, flowers, and a garland. As a mark of surrendering all that no longer served me, such as old beliefs, thoughts, and behaviours, I placed a single pink orchid in the stone lap of this divine being. I felt utterly grateful for being here, and made a humble offering of a ripe mango.

My relationship to Lord Ganesh was anything but stony. My experience of him was palpable—a being of sharp intelligence, wit and compassion. Hands joined at the heart centre, I bowed with a heartfelt greeting of *pranaam*, and connected with Lord Ganesh. "Less than six months ago, the doctors told me I had a life-threatening disease, and less than eight weeks ago I had my second four-hour surgery. I feel so much gratitude to be alive and well again, and to be free of the excruciating pain that I've had to live with for a couple of years. Thank you for giving me a new lease of life! I feel so blessed." More than ever, I understood that good health was the most precious gift of life and I would not take it for granted ever again.

To the left of the statue of Lord Ganesh was the entrance proper to the temple, under a carved stone arch, beyond which lay a long, painted, red pathway, lined with ample forest ferns and flowering trees. A few paces ahead, I couldn't help feeling surprise and delight at seeing the enormous canopy of a large banyan tree just on the left of the red pathway. Under the banyan stood a tall stone statue of a six-headed deity, carved in unmistakable and intricate South Indian style. I was not familiar with this deity, and yet I felt intriguingly drawn to this spot. I made up my mind to return to it later.

A few more paces on, to the right of the red pathway, stood the temple building, its huge, heavy wooden doors wide open for all to enter. But the side of this building drew my attention, where the pathway continued to open into a clearing. Ahead were views of vast, scenic, breathtaking gardens while a steep, unexpected valley dropped quite abruptly to the left of the temple. In this majestic sprawling valley stood enormous green bamboos, maybe eighty, one hundred, or two hundred feet in height. You could only just peak at the spectacular view of the River Wailua gushing through the distant bounds of these sacred grounds.

Carefully positioned stone features around the temple building allowed water to flow over large rocks, crystals, and glass clusters. The magnificence of the lush green tropical forest that made up these grand temple grounds overwhelmed me with awe. Acres of beautifully kept gardens and groves sprawled with vibrant flora and rich fauna, typical on these islands. Trees in blossom, tree ferns and mosses, fragrant vines, exotic tropical flowers that unabashedly expressed their beauty through an explosion colour, scented plumeria, hibiscus, fruit orchids, heliconia, and ginger, all grew in abundance. A stream further below boasted delicate, pastel water lilies and lotuses as it meandered through these monastic grounds. Coco and other tropical varieties of palm, breadfruit, taro and passion fruit, or *lilikoi*, gave a seal of approval to the majesty of this tropical natural beauty.

A few days later, when I was granted permission to walk around the monastery grounds, I would go down to the edge of the river that flowed through here. I found a spot to sit on at its grassy verge so that I could dip my feet in the pristine, crystal clear waters of the Wailua that weaved its way down from the virtually impenetrable wilderness of Mount Waialeale at the very heart of Kauai. The experience was as enchanting as taking a dip in the River Ganges. Only now, I was on the awe-inspiring grounds of a sacred Shiva temple on a tiny island in the middle of the Pacific Ocean, which had its own unique magic. I saw plants and fruits native to India and that were used for healing in *Ayurveda*; curry leaf or *neem*, Indian gooseberry or *amla*, frangipani flower or *champa*, sandalwood. Even fruits, such as *chiku* or sapodilla, were cultivated here. I became less and less surprised to see all kinds of verdure vegetation thriving in this rainforest of an island. Even desert dwelling cacti and succulents flourished here.

Seduced by the spectacular beauty of these surroundings, I almost forgot that it was the temple I was here to visit. Surely it could not get better than being in this Zen haven with its dramatic, lush rainforest valley. Summoned by the tinkling of the temple bell, I walked past a lava rock podium housing a towering black granite statue of Nandi, the bull, protecting the temple entrance.

Walls on two sides framed the impeccable space in the room, and displayed rare, sixteen inch bronze statues, 108 of them, each with different dance poses of Lord Shiva's *tandava*, the divine dance of creation, preservation, and dissolution. The purity of this space felt palpable.

The main sanctum of the temple enshrined a large statue of Lord Shiva in his form as the dancer, Natraja, in front of which was his symbol, an enormous Shiva *lingam*, made of a tall, six-sided quartz crystal that was at least three feet high. It was a symbol of

Lord Shiva's pillar of fire or light that is said to pierce through the earth into the higher realms when Shiva attained the highest spiritual level. Representing enlightenment, peace, and harmony, it integrates the male and female. It encapsulates the creative energy of Shiva, the manifest form of highest consciousness and Shakti, the primordial cosmic energy, Shiva-Shakti—consciousness and feminine creative power, male and female. When integrated as one, they form the supreme intelligence from which springs forth the universe.

Two six foot tall black granite statues stood either side of the central sanctum. Lord Ganesh was easy to recognise, but I was less familiar with the other representation whose plaque declared it to be a deity called Lord Murugan. I had never heard of Murugan. Perhaps the name here was of South Indian origin—in the north of India, we often had altogether different names for the same deities. I decided to ask one of the monks about him later. I was curiously magnetised to the energy of this being, looking again and again at this statue. Then I noticed that the deity was riding on his power animal, a peacock. Something about the peacock niggled me. It felt eerily familiar.

On the left, towards the entrance of the inner sanctum, I was surprised to see the man I had just been talking to at the Java Kai café, John. He must have just walked in before me, while I was absorbing the scenery outside, and was greeting a thin monk in an orange *dhoti* wrap. The monk had pale white skin with a longish, white beard and hair, a portion of it tied into a tiny knot at the back of the head. He wore a large red dot at the third eye and three stripes of *vibhuti* or sacred ash pasted across his forehead to denote that he belonged to the Order of Shiva. Though clearly not of Indian origin, I was tickled pink to note that the monk looked every bit as authentic in his appearance as any Indian monk that I had seen on my travels across India.

"*Namaste*, Swami Ceyon," John greeted the monk in a familiar tone.

"Dear John, what a surprise! How wonderful to see you again. After the last time, I wasn't expecting to see you here so soon. Welcome back," Swami Ceyon said in a soft voice and an American accent, his sky blue eyes twinkling as he greeted John.

Two more bare-chested monks with orange cloths wrapped from the waist down were working in the inner sanctum of the temple. They were busy making preparations for the morning ceremony that was about to start. One monk dressed the huge quartz crystal Shiva *lingam* with a long red and orange flower garland. The other stepped out into the outer chamber where

John and others stood. I looked at this monk and then the other and back to the first and then at Swami Ceyon. Was I seeing in triplicate? The two monks looked almost identical to Swami Ceyon. Each one of them had a slight, slim build with translucent skin and not an inch of body fat more than was necessary for vital functioning, long blondish or white hair and beards, piercing blue eyes, all bare-chested, wrapped from the waist down in orange renunciate's homespun cotton cloth. They all resembled the poster images I had grown up seeing of Lord Shiva, the ultimate *yogi*. It was as if Shiva had jumped off the wall poster of an Indian household, made copies of himself, and started living and breathing, in the form of Hindu monks, on the island of Kauai. Their manner was gentle. They had something innately joyful about their being that reminded me of the playful spirit of the spinner dolphins I had swam with just a few days ago.

"Ah!" John's wide eyes suggested surprise, as he turned around to see me standing behind him inside the temple. "What a coincidence. I didn't know you were coming here too. It sure is a small world." Then he turned again to Swami Ceyon and said, "Swami Ceyon, meet my new friend, Smita, whom I met this morning. She's come all the way from London, England."

"Welcome, Smita," the American Hindu monk said. "How wonderful that you found your way to our temple all the way from London."

"*Namaskaram*, Swamiji," I said, and joined my hands to my heart in greeting. "Thank you so much. It's quite a story how I've come to be here." I smiled.

"You must tell me all about it," he said. "It's time for the sacred ceremony. Please, take as much paper as you like from the entrance over there and write down all the things that you would like to pray for. We will come round in a little while and take the pieces of paper, and then they will be offered up to the *devic* realms in the fire ritual."

12

Cosmic Postbox

To my surprise, by the entrance door of the temple was a small wicker basket containing pieces of paper and pens. Next to the basket, a notice told visitors that they could write down and ask for anything they wanted and it would be granted to them. The prayers were then given to one of the monks for burning in the consecrated fire, and the priest recited appropriate *mantras* to the *devas* who were guarding the temple from the other side of the veil, and the impressive quartz crystal Shiva *lingam*.

I was astonished to find that the uncommon practice I'd been taught in a meditation some years ago by my Inner Diamond was also being done on a daily basis at this temple. For years, I had developed this practice, using a specific method of writing down exactly what I wanted to manifest in my life.

In the days when I had first started doing this practice, my Inner Diamond had given me this instruction. *"Be crystal clear about what you are asking for so that even a child cannot misunderstand you or your intent. Describe it with simplicity. You must also examine that your ego-mind and heart are both aligned in having what you are asking for.*" This, my Diamond had said, was because *the universe was indiscriminate.* It wouldn't interpret what you said or asked for, but it was keen and ever ready to deliver on your desires, conscious or unconscious. It had also emphasised this: *Always ask that what you desire be given to you will harm none. Else you bind yourself to difficult karma.*

I would take my time to get clear about what I wanted to ask for and articulate it with utmost clarity, which sometimes took several days. Once I'd done this, it was then time to perform the fire ceremony in which I would offer the pieces of paper containing my requests.

This practice became invaluable because it forced me to get not just clear but committed to what I said I wanted. It made me get specific about the thing I was asking for in terms of not so much the exact form it would take, but its essence and qualities—what would be different in my life by having it, how it would make me feel, how it would make others feel or benefit them, the manner in which it would show up in my life, for example, with ease and joy.

I applied this practice for creating almost everything in my life: new relationships, whether personal or business, altering the dynamics of existing relationships, business deals, holidays, car, house— pretty much everything that was important to me. It became a means of *creating* my life in a conscious way instead of hopelessly hoping that, somehow, I would stumble upon the things I deeply desired. The more I used this practice, the more I became aware of anything that was in the way of my attaining an authentic desire, blocking me from receiving it. Then it was down to me to find ways of clearing my path so that I could receive and manifest my request.

Tongue in cheek, I called this my 'cosmic post box'.

There were certain perils in doing a ceremony such as this at home. If the person conducting the fire ceremony, normally a priest, carried anger or any other overwhelming negativity, instead of attracting the *devas* or benevolent angelic beings, there was the danger that you might call up dark, *asuric*, forces instead. Performing a sacred ritual was no small responsibility and could not be undertaken without clear intent and high conscious awareness.

Later, I shared with Swami Ceyon about this practice. I explained to him my process and its astounding results, as well as how I had come to learn it.

"I've not known, until today, of anyone else doing this," I said. "I thought it was just me, you know, being whacky and weird!" I laughed. "Burning prayers written on paper is not normal practice in Indian temples, is it? How did you come to adopt this practice here, of giving prayers in writing using fire ceremonies?"

"It's true that this is not a normal practice in most temples," Swami Ceyon said. "One day, in a vision, Gurudeva [Satguru Sivaya Subramuniya Swami who founded the Kadavul Temple in Kauai] was told by the *devas* that in the inner world they could receive written prayers through being burned in the sacred fire inside this temple."

"Really? Interesting," I said. "Have you found that people do receive what they ask for when their prayers are burned in the temple's fire rituals?"

"We've heard of some intriguing results that have come about for people through the burning of their prayers," he replied. "There's every reason to believe that this practice is a powerful one.'

"How fascinating."

"Writing and delivering prayers to the realms of the *devas*, or *Devaloka*, through the sacred fire comes from the lineage (*sampradaya*) of the ancient *Natha*, a tradition that is perhaps more than a thousand years old," Swami Ceyon said.

"I see," I said thoughtfully. Then, somewhat tongue-in-cheek, I asked, "Something puzzles me. Surely the *devas* are busy with more important issues to take care of in the world and the wider universe? And let's say that they do respond, some people's handwriting is just rubbish. How can they read these prayers, in cinders too, after being burnt. Can they get it wrong?" I asked, genuinely concerned.

Swami Ceyon laughed. "I can see that this could happen, that's why it's important to be clear and crisp about what you're asking for. As the paper with the written prayer burns, the astral double of the prayer appears in the *Devaloka* realm. The prayer is then read by the *devas*, who proceed to carry out the requests. These temple *devas* are fully dedicated to assist all who come through the temple doors, whatever their problem. That is their purpose for existence. That's what they devote themselves to, assisting humanity."

"I see. Do they have their own language or do they understand ours, whatever it might be?" I asked.

"Gurudeva was taught by the *devas* the script that they use and to which all prayers are translated," he said in patient tones.

"Why Kauai and not another place to establish this monastery and temple?" I asked.

He replied, "That's a good question. Gurudeva believed that our inner life is more important than our outer life and he felt it necessary, therefore, to be cloistered away from the world. He felt strongly that had we been in San Francisco, New York, Singapore, or New Delhi, we could not do this same work as a contemplative order of meditators and teachers because we would primarily reach the world through publications and the Internet. So he searched deep and hard for years for the right spot and he found it here. He said that Kauai was a spiritual place, a vortex of healing energies emanating from its sacred Mount Waialeale, and the pristine air and ocean. So here we are." Swamiji gave a smile of satisfaction.

"Ah, that's what it feels like to me, a portal into other worlds—the material and inner," I replied, lighting up within. "I'm sure that the worship you do for the benefit of others has its own benefits."

"Yes, it's called *parartha puja*, worship or devotion that transcends the self-centred focus or the material," Swami Ceyon said.

"It's so different to any other temple I've ever visited. There's an atmosphere of peace and, I want to say, *purity*, in the space here. Is that *all* due to Kauai being an unspoilt tropical rainforest, and Mount Waialeale, or is there something else as well?" I asked.

"Well, this beautiful setting certainly helps. Now I don't know about elsewhere, here we perform vigils every three hours round the clock. For example, at three in the morning, we do an offering or *abhishek* to Lord Ganesh, at six o'clock to Lord Murugan, and the nine o'clock ceremony is dedicated to Lord Shiva. Then, for the rest of the day, we perform different sacred rituals. We've never missed any of the three-hour vigils yet since the temple opened in 1973. Every ceremony serves to clear away stagnant or negative energy and bring in the vital force, *prana*. The consecrated fire is also the medium that connects the material world with that which exists on the other side of the mystic veil, the divine realm. So that could well be something that perhaps you have tuned into," he said with humility, examining my face.

"You keep the energy of the space impeccable." I could feel this clearly.

"There's also the three foot high quartz crystal Shiva *lingam*," Swami Ceyon said. "It weighs a colossal seven hundred pounds and is one continuous piece. That's a unique feature of our temple. You know, in the Hindu scriptures, a Shiva *lingam* of crystal is considered to be the highest."

"Really? No, I didn't know that. I've only ever seen ones that are granite or dark rock, at best, marble," I said.

"This crystal is known as an Earthkeeper," Swami Ceyon said.

"Hmmm. Very interesting. What's an Earthkeeper?" I asked.

"It is said that these crystals were devices for storage of planetary knowledge, that they had capacities to generate psychic power, and were even microcosmic homes for *deva*-beings, even Gods, living in interior universes to ours. Of course, we don't know if that's just folklore or if it became myth over thousands of years and there was some truth to it. What I can say is that the presence of the quartz Shiva *lingam* amplifies the ancient spiritual rituals and daily sacred fire ceremonies that we perform here. Perhaps, you're not too far off in calling this place a 'portal' into the inner and divine realms." Swami Ceyon's face beamed.

"How fascinating. As you probably know, Swamiji, at the heart of every radio or transmitter, every mobile phone, there's a tiny quartz crystal, the size of a grain of salt. It vibrates with the electromagnetic fields around us and picks up even the tiniest of signals. Just imagine the sensitivity and power of this massive quartz crystal! Even from a scientific perspective, you could say that it's listening to and transmitting into the entire universe. It's literally vibrating in tune with the universe."

"It's certainly a thing of wonder, for sure," Swamiji agreed.

"The individual is,
in truth,
the Universe."

13

Sacred Ceremony

At least twenty or so people gathered in the temple for this morning sacred ceremony. Some were local regulars: men and women wearing Indian suits that looked like they had been bought on their travels in India. The women wore coloured dots on their foreheads and bangles on their wrists. Several Indian families visited from different parts of America. As was typical when visiting a temple, the mothers made a point of wearing beautiful *saris* and made their children dress in Indian clothes too. Everyone, as they came in, went one by one, to the deity statues and bowed or kneeled reverently before them, placing their offerings of fruits and flowers. I took my turn to do the same. The monk priests took the flowers and garlands away to adorn afresh the gods' statues.

As I sat on the floor to the left of the temple, I watched the monk priests at work. They placed every flower just so on the statues of the deities, 'dressing' them with tender, loving awareness and focus. They applied a red-yellow dot, using a paste of red *kumkum* and yellow *sandalwood* powder to their foreheads. Scarves of gold, silver, yellow, red, and green cloth were carefully wrapped around the deities, which looked so lifelike that they might walk off their podiums at any moment and start chatting to us. One priest waved the lit, clarified butter *ghee* lamp in circular motion, offering the light to each of the statues, and chanted a string of *mantras*, specific for invoking the different deities in the temple. Meanwhile, a cacophony of angelic and mystical sounds were generated as another priest rang a handheld metal bell and Swami Ceyon blew into a large conch shell—Shiva's quintessential instrument. The delicate aroma of *sandalwood*, floral incense, and burning *ghee* filled the temple while the sound of chanted *mantras* and accompanying handheld bells made a feast for the ears. The beautifully decorated deities and undulating light from the *ghee* lamps enhanced the mystical experience.

Every part of the preparation was performed as per the strictest code prescribed by the requirements of this ancient ritual. And yet, though the priests followed these ancient rituals to the letter, they made it their own heartfelt action.

With the *puja* ceremony underway, burning incense lightly filled the air. As though God himself were standing in front of us, the monk priest offered to the symbolic statues flower petal after delicate flower petal, bloom after beautiful bloom, along with fluently chanted Sanskrit *mantras* that sounded just like the sweet poetry they were meant to be. Every action, every movement, was intentional and essential to this ancient ritual.

Swami Ceyon had consciously connected with the inner realms through this ceremony, and it was now his turn to begin the consecrated fire ceremony in the main temple room where we sat. In a square copper container, the monks had arranged pieces of wood to allow air to circulate, and inserted this into the purpose-built three-tiered brick container, similar to a backyard barbecue grill. Surrounded by carefully arranged, small shiny metal containers with essentials for the ceremony, such as rice grains, clarified butter *ghee*, powders of red, yellow, vermilion and white, water, Indian rice pudding, sugar cane cubes, dried fruits, fresh fruits, and an abundance of flower petals, Swami Ceyon poured a couple of spoonfuls of liquid clarified butter to the dry wood and initiated the fire.

As the fire ceremony got underway, the familiar smell of fresh *ghee* burning the wood wafted around the main room of the temple. Since childhood, these aromas had signalled to my senses that something special and sacred was taking place. A symbolic messenger to higher consciousness, the fire carried our prayers into to divine realms on the other side of the mystical veil, where microcosm and macrocosm met and became a manifest new reality.

Swamiji then flicked grains of rice into the flickering flames, more spoonfuls of *ghee*, and other select items. A relevant *mantra* accompanied each action, with each sacrificial offering being made with purpose and devotion.

I was only too aware that one could easily write this off as mere ritualistic rigmarole, as religious hocus-pocus. It was, however, important to remember that all Vedic philosophies, ceremonies, and rituals were intended to remind and connect us to one thing and one thing only, and Swami Ceyon captured it by saying, "The individual is, in truth, the Universe."

In one of his many writings, the Gurudeva who established this monastery and temple, explained, "To be fully anchored in the knowledge of the Source of our being, the eternal now can and must be a constant experience. It's easy to live in the now if you work with yourself a little every day and concentrate on what you are doing each moment."

These sacred ceremonies, through evoking each of our human senses, were merely opportunities to become increasingly conscious of, and to draw upon, *who we are in essence: pure intelligence.*

I had filled every single piece of paper provided with requests of good health, wealth, and prosperity for my family and friends, naming each one and asking for that which I knew was close to their heart. Not to mention, of course, for myself too. After all, I had a whole new life to create. Swami Ceyon went to every person in the room with a wicker basket to collect their written prayers. I let out an embarrassed giggle when I handed mine over, as it took several handfuls to get my reams of paper into the basket. Thankfully, he didn't judge me and, even if he did, he certainly didn't show it.

I watched each piece of paper being placed by the priest into the fire, feeling goosebumps on my arms as I contemplated all that I had intended actually becoming reality. The question now was, *how awesome can you stand life to be?*

"Eka brahma dvitiya nasti—
there is only one God."

14

One

After the fire ceremony, I went back to the banyan tree under which the South Indian stone statue of the six-headed deity had been erected. The minute I stood under it, I had goosebumps. A small plaque named this statue to be that of Lord Murugan. Here he was again! This time, I heard the same flutterings of wings that I had heard for the first time in the vision in my meditation room at home when the angel-bird showed me the words Hawaii, and then again at sunset atop the crater of Kilauea. Once more, as I stood beneath this banyan, in front of this statue, I had a vision of the peacock come alive, lower half bird, upper half angel. *"It was I who guided you to come here. I am Murugan, I am Michael."*

Just then, Swami Ceyon appeared and joined me at the statue.

"Swamiji, I've had the most surreal of experiences. Just after my operation, about eight weeks ago, I was meditating at home one evening and this enormous peacock half-bird, half-angel, appeared in my vision. It came and sat down right in the centre of my room. At first I thought I was dreaming, so I opened my eyes. But the vision of this massive angel-bird was still there. I realised that I was seeing it through my third eye, and opening or closing my eyes didn't make it go away. I asked it to tell me who it was, and why it was here. It communicated silently, 'I am Michael.' Then, taking the smoke emanating from the *ghee* lamp, using the tip of one of its wings, the angel-bird wrote in thin air the word 'Hawaii'. *'Go!'* it proclaimed."

I paused, caught my breath, then carried on—dying to share my mystical experience with someone who might understand. "Then it just sat there with me until I could hold the vision no longer. The vision was so real, he was sitting as close to me as you are standing here right now."

I looked at the Swamiji, animated. "Then, that night, a goddess in a green and gold *sari* appeared in my dream and told me to retreat, swim with dolphins, and heal myself."

"Gurudeva often had experiences of talking with Lord Murugan. He said that Murugan, like Ganesh, is a real being," Swamiji said.

"Really? How extraordinary," I said. "It happened again at the crater of Kilauea. I sat for a few minutes with my eyes closed and I heard three quite distinct flutterings of what had to be a bird with large wings. With each fluttering came a whispered message. And then this morning, I saw the peacock in the temple sanctum and something about it niggled me. Just now, I heard the words *'I am Murugan. I am Michael.'*" I looked at Swami Ceyon, with bafflement on my face. "I've never heard of Murugan, and yet could he have directed me to come here? Does he have another name?"

"Of course. Yes, he is known in North India as Kartikeya, the older son of Shiva," Swamiji said.

"Oh. That name I recognise," I said, somewhat relieved.

"He's also known as Skanda, the God of War, Commander of the Gods."

"And his animal is the peacock?" I asked.

The Swamiji nodded. "Yes."

"His colours, are they indigo and does he carry a staff or a spear?" I asked.

"Yes, and it's called the *vel*, the divine spear, with which he wields *Shakti* or creative power. That is his weapon. The peacock signifies the destruction of ego," Swamiji Ceyon said.

Of course. Now it made sense. This was Kartikeya, the warrior brother of Lord Ganesh, and elder son of Lord Shiva.

"Just now, I heard the words, '*I am Murugan, I am Michael*'. Could it be that Murugan or Kartikeya and Archangel Michael are all one and the same? Isn't Archangel Michael also a warrior? Doesn't he also have indigo as his colour—the primary colour of peacock feathers? And isn't his weapon also a spear-like sword? To fight the darkness and cut the bonds of attachment?" I said, almost squealing as I made the connection.

"Well, there is only one God that shows himself in his different forms, be it an angelic form or its feminine divine form or any other. The Vedas say *Eka brahma dvitiya nasti*—there is only one God. There is no second. Anything else is a great misconception, a delusion," Swamiji replied.

"Why, then, did I see the big angel-bird and the Goddess in Green? Why not, say, Mother Mary or some other prophet?" I asked.

"What you see and relate to very much depends on your frame of cultural reference. While Kartikeya is recognised by the Hindus, he is by no means exclusively a *Hindu* god. There is only one God. The Vedas explain: *Self-resplendent, formless, unoriginated, and pure, that all-pervading being is both within and without. He transcends even the transcendent, unmanifest, causal state of the universe.* It's universal and one that encompasses male and female gender. It transcends religion, creed, and language. So, Kartikeya can take the form of Archangel Michael in the Christian pantheon."

This series of synchronicity were magical to me. Something felt right about it, as if dots were being connected.

"You were assisted by Murugan to come here for your healing. He often appears to help behind the scenes, even though you may not be consciously aware of it, when your soul is at a certain juncture of its evolution. When it is ready to clear *karma* that has kept you entrenched in stubborn patterns and to dissolve a part of your ego, so that you can merge with your higher Self," Swami Ceyon said. I was immediately reminded of my mystical experience the previous day at the cliff head, when I did exactly this. Swami Ceyon smiled warmly at me, as if he could see what I had witnessed yesterday. He looked into my eyes, as though he could somehow sense the mystical experience that I'd had at the top of the cliff.

He said, "To do that, your *chakras* must be awakened and become properly functional. That requires the *kundalini* energy to awaken, and what most people don't know is that awakening kundalini requires Murugan or Kartikeya's help."

"No kidding. In the last months, I've had several occasions where I've worked to open the *chakras*. For example, having the vision of the angel-bird was a potent third eye experience. Then a shaman woman on the Big Island did some *chakra* clearing using her voice and, again, I felt the presence of the same angel-bird at the Mount Kilauea crater," I said, fascinated.

"That would make sense," Swami Ceyon said. "These are all experiences that require the creative force *kundalini* to awaken in us. When this creative force awakens, the ego or darkness within shrinks, and we gradually become more and more aware of the light of our higher nature. Murugan is the God of Love and War. When you're ready, he helps to slay your inner demons that act as blockages— anger from thwarted intentions, disappointments from unfulfilled desires, resentments and jealousy, unhealthy attachments. As the emotional body clears, we become more and more capable of delving into our true nature."

"How very interesting. It's true I've spent a huge amount of effort over the years clearing away what's probably lifetimes of emotional pain and trauma and tying up loose ends from the past. I felt heaviness from it and my view of what's possible in life was blurred by it. It seems to me that even the illness for which I recently had surgery was a clearing of *karma*."

"Literally, on a physical level," he said with a smile. "It seems you have gone through a series of initiations—you know, tests, that you've had to pass. Then you attract and get granted access to divine or higher assistance in ways that you can see and experience. Clearing away the inner debris increases your awareness and vibration. As this happens, you can actually interact more lucidly with the *devic* beings and avail yourself of their help in your daily life," Swamiji said. "That is when you know that you have grown up, spiritually."

I fell into a humbled silence as a few more of my defences blew away.

"Bhava, that deep,
authentic inner feeling,
is the seed that will bear
the fruit of your spiritual effort.
Without cultivating
the right inner feeling,
that which comes from the heart,
your effort will fall
like stone in an arid desert."

15

Goddess

Swami Ceyon and I parted company shortly after our conversation. I walked down the path to leave the temple premises, but from the corner of my eye, I caught sight of a smallish shed to my left. Through the open door, I could just see a few crystals and a shelf with books. It was the temple shop. I wandered in to browse. From the corner, I heard a voice, "Pretty special here, huh?" It was John, the man I had met earlier in the coffee shop.

"It certainly is. It's a spectacular place, this temple," I replied, picking up a rather handsome looking rosary *mala* of 108 *rudraksha* beads.

"Those beads are from right here on Kauai. Have you been to the Rudraksha Forest?" he asked.

"Really?" I asked, perplexed, wondering if this guy was a bit odd or if he was pulling my leg. "They make *rudraksha* beads here, in Kauai? I've only ever known of them growing in the plains of the Ganges in India."

These beads were believed to have special healing properties and were considered the most sacred of all in India.

"That's right. Right here, in Kauai. Have you been to see it yet?"

I knitted my eyebrows together, looking confused, "Are you having a laugh?"

"No, I'm serious. It's just a mile or two up the hill, left off the main road."

According to legend, the *rudraksha* tree sprung up from a tear shed by Lord Shiva. A tear of fulfilment experienced by Shiva after being in deep meditation. Rudra, or 'one who weeps', is one of the names of Lord Shiva. *Rudraksha*, in Sanskrit, literally means Rudra's eyes and 'askha' is to give and receive. So *rudraksha* is one that has the ability to wipe away tears and provide fulfilment. Holy men all over India wear these beads as a necklace, which doubles up as a rosary.

"I'm going there now, if you'd like to join me," John said.

I hesitated. Though the sense I had of John was that he was a 'gentleman', a good guy, I was not in the habit of accompanying strange men I had just met into forests, in lands to which I was an absolute stranger. I had barely met him a few hours ago and I wanted to smoke him out first, to get to know a bit more about him and see if he was a trustworthy character.

"Now that you've told me about this forest, I'd definitely like to go there. But right now I'm going to grab a coffee down at the Coconut Marketplace in Kapaa. You're welcome to join me."

"Sure. Why not? I can always go there a little later," he said.

"Okay, well, I'll see you down there." I walked to the shop door.

Just then, something fell out of John's wallet as he stood at the counter to pay for a purchase. It was a piece of paper. I walked towards the counter and bent over to pick it up and return it to John. As I crouched down, I caught sight of a colourful, almost kitsch-looking image on this tatty, crumpled, glossy card the size of a cigarette packet. The card, its once white edges now browning with the passing of time, curled at the corners and creases, from being stuffed along with the contents of a bulging wallet, lined its surface.

Despite its wear and tear, the picture on the card was still vivid and I gasped on seeing the image of the woman depicted. Adorned with abundant jewels, she wore an old-fashioned, rich golden-bordered green *sari*, worn in typical ancient South Indian style. A beautiful green parrot perched on her right shoulder.

John, now also crouching down, joined me in staring at the card. "It's a mesmerising image, isn't it?"

I was gobsmacked. My mind raced with so many questions that I couldn't string any one of them in a coherent sentence. "It's the one I call the Goddess in Green! Who is she?" I managed to ask.

"Why, it's Goddess Meenakshi, of course."

"Who? ... Meenakshi? ... But she's the one I saw in my dream. The same *sari*. ... She told me to come here ... the same green parrot on her shoulder. Who is she? But she looked younger in my dream ... and she had three breasts ... ," I muttered, my mouth agape with disbelief. "I saw her just yesterday when I was sitting, enjoying the breeze, at the top of the cliff on the seashore, and she suddenly appeared in a vision, or should I say, an epiphany. She just blew me away."

"Well, that doesn't surprise me," John said. "She's pretty special. That's why I take her everywhere with me." His tone was lighthearted. "She's the real McCoy."

"But who is she? Apart from in my dream and again yesterday, I have never come across her," I said, desperate to learn more about her.

"Oh. Being Indian, I thought you would know her."

"No. I have no idea who she is. India's vast, you know. It's a subcontinent. There are so many subcultures and deities in India, and I grew up knowing only the main ones and those that are well known in Gujarat and in the north of India. Who is she, John?" I asked. Now that I had seen this goddess again, I knew it was no accident.

"Well, that would explain it. She's better known in the south of India. She's Goddess Meenakshi, an *avatar* of Parvati, the consort of Lord Shiva."

"But why did she have three breasts in my dream and again when I saw her yesterday? I've never heard of Parvati having three breasts. Or was that just some sick Freudian warp in my psyche?"

"Ah. Yes. Meenakshi, granted as a boon to her father, King Pandyan, was born with three breasts. The legend goes that when she found the man she would marry, her third breast would disappear. After the king died, she took over ruling the kingdom. On a visit to the Himalayas, she came across Shiva, the man she would marry. On seeing him, her third breast disappeared."

"No kidding. So, it was Goddess Parvati who appeared in my dream and directed me to make this journey. But why would she fill my hair parting with the orange-red powder? That's something that married women wear," I said, still in disbelief.

"Oh, that's easy. Parvati's the eternal Mother. She's the Goddess of Relationships. That red powder, isn't that something the groom puts in his bride's hair parting in a marriage ceremony? I take it you're not married?" John said.

"Goodness. Yes, I mean, no, I'm not married," I mumbled.

"Sounds to me like she's given you the heads-up for a forthcoming marriage, symbolically, I mean. From what I've learnt, the Goddess is a hard taskmaster and her grace is not easily attained. You must have been doing a hell of a lot of work on yourself spiritually, possibly over many lifetimes, that you have now stepped into the view of her light and invoked Parvati Devi's grace."

I joked to conceal my despair. "Hmmmm ... that all sounds very nice. But it's handy to have that essential prop first, surely, I mean the groom, or even any groom."

"Expect to meet the perfect man for you within the year." John laughed. Despite his casual manner, he was serious. "If she has appeared in a recent dream, chances are that you've already met him somewhere along the way."

I was stunned and silent. Could this be true? Event after event was strung together by elegant, effortless synchronicity that I could not discount even the most outlandish of possibilities.

"You see," John said, "I went to India ten years ago after a horrible divorce. I lost everything, my business had crumbled and around the same time I found out that I had a particularly bad form of cancer. Doctors gave me less than a year. With nothing to live for at home, and even less to lose, I decided to go to India to make the most of my last days and to salvage something of myself and of my miserable life. Someone told me about the Goddess Meenakshi and the blessings they had received from connecting with her, so I went to her temple in Madurai. Not only did I outlive the cancer, but my life has gone from strength to strength ever since. You could say I've been granted a new lease of life." He looked at me. "They say that once Meenakshi Devi's gaze falls on you, your suffering disappears and you can begin to live, really live."

"She absolves your *karma*," I said, somewhat stumped. "But why me? I know people far better than myself who pray religiously and do rigorous daily rituals. I don't do any of those things."

"It's not about how much you do, or even what you do. It's all about your *bhava*, the depth of feeling and the purity of your being with which you do whatever you do," John said.

"That was exactly what a *guru* told me when I was in India," I said. "'*Bhava, that deep, authentic inner feeling, is the seed that will bear the fruit of your spiritual effort. Without cultivating the right inner feeling, that which comes from the heart, your effort will fall like stone in an arid desert,*' he said."

"It's all about the *quality* of your awareness. And you seem to have hit the mark on the head," John said. "It's not a journey without challenges and tests of the mind, body and spirit."

"What's even more curious is that the same *guru* wrote to me some time after that visit. He said that in a dream, Parvati Devi had told him to give me a particular *mantra* to repeat 108 times for 108 days. After doing it for those 108 days, I continued with it as part of my spiritual practice," I said.

"There you go. The Mother Goddess has a soft, tender heart and she responds when you reach out to her with a genuine affectionate state of being—purity of heart, if you like. She clears away all the obstacles, no matter how sticky, and that's when life flows with fulfilment."

I looked at him, tears welling up in my eyes. I knew what he meant by 'genuine, affectionate state of being, and purity of heart'. I realised that what I had experienced at the top of the cliff yesterday was exactly this. The state that John was referring to came once I had been willing to sacrifice the right to hold on to my anger and grief. It came only after authentically forgiving those whom I felt had rejected me or hurt me in some way. It came after I had forfeited my right to demand that I be treated in this way or that. It came after I had been able to let go of believing that my judgement—of others and myself—was the only correct view. It came once I could let go of the notion of who I believed 'I' was and surrendered to being led by the wisdom of my innate Self, aligning even my stubborn, arrogant ego with it.

Somehow, I had been able to make this 'sacrifice' because like John, little by little, I too had reached the realisation that there was nothing of real value and no one left for me to lose.

What had felt then like a sacrifice, in hindsight, had been nothing more than becoming conscious of the mental and emotional clutter that I had believed was the real me. It was clutter that I no longer needed or wanted. Just as when you clear out years and years of 'stuff' that you had accumulated and that littered your house, clogged up your attic, garage and even the basement, things you thought somehow defined you but actually, all they did was keep you from seeing the real you—from being free to be that real you.

In other words, when I could let go of the illusion of what my life was, of who I was, and even of my interpretation of the events that had shaped my life, then the Mother Goddess appeared. Before that, my ego's version of me and the world ruled, and nothing else could penetrate through its solid, well-constructed walls.

What was more, this awareness, the courage to let go of the inner state that in part defined me, and the experience of my own true being—these were all possible because of divine grace that in my case, had shown itself as the Goddess in Green, the Mother Goddess Parvati.

"If you take one step
towards your higher Self,
your higher Self
will take a thousand steps
towards you."

16

Rare Blessing

That afternoon, after having coffee with me, John received a call from a friend in distress and rushed off to meet her in Kapaa. I welcomed the opportunity to go the Rudraksha Forest on my own as I suspected that it would be the perfect place to absorb what I had discovered earlier in the day. Rather than walking through the vast monastery grounds to gain access to the forest, it was easier to drive from Kapaa along the Kuamoo Road, which had a direct entrance. I drove slowly, being vigilant so as not to miss the small enclave John had told me about, just in front of the forest, where I could park my car.

A large stone statue of a flower-garlanded Lord Ganesh guarded the forest entrance, and the sunlight that streamed through the canopy gave just enough warmth to the coolness from the awning of greenery that sheltered the entire forest. It was not a vast forest and I was still close to the main road. So, even though I was the only one there, I felt safe.

Crowned by verdant green leaves, the slender trees, with their tall lanky trunks, fifty to a hundred feet high, filtered the bright rays of the afternoon sun, drenching these woods with enchantment. The bright, cobalt blue rudraksha berries bejewelled the forest ground, their bold ripeness enticing you to pick a few up, and daring you to savour their fruitiness in your mouth. I wished I'd brought a water bottle with me so I could wash and eat them there and then. I gathered a few instead to enjoy later at my hotel.

Time stood still in this haven of a place. There was nothing to do but embrace the cool summer breeze that whispered between the gaps of the tree trunks, soak in the murmur of the rustling leaves, and enjoy the sweet twittering of bright scarlet or olive green honeycreepers, small thrush songbirds, and other vibrantly coloured birds that made the rudraksha trees their home. Seated at a wooden bench provided by the thoughtful temple folk, I closed my eyes and breathed long, slow, deep inhales, soaking up the still, pure richness of this sacred forest, trusting that it was safe to let go of any remaining heaviness to which my subconscious may still be clinging.

After simply sitting, still as the tree trunks in this forest, for what must have been at least half an hour, I got the sense that my head had been washed with some of the cleanest air I had ever breathed. It made me almost giddy. It wasn't just that I was used to living in the pollution of London and that fresh air was rare for me, but more that there was something else in the air here. If there truly was some reality to mystical phenomena, it infused the air in this forest. Whatever it was, it lifted the fog that had become the 'norm' of my mental landscape, unbeknownst to me, and new insights about who I was beyond my identity and inspiration for new possibilities popped up like bubbles in a clear fizzy lemonade. My body filled with energy and lightness, which set my mind ablaze.

I reached for my notebook and jotted down these insights and inspirations, one after the other, so I could capture them into my future reality, declare them as intention, and 'post' them in the next day's sacred fire at the temple. When I finished writing, a further hour, that felt like just minutes, had flown by.

Perhaps for the very first time in my life, I was at peace with myself, with the events of my past, and all the people in it. The mysterious ways in which the Inner Diamond worked and revealed its presence was awe-inspiring. It begged that you remain humble, open, and present so that you could see new possibilities unfolding and becoming accessible to you.

I visited the temple again the next morning, and there were just four visitors, two of whom were local people that came regularly. I had brought with me the ream of paper I'd written on. All the visitors were mesmerised, watching the monks at work in the inner sanctum. Just as they had done yesterday, they prepared the statues and the quartz crystal Shiva *lingam* with beautifully exotic and vibrantly coloured flowers and garlands, placed with utmost focus and consideration.

The visitor sitting next to me, a young American woman called Marie-Jo, turned to me and said, "They look so absorbed in what they're doing. It's as if they're dressing the person they love the most."

"Look at how nimbly they select each flower and place it with tender care, in just the right place. Pure devotion," I said. "They're so present in every action."

"They're so into what they're doing, it looks like they're in a trance," Marie-Jo said.

After the *puja* ceremony, Swami Ceyon came over to take our pieces of paper for burning in the consecrated fire. Today, however, the purpose-built brick fire hearth in the centre of the main room was covered, and a copper container had been placed in a smaller fire hearth in front of the statue of Nataraja (Shiva) performing *Tandava*, the Dance of Life.

I felt pulled towards the six-sided crystal column in the inner sanctum, but a cordon with a sign reading 'no visitors beyond this point', prevented me from going closer to it. I resigned to connecting with it from afar by simply holding it in my awareness in meditation after the sacred ceremony was complete.

Here, the energy was so crisp and clean that it was easy to drop into deeper awareness. Magnetised, I could not take my eyes off the large 700lb. crystal and I kept staring at it for a minute or two, so that when I closed my eyes, it became visible through my third eye. I simply sat observing it, absorbed in inner space, hearing nothing, for what must have been about thirty minutes. When I opened my eyes, I was the only visitor remaining in the room, with Swami Ceyon sitting at the centre of the main temple.

He walked over to the red cordon, unhooked it from the wall, and beckoned me to come over to the crystal Shiva *lingam*.

"Take a look," he said, kindly. "You know, I'm not supposed to do this but I'll make an exception today." He smiled.

I placed my hands a few inches away from either side of the crystal only to suddenly expand my arms open wide on feeling the force of energy emanating from it. It was not a gushing force but more of a subtle force-field, similar to a person whose body heat you could sense several feet away.

"Take a seat and close your eyes. Then tell me what you feel," the monk said.

I had barely closed my eyes when a cold, sharp, freezing gust of wind, more like a gale, blew into the front of my body and knocked me back towards the wall behind me. My chest and belly curled back as if a round football had been pressed into me.

"Oof!" I cried, in shock. "Goodness! Did you feel that?" I asked Swami Ceyon.

His eyes twinkled. "Yes, I did."

I braced myself, crossing my arms over my chest to bear the ice-cold shivers going into my heart centre and down my spine. "I can't see any windows or open skylights in here. Was that from your air conditioning vents?" I asked the monk.

"No air conditioning vents here," he said, laughing. "We do have air vents that we open during fire ceremonies but they're closed now. We make a point of closing them shortly after a fire ceremony to avoid creepy crawlies rolling in."

"Are there doors open at the back, maybe?" I asked sceptically, looking around.

"Nope!" he replied, certain.

"But then where did that gust of wind come from? It was arctic cold," I said, perplexed. "How can you have freezing cold wind in these clammy tropics? I was sweating just a few minutes ago sitting over there, just a few feet away."

"The icy gust was symbolic. It was a blessing for you from Lord Shiva, communicated by the angelic messengers, the *devas*, on the other side of the mystic veil. I've only known it happen once before, many years ago." He looked at me. "It's a rare thing. Receive the grace well. Whatever you've asked for, it shall materialise."

Just as I had experienced melting away of my being as I knew it at the cliff top, so again today, here in front of this quartz crystal pillar, I again felt myself dissolve into a humble speck of light, into the tiniest diamond of my higher Self.

Swami Ceyon and I sat in front of the tall quartz crystal Shiva *lingam* for a few minutes longer as I absorbed this extraordinary mystical experience.

A little later, Swami Ceyon walked out of the temple with me and said, "Come, there's something you should see." He beckoned me to walk with him down hill of this tropical garden, behind the temple building, that opened to a sprawling, spectacular vista. I gasped with surprise at the steepness of the valley dropping to the left of us, hosting tall, magnificent, mature bamboo trees.

As we walked, I told Swamiji about the synchronicity of yesterday, when a tattered picture of the Goddess in Green had fallen out of John's wallet and I learnt that she was the same goddess who had directed me in my dream to come to these islands.

"Swamiji, can I share with you the confusion that I feel about the series of synchronicities that I've witnessed?" I asked him.

He stopped walking and turned to give me his undivided attention. "Sure."

"Today, you said that the chilly gust of wind was symbolic of blessings from Lord Shiva. Yesterday, I discovered that the Goddess in Green, who had directed me to come to these islands, was an avatar of Goddess Parvati. The swamiji I travelled with in India had sent me a *mantra* to repeat 108 times every day for 108 days. Then, in a meditation, a massive angel-bird, who told me his name was Michael, appeared in a vision, and he spelt out in bold smoke coming from my *ghee* lamp the word 'Hawaii'. Then, that same night, I had a vivid, lucid dream in which I saw the three-breasted Goddess in Green. She told me to take a retreat, heal myself, and go to the Hindu Monastery. The angel-bird appeared again at the crater of Kilauea on the Big Island. Then, for the first time, I discovered Lord Murugan, known also as Kartikeya, at your temple. Yesterday, quite out of the blue, a picture of the same Goddess in Green falls out of John's wallet and he tells me she is a form of

Goddess Parvati." I looked at the Swamiji with a look of perplexity, somewhat sceptical. "How can this be? Am I making all this up?"

"Well, don't you see, Smita?" He looked at me with a wide smile. "The Goddess in Green, as you call her, is Meenakshi. She's another form of Goddess Parvati, who is the wife of Shiva. Murugan or Kartikeya, is their elder son, while Lord Ganesh is the younger one. You, in this scheme of things ..." He turned to me. "... are the seeker, a true householder *yogi*, who has been working diligently to discover her innermost essence. And you've done that, from all that you've told me, through journeys, study, and first-hand experiences. Many of those have demanded that you make sacrifices that human beings normally do not want to, such as letting go of attachments to people, habits, and emotional patterns that keep you seeing the deeper, mystical reality—"

I interrupted him. "You mean the nature of what some people call God, in all its manifestations, like consciousness and the creative power? The higher Self, whose spark that we are?"

"Yes, exactly. Let me ask you a question. What is a seeker or a *yogi*, ultimately?" He looked at me for the answer, but I kept on listening, knowing it was a rhetorical question.

He continued, "A *yogi* is someone who is seeking to merge their humanity with the higher Self. You are a *yogi* who is looking to bring together and integrate your material existence with the spiritual. Lord Shiva is the ultimate *yogi*, while Parvati Devi is the quintessential *yogini*. Where does Murugan or Kartikeya come into the picture? Well, you see, we need Murugan's grace to stimulate and realise the *kundalini shakti*, the divine creative power that resides within us. When this creative power moves freely within us, then we can experience the higher states of being. Some, such as the Buddhists, call it enlightenment. We call it liberation from being at the effect of *karma*."

"And Lord Ganesh rubber stamps that your endeavours will bear fruit," I added.

"Yes. Such is the power of Lord Ganesh," Swami Ceyon replied. "You have to understand this: if you take one step towards your higher Self, your higher Self will take a thousand steps towards you."

"I see," I replied, trying to understand. "So, the ability to invoke the grace of the universe and evoke these types of synchronicity is possible for everyone? Even the privilege of all?"

"Indeed. Consider that learning to align with higher intelligence, and becoming one with it, is our life purpose, our *dharma*," he told me. "So, it seems, you have invoked the grace of the entire Shiva clan through your spiritual efforts and are becoming more and more aligned with your higher Self."

"I see. It's mind-boggling, humbling, and moving all at once," I said. "But you don't have to be a Hindu to benefit from these beings, do you? I mean, I know that as a Hindu, I can relate to these gods and goddesses in the forms and philosophies that I grew up absorbing, like osmosis. But they exist in their own right as beings that are completely free of cultural or religious frameworks, right? I mean, if I were Christian then Murugan would show up as Archangel Michael, or Mikail if I were a Muslim? They would occur for me in the context of that belief system, right?"

"As I said, there is only one God, the infinite intelligence." Swami Ceyon seemed completely at peace with himself.

I had an insight and ventured, "So, we each relate to this infinite intelligence through the lenses of our own backgrounds and systems?"

"Yes, we see things from the lenses of what we know and recognise."

"Is it that the many manifestations of this ultimate intelligence is available to everyone, without exception, should they wish to open their hearts and mind to it?" I asked, waiting for affirmation. Swamiji nodded in agreement. I asked further, "Be it in the form of a deity or a disincarnate being, or merely as archetypes that live in our collective consciousness?"

I felt more at peace with my mystical events and experiences, and the feeling that I was imagining these 'far-fetched' things lifted even in just talking to this wonderful monk with a shining soul. I began to realise that the more I reached into the higher intelligence, which I had first become aware of at the age of seven in front of my Grandma Motima's home shrine, the more it revealed its secrets to me, many of which had yet to be understood by man.

Swami Ceyon stopped by a sapling, which wire gauze supported. "This is what I wanted to show you," he said, pointing to the unremarkable sapling. I hid my disappointment, wondering why on earth he would make me walk almost half a mile on these grounds to show me a twig of a bush.

"I see," I replied, bewildered. "What is it?"

"Well, *this* is a Bodhi tree and we recovered a sapling of the very Bodhi tree under which the Buddha became enlightened in Bodh Gaya, India, all those years ago," he said, his blue eyes dancing.

"I see. I would have thought that specific tree would have died by now?"

"Quite fantastic is its story, Smita. That tree was cut down by many a queen or king over the centuries but, every time it was cut down, it grew again or a new one was planted in its exact place and it flourished. This sapling was cultivated from the Bodhi tree in Bodh Gaya and planted here." Swami Ceyon told me the story with such pride. "Offer your prayers here, Smita, since you have been brought here by divine intelligence."

I knelt down on the cool, lush grass and closed my eyes. With a heart overflowing with gratitude for the amazing experiences and the wonderful people with whom I'd had the privilege to share my life so far, my only prayer: *Thank you! Thank you! Thank you!*

Just as I got up, a tender green heart-shaped leaf of the Bodhi tree floated down, zigzagging and landing at my feet. "There you go. Your prayers have landed. Consider that another blessing," Swamiji said, and laughed.

I picked it up and looked at this interesting piece of history. "Can I keep it?"

"Yes, of course. Consider that the *devas* have given it to you," Swamiji said.

For me, there was no going back.

The person who had landed on the Big Island was a different person to the one in this moment, here at the Hindu Monastery in Kauai. With the multiple surgeries that had lasered away the diseased parts of my physical body, to a series of mystical discoveries, realisations, visions, and blessings that I had been graced with, I was altered forever.

My relationship to having to suffer in life had also altered. I even came to the Buddha's Bodhi tree with my heart free and full of gratitude.

In allowing my Inner Diamond to step into the driving seat of my life and take the steering wheel, my outlook to life had transformed.

Life had been granted afresh. It would not be the same again. It was time to stop fighting for survival and start receiving, to start truly living, and enjoy the gift of being alive.

" ... just a few drops of kindness
are a blessed balm
on an aching soul."

17

Soul Call

"My spiritual adventures on the Hawaiian Islands had left me awe-inspired and humbled. More than ever, I was certain that once you can get out of your own way and trust yourself to live life connected to your greatest self, your Inner Diamond, even your stubborn ego comes on board, gets excited and wants to join in. I realised that the shift that this brings about is so profound that your ego gets aligned in helping you to create the most gorgeous life.

Eager to take my health and work into waters as yet unchartered, I was becoming more open to allowing the most exquisite relationship I had ever experienced. Surely, even I couldn't have any more sticky karma left to clear now?

Four months later, quite out of the blue, I got my answer.

"Mum? It's me. I'm going to go and see Motima this evening. I think you should come with me," I said, speaking from the office phone, urgency in my tone.

"Why? Is something wrong?" Mum asked, concerned and also surprised to hear from me at five in the afternoon. With my work and frequent travel, it wasn't often that I was able to take my mum to visit family.

"No. Maybe. I don't know. I just have a strong feeling that we should go and see Motima this evening, as soon as possible," I replied. "Please, be ready. Traffic permitting, I'll be with you in just over an hour. But we have to hurry so I won't come upstairs to the flat to get you." I hung up the phone and shut down my computer. Then I stuffed the pile of papers with my handwritten notes, including those from client meetings, into my desk drawer, and made my way to the car park. A few of my colleagues, having a smoke outside, called out to me to pop over and chat to them. "Got to jet. Emergency!" I shouted, as I hopped into my car and waved to them, then sped away.

About an hour earlier, just as I was finishing a conference call with a team of my colleagues at our Bangalore offices, I had the clearest intuition that I needed to make my way to see Grandma Motima *now*. Something told me that time was of the essence and that I had to leave instantly. Grandma Motima, now somewhere in her eighties, having suffered from excruciating pain in her legs, had just come out of hospital where I had been to see her two days ago. Apart from the worsening leg pain, she had been fine and in reasonable spirits. Still, my intuition was insistent that I absolutely had to go and see her as soon as I could.

I picked up Mum from her flat, then drove to Grandma Motima's. As I pulled into the car park of the block of flats in which my grandparents lived, we saw an ambulance with flashing lights in front of the building entrance. Some people, whose faces I couldn't make out in the twilight of the October dusk, scurried around while the paramedics manoeuvred a loaded stretcher into the ambulance. A rush of adrenaline shot through me as I had a horrible feeling that it was Motima on that stretcher. I rushed out of my car, and ran to see who it was. As I came closer, I caught sight of one of my dad's brothers and his wife—my uncle Hari Kaka and aunt Usha Kaki. My grandfather Bapuji was just behind them. I knew then that it had to be Motima.

"What's happened?" I said, panting with panic. My uncle and aunt, looking beyond worried, mumbled something but I didn't understand what had actually happened. "What's wrong with Motima? Did she fall? Has she collapsed? What's wrong?"

"Don't know. She's just been crying out incessantly. We can't tell what's wrong, but I think she's in a lot of pain," Usha Kaki said, distraught. Granddad Bapuji stood stock still, stunned and sorrowful. In shock. Grandma Motima cried out in agony from inside the ambulance as the paramedics were closing the doors.

"Which hospital are you taking her to?" I asked them. One of them shouted to me the name of a nearby emergency department.

"Okay, we'll follow you there," I answered. "Kaka," I said, turning to my uncle, "would you all like to hop into my car, or shall we meet you at A&E?"

"Let's take both cars," he said. "We'll see you there."

My grandfather went with my uncle and aunt, while Mum came in my car as I followed the speeding ambulance, with its flashing lights and ear-piercing siren through the dark streets at the tail-end of rush hour. While the ambulance went on to the Accident & Emergency entrance, I drove into the visitors' car park, followed by my uncle. We rushed into the hospital building. Motima had been taken into the emergency ward, gasping for breath, disoriented and in distress, calling out as if to someone she could see but we could not.

"Motima, are you in pain? Where does it hurt? Can I get you something?" my aunt asked. Motima didn't register my aunt talking to her and continued to wail with agony. My aunt and mum stood around Motima's hospital bed while my uncle and grandfather remained some way away as the nurses scurried around the bed, doing their best to make Grandma Motima as comfortable as they could. Meanwhile, we waited for a doctor to show. The nurses did their preliminary examinations, taking Motima's temperature, measuring her blood pressure, and so on.

She was clearly confused. Her distressed and continuous groans became louder. Was she in pain, or was it something else altogether? Her eyes were closed and it seemed to me as if she was plugged into some other reality that caused her to be afraid and scared. I took hold of Motima's hand. "You're safe now, Motima. We are in hospital. The doctor will be here soon to help you. Tell me, what are you feeling? Are you in pain? Where is the pain?" I tried to bring her awareness into the present, into this emergency ward, but she just continued to cry out loudly, oblivious to her surroundings.

Then, as if there was a delay in registering what I had said, she asked, *"Meeta, tu che? Tu aavi gayi ne? Saaru thayu ..."* (Meeta, is that you? Are you here? It's good that you're here.) She gripped my hand tighter and then carried on groaning in distress.

"Motima, breathe. Breathe slowly, Motima." I tried to use her breath to bring her back into the present, to plug her into a different reality to the one that appeared to have hijacked her attention and peace of mind. "Take another breath, Motima," I said, holding onto her hand.

Meanwhile, my aunt and mum looked on, worried and helpless. My uncle and grandfather paced back and forth, and then, seeing there was nothing they could do to help, went away again to the other end of the long emergency ward and took a seat for a while. No one seemed to have any idea of why Motima might be feeling this way and looked worried out of their minds. The nurses were doing their best but the doctor, sucked into a cubicle nearby with two profusely bleeding patients who had been extracted from a car accident, still had not been able to see to Motima.

In between moments of calming down with the odd conscious breath, Motima was now inconsolable and her groans grew louder. Grandma Motima was a tough cookie with an extremely high threshold for pain. In all the years I had known her, even with her severe rheumatoid arthritis, I had never known her to groan and wail like this. Something was really, really wrong. I ran over to an Indian-looking doctor in blue scrubs and matching plastic cap who had come out from behind the curtain of the cubicle opposite. I intercepted him by almost jumping into his path and pleaded frantically, "Please, I understand that you've got patients bleeding in there, but can you *please* get one of your colleagues to take a look and see what's wrong with my grandmother? We've been waiting for over twenty minutes to be seen. I'm afraid she might have internal bleeding or something and be getting worse every second we're waiting for you!"

"Yes, okay. We're short-staffed this evening, but I'm going to call over a doctor from another ward to come and see to her. Just keep her as comfortable as you can." The Indian doctor rushed off and spoke to someone on the phone, while I stood right behind him, waiting for an answer. "Someone will be with you soon," he said.

"A doctor, right? Because she's already been seen by several nurses."

"Yes, yes," he replied, stressed but polite, and rushed off to continue with his original mission.

My family members looked resigned and utterly helpless. My aunt and mum were close to tears at seeing our Motima in such distress, while the men simply did not know what to do for the best, now and then trying to reach out to Motima with their words, suppressing their own emotional turmoil. It was clear that whatever was ailing Grandma Motima, none of us had dealt with it before.

I looked at Motima and noticed how she had shrunk, almost over the course of days—her formerly round face and full cheeks now bony and hollow. As time went by, she appeared to become less and less present in the room and more drawn away by something else that had grabbed her attention. All the while her eyes remained closed, as if she was seeing something in the inner realms that was only visible to her. Whatever it was, it was causing her unbearable anguish and vexation. "Meeta, where are you? Hold my hand," she cried out, as if from within the suffering of a harrowing dream.

"Here I am, Motima," I replied. "I'm right here. Let me hold you, Motima." I cradled my arms around her, so she was leaning into me, comforted. "It's okay, Motima, we're all with you." I told her who else was present from our family and kept talking to her in soothing tones. It seemed to calm her down—to pacify and relieve her of the fear that appeared to be gripping her.

"That's good, stay here with me," she muttered. "Stay with me."

The emergency ward was well organised and clean but chaotic, with each and every available bed occupied by patients recently treated or waiting to be diagnosed. More patients with all manner of ailments queued outside in the reception area, waiting to be seen by a medic. When I popped out to buy bottles of water and a coffee, I noticed a girl who looked like she had a hair dye disaster, with burn marks flaring her hairline and parts of her face. Another woman was arguing with the receptionist that her false nails had stuck and taken root permanently and yes, hers was indeed an emergency. There were seriously worried people too, a man who reported at reception that he had brought in his mother after he suspected she had suffered a stroke. A man who complained of heart murmurs as a result of eating a red-hot curry was being given a ticket number to wait his turn in the growing queue.

Just as I went back inside to Motima's bed, the doctor arrived and examined her. "I'm not able to find anything obviously wrong with her," he said. "We'll keep her under observation for a while down here and see how she's doing."

"But is she in pain? Why is she so distressed? Does she have internal bleeding or something?" I asked.

"From what I'm seeing, there's nothing obvious."

Argh! This wasn't good enough. "Can't you do a scan? What if something's ruptured inside? She came out of hospital a couple of days ago. Maybe something's still aggravating her legs?" I asked, frantic with worry and not willing to be fobbed off by the British National Health Service.

"Okay. I'll request a scan for her but I really don't think it'll show anything," he replied.

"Thank you," I said, wondering how on earth he could be so sure without conducting the proper scans. What was the matter with these people? Wasn't it obvious that they'd have to do a scan to see what might be wrong with her?

Little did I know that the doctor already knew what was happening with my grandmother.

Almost two hours had now passed by. We were still in the emergency ward of the hospital and Motima's condition remained constant. The nurses took her in for a scan and brought her back. The doctor came by with the results and told us that the scan had not shown any internal ruptures or bleeding, but that they wanted to keep Motima in anyway and monitor her throughout the night. As I held her in my arms, as though she were a child, cradling and comforting her, she became somewhat calmer. I kept talking to her about this and that, not sure if she heard what I was saying, but it seemed to comfort her to hear my voice. When I popped away for a few minutes to go to the toilet, I came back to find her once again wailing and groaning, almost hysterical. It seemed that somehow, I was able to reach her in her innermost awareness and soothe the fearful torment that made her frantic.

"It looks like there's nothing we can do for the moment," my uncle said. "Usha, why don't I take you and Bhabhi [my mum] home and drop Bapuji off also. It's ten thirty now and there's little any of us can do."

"Let Meeta stay with me!" Motima said loudly, lucid as the light, trying to lift her head and moving it from left to right and back, so as to try and see me with her eyes closed. "Meeta, eh Meeta, you're not going anywhere, are you?"

"I'm right here, Motima," I said, squeezing her hand tighter now. "I'm here. I'm going to stay right here with you until you're better, Motima."

What on earth was happening to my Motima? I felt upset, unable to see Grandma Motima caught up, beyond control, in this anguished, agitated state. Seeing her like this, the one who had given every ounce of herself to our family, ripped my heart out. What could I do to make her better? How could I take away her fear? What was she seeing or feeling that agitated her so much?

I kept telling her that she was safe, that she was looked after, that we were there with her, and that the nurses and doctors were taking care of her. All the while, what I really wanted to do was burst into tears, but I did everything to put aside my own feelings and concerns. Now was not a time to indulge in personal feelings and emotions. This was a time for being present, vigilant to how I could best serve this vulnerable old woman, this woman whom I had grown up calling my second mother, this woman who had raised me with such care and tenderness when I had been the vulnerable one. She needed me now, and I wasn't going to let up in being there in her greatest time of need.

"Don't go anywhere! Stay with me! You stay close to me!" she said again, as my uncle explained to her that he would drop the others home and return in a short while. My aunt and my mum looked devastated as they left Motima with me. "Meeta's staying with you, Motima," my uncle reassured her. "I'm going to take the others home and then I'll be back with you."

I kept myself together, strong, solid. As I sat on her hospital bed, holding her, caressing her forehead, wiping away the beads of sweat that came and went, I knew very well that nothing I was feeling could be a patch on what this extraordinary soul was going through in these hours. She, who had given me such love in my fledgling years, who had taught me the values of our ancient culture, and ignited in me the yearning to be the best I could be. She, who had planted the seeds of that which would make me into a woman of depth and substance in my later years. When tears welled up, I wiped them away with the back of my hand, not allowing Motima to sense that I was falling to pieces inside.

I realised just how inadequate I had felt all those years when, knowing that I could never really repay what she had done for me, I would give Grandma Motima the *sari* I had brought back for her from India or insist that the new toaster I had bought her would be much easier for her to use. After all, what gift could you possibly give to the woman who had raised and shaped you? How could I ever repay her?

After the others left, I continued to talk to Grandma Motima through her distraught state, bringing her mind back from wherever it was wandering and into the present. I kept making her focus on her breath, telling her again and again to take slow, long breaths so that her rattled mind would become less agitated and her frazzled nerves calmer.

By the time Uncle Hari had come back, she was more settled and quieter.

"We're going to move her to another ward now," the Head Nurse said. "We'll keep an eye on her overnight and call you if anything changes."

"Meeta, are you still here?" Motima tightened her grasp on my hand, like a fish out of water gasping to stay alive.

"Can we stay with her, please? She's asking me to stay near her. She's obviously deeply disturbed and not ready to be left on her own." I worried that the nurse would enforce hospital rules about when visitors were allowed.

"Yes, yes. By all means, stay with her, if it helps her," she said with kindness. In moments such as these, even just a few drops of kindness are a blessed balm on an aching soul. "If she makes it through the night, who knows what might happen."

Alarmed, as the nurse's words dropped into my head with a thud, I said, "*If* she makes it through the night? Whatever do you mean? The doctor said there was nothing obvious that was wrong with her. Presumably, then, she's just in pain with her rheumatoid arthritis?"

"Well, yes. Didn't the doctor tell you?" the nurse asked, surprised.

"Tell us what, exactly? He said he could find nothing wrong with her and just wanted to keep her in overnight for observation."

"Ah. I see." She looked uneasy.

"Are you saying she's dying or something?" I was beside myself with worry.

She pulled me away from Motima's bed and indicated to my uncle to follow us. Outside the ward, in the corridor, she said, "I'm afraid the groans and wails you hear your grandmother making are indicative that she may not be with us much longer. I'm so sorry." My uncle and I looked at each other, unable to take in this morbid message, unwilling to accept this possibility as being true.

Of course. The doctor must have recognised the signs straightaway and that was why he didn't feel the need for a scan. He could see and hear that Motima was in her final stages, facing death. She probably sensed this and that was why she was so shaken out of her skin, so terrified.

My uncle and I stayed at Grandma Motima's bedside after she had been moved to a new ward on the fourth floor. It was almost eleven o'clock at night, the lights had already been dimmed, and the other patients were asleep. In the otherwise pin-drop silence of the sleeping ward, Motima was still crying out, unable to control her reaction to whatever she was confronting her in her inner world. I kept comforting her, whispering to her so as not to disturb the other patients too much, bringing her attention again and again to her breath to refocus her into the external reality. My uncle said little and I could see he was devastated at the possibility of losing his dear mother. It seemed to me that he had already prepared himself, resigned to her fate. No longer able to see her suffer, he said that he would wait in the visitors' room across the hallway.

18

Squaring the Circle of Life

Until this moment, I'd been sure that Motima was in some sort of pain that she was unable to communicate but, now, the gravity of her condition slowly dawned on me, as I sat beside her bed at the end of the evening. The thought of life without my Grandma Motima was something that I had never ventured to contemplate. My heart filled with even more compassion for her as I watched her fighting to stay with us. It made me appreciate her all the more for the struggle that had been her life, for the sacrifices she had made on behalf of each and every one of us, her nine children and me. And for my mother, too.

The hours ticked by, slowly but surely, as I did my best to make Motima comfortable, adjusting her pillow here, offering her sips of water now and then. I focused on her as she lay there holding on to these precious hours into the night, and thoughts of who Motima had been for me flooded my mind. While I regretted that life had presented me with choices that may not have been to her liking, much less her approval, nothing she had done for me had passed me by. I may not have been mature enough to have emphatically let her know just how much I loved or appreciated her, but not for a second had I ever taken Motima's kindness or sacrifices for granted.

Her light blue cotton *sari* had bunched up under her thighs, and I freed it, as if a reflex action, and pulled it and smoothed it with my palm over her ankles, just like I used to for her every day when we lived together in India. "Pull it gently and make sure you can't see my ankles," she would say. "*Saris* are elegant only when they cover your feet." Memories of just how much I adored her then resurfaced, and I had to take a gulp so as not to turn into a blubbering mess.

Memory after sweet memory arose as I tended to her. Here, in this emergency ward, even though it reeked of disinfectant, I was suddenly overwhelmed with the flowery fragrance of Motima's skin that I had so loved to be close to in my younger years, kneading her skin as though it were dough because it was so butter-soft. Or I would sit by her side and count the design of dots that she had tattooed on olive skinned arms. "Motima, you are so *gori gori*," I would say, referring to her light, fair skin, making her break into a smile, melting her with charm.

The nurse came by again and asked, "How is she doing?" I told her that Motima was a little calmer now but still obviously distraught.

"I'll be dropping by every hour to check in on the patients but if you need anything, here's the button to press to call me," she said. Another hour must have passed by since I had seen the nurse last. Time seemed to have taken on some other dimension. There was a surreality about what 'time' meant, as I waited with Motima in these hours. Now a little calmer, she weaved in and out of moments of rest and agitation.

As a little girl in India, I had watched her go every week to the market in Porbandar town centre and bring back, single-handedly, heavy loads of groceries in the afternoon Indian sun, dripping with so much sweat that she would have to shower immediately on reaching home. I remembered how she would get up early six days a week and begin cooking for us so that my aunts and I could go to college or school after having a hot breakfast, and take a packed lunch freshly cooked by our beloved Motima's own hands. I remembered how, every summer, she would insist on making a whole year's worth of several different types of mango and *gunda* pickles, each one complicated and requiring a master chef's skills. Why? Because she knew that each one of us, me and my three aunts, we each had a different favourite pickle to the other and she wanted to keep us all happy. I remembered how on that awful day, when I was seven years old, she took special care of me when I was in deep shock after my mum had tried to take me back with her to Granddad Motabhai's. I remembered how on that very day, to console me, she had told me that *she* would be my mother.

The nurse was back again. How many times had I seen this nurse come by now? Four, maybe five times? I looked at the round white clock on the back wall of the ward and saw that it was already five o'clock in the morning. After checking in on Motima, she said, "Gosh, you've been here all night. You could probably do with a cup of coffee." I shrugged. "Why don't you come with me to the staff room? We have freshly brewed coffee there, as the new shift will arrive soon."

I sat in the nurses' staff room, my hands cupped around the mug of hot coffee, as the nurse remarked, "How's your grandmother doing? I can see that she means a lot to you, and you mean a lot to her."

"Yeah," I said. "That's because she brought me up. It was at a time when my mum wasn't well."

"Yeah, when you share an experience like that at a young age, it stays with you. It continues to mean a lot throughout your life," she said. "Isn't it great if you can do something for them, when it really matters?" I smiled a little as she said that. "I'm sorry, I'd better get on. I need to prepare for the next shift to take over. You carry on drinking your coffee."

"Oh sure, no problem. Thank you for the coffee and chat," I replied.

Back at Motima's bedside, seeing her lying peacefully for the first time since she had been admitted, those months that I had been without her in India flashed in front of my eyes as though it was yesterday. How desolate I had been in that one year when Motima had left me behind in India. How lonely had I been without her and how I had missed her. As the minutes and hours tick-tocked into the dead of the night, perhaps towards the final hours in the life of this special soul, she who had been the true centre of my world for the first seventeen years of my life, my heart was awash with love for and gratitude to her. I knew that, as much as she loved all her children and grandchildren, she had nurtured a tender, soft spot in her heart for me since the day I was born.

After all, just look at how our higher Selves had conspired to have she and I be together, alone with each other, granting me the privilege of taking care of her, giving her the strength that she needed, in her most vulnerable condition in those final precious hours. Sometimes holding her hand, sometimes stroking her butter-soft olive skin, sometimes holding her in my arms, sometimes feeding her sips of water, I yearned to tell her just how much she had meant to me. And yet, I knew that she knew.

Now, with more nurses arriving to take over the morning shift, the corridors were fully lit, and the white light poured in and brightened up the ward in which Motima was lying. A clinking of cups and cutlery could be heard as the trolleys for the patients' breakfasts were being prepared. It must have been around six o'clock. Motima sprung to life, fully back in her body. It was as if this were her inherent reflex, her whole life, devoted to waking up each morning to nurture and prepare nourishment for her loved ones. She said in a soft voice, "Meeta, you are still here. *Saaru thayu ke tu maari saathe hati. Taraa ma khari shakti che. Mane saaru laaigu tu ahiya hati to.*" She said that she appreciated that I was with her all this time, that I had true strength and courage in me, and that this helped her through those difficult hours.

Coming from Grandma Motima, who was not given to sentimentality, these sweet, affectionate expressions of her feelings were a treasure to me. I burst out with the tears that I had been suppressing during the night and all these years. I wanted nothing more than for my Grandma Motima to know just how dearly I loved her, no matter the challenges we'd had to face. I didn't care about any of what had gone on in the past. All that mattered was that she acknowledged and received the love that I, from the depth of my soul, had always felt for her and always would.

Something told me that Motima knew that this morning would be her last one and that she had precious little time left. Still seated at her bedside, I leant over towards her. When I laid my head on her chest, I whispered just loud enough for her to hear, "Oh, Motima! I have always loved you, Motima." I blubbered the best I knew how in Gujarati, "Please forgive me for my mistakes, for when I have caused you pain. I didn't mean to hurt you, Motima. I've always wanted to make you proud."

She, now more lucid than I had known her to be in the last months, reached out to put her hand on my head and whispered, "Since when have you learnt to cry, you silly girl? Remember, you're the strong one, like me. We don't cry at the little things of life, do we?"

"What will I do without you, Motima?" I sniffled. "Who will I call when I need recipes, the ones you make best? Who will tell me off if you're not there?" I said, tearfully, making a pathetic attempt to inject humour.

"What time is it?" she asked. I told her it was now coming up to six in the morning. "Go home now," she said. "You have to go to work soon, don't you?"

"No, Motima, I'm not leaving you. It doesn't matter about work," I replied, surprised to see her recover right in front of my very eyes.

"Go now. Come back later. I'll be waiting for you. I will be waiting for you," she said, commanding me in her usual manner. "Go! I'll be fine."

"All right, Motima. But I'll be back straight after work, okay?"

Uncle Hari had dozed off in his chair in the visitors' room, so I woke him gently to tell him that Motima seemed to have pulled through the night. Just then, a lonesome-looking Granddad Bapuji arrived saying, "Are you still here?"

I explained that I had sat with Motima throughout the night and that she appeared to be much better now.

After showering at home, I went straight to work. The meetings lined up for the day were important, including one that I had worked for a year to get with the chief executive of one of the largest insurance companies in Europe. He had agreed to do our first meeting at his company's offices in central London. Though I had not slept at all, I was more awake and alive than I had been in a long time. In Grandma Motima telling me to stay with her, in her allowing me back into her world in an intimate and meaningful way, I had been able to give her something. In my giving and in her receiving, something between us had been restored— our ability to express the love we so deeply felt for each other. Balance and harmony had been restored between our inner being as well as in the outer world. This was more precious than anything else I could imagine.

After the meeting with the chief executive of the insurance company, I went back to our offices in Euston. With no appetite for food whatsoever, I must have been on my fifth cup of coffee by lunchtime. I got through my various meetings and calls as best as I could that afternoon, then rushed out of the office as quickly as I could and zigzagged my way through rush hour traffic, straight to the hospital. I couldn't help wondering what Motima had endured throughout the hours since I had left her. "I'll be waiting for you," she had promised.

When leaving the hospital that morning, I had bumped into the doctor who had attended to Motima the previous evening in A&E. I had been perplexed throughout the night, after I realised that the medics' prognosis was that Motima was dying.

"How could you tell that she was dying?" I asked him.

"Oh, we see several patients a day with your grandmother's predicament," the doctor said, matter of fact. "Often, when a person is in their last stages, they have a sudden deterioration. Their body starts to shut down rapidly, making them deeply distressed. They don't realise what's going on until much later. They're not able to have any control over their bodies or their reactions and so they're terrified. It's really important in those last hours to stay with them and comfort them. I've heard from the nurses that you've done this very well, to help your grandmother with the preparation of her journey." He said that in an objective, diagnostic manner, as if it was some sort of a clinical observation. He must have realised he sounded scientific and cold, because he tried clumsily to compensate by adding, "Sorry for your loss."

When I reached Motima at around half past six that evening, the whole of our clan was there, surrounding

Motima's bedside—my grandfather, my parents, three uncles and aunts, and eight cousins. My spirits perked up with hope, remembering what the nurse had said: "If she makes it through the night, who knows what might happen." Motima appeared calm, lying still as though she might be napping, as I caught sight of her through the crowd of the clan. I was the last one to arrive. I made my way to her immediately, past my aunts and cousins and, smiling, uttered just one word: "Motima."

"Meeta? *Tu aavi gayi ne?*" She asked if I was now there, with her, and raised her hand slightly and moved it on the bed towards me. I took her hand in mine and she clasped with what little strength she had. *"Tu aavi gayi ne?"* Then she repeated her question in English, "You're here now, aren't you?"

"*Haa, Motima,*" I confirmed, taking a seat on the empty chair beside her, at the top of the bed. My emotions melting within, I held on to her hand ever so firmly, my belly quivering, shivering inside with the strangest, icy nervousness. She had pulled through the last twenty-four hours but her condition had deteriorated considerably during the day. She lay there with her eyes closed, motionless, her breathing short and shallow. Pale and lifeless, her complexion almost grey, she looked a mere shadow of the person that I had left earlier that morning. An air of impending inevitability loomed thick and heavy around Motima's bed, as if the angels were preparing to lift her large motherly spirit out of her well-worn and exhausted body.

Surrounded by her loved ones, relaxed, Motima smiled ever so slightly. A few breaths later, after squeezing my hand, she let out a gentle sigh, her final one, surrendering the *prana*, vital force, over to the angels. With this, the essence of her soul left her body, taking her from this life into a time and space beyond. Her hand, still warm in mine, had let go of her grip, but unwilling to let her go, I squeezed it harder, as she slipped away and upward, continuing on her soul's journey into divinity. Her physical eyes closed to the world while, no doubt, her inner eyes opened to embrace a soulful peace and bliss that she had so much earned.

"Motima! Motima!" I screamed. "Open your eyes, Motima!" Tears of grief unleashed from my heart. Other family members, my cousins, aunts, and my mum, all wept too as they realised Motima had passed away, unable to bear such great loss. I surrendered and cried irrepressibly for the next while, as others also shed rivers of tears or walked away into the corridor to avoid breaking down. I gazed at Motima, who, having come into the hospital disoriented and distraught, now lay on her deathbed with an expression of absolute peace. Her face, in its heyday considered remarkably beautiful, conveyed contentment of one who had the satisfaction of knowing that she had given her all, everything she knew how. I pushed myself heavily from my chair, bent towards her cheek, and kissed it, stroking her other cheek softly with the back of my fingers. Still sobbing, I rested my head on her left shoulder for a moment or two, as a whirlwind of gratitude and sorrow whizzed within me.

My cousin Rakhi, standing next to me, turned to comfort me with a hug, as other family members turned to each other for consolation and support. A sudden ache in my gut began to uncoil. I had a sense that a deeply rooted cord that had connected me and Grandma Motima all these years was being wrenched out of me as her soul drifted away from our physical world.

I realised that Grandma Motima had been waiting for me to arrive, so that we could say our final 'adieu', after which she could step out of this world at peace. She, the personification of Mother, wanted me to know before she left that she loved me, that she had always loved me, and that we were parting from each other in this lifetime, also in love.

The *karma* between us, which that day when I was seventeen had come to an abrupt full stop, was now bountifully whole, granting both our souls the peace and oneness with each other that we secretly yet profoundly yearned but were too proud to show.

Motima, my grandmother and mother both, held nothing back in giving of herself when I needed her most and in teaching me those things that would be the making of me in this lifetime. I shall always thank God for the grace of having had her in my life.

May her soul receive, multiplied, the magnanimity with which she nurtured others.

May her soul, protected by angels, remain steeped in peace, returning liberated into Divinity.

May the light of her soul shine ever luminous in a stellar constellation ruled by her beloved:

Mahadev—Lord Shiva, the Transformer.

19

Taking Flight

After Motima's funeral, work got much busier. I was secretly thankful for this, because it gave me some space to slowly process the grief of her loss. My clients awarded me larger and more exciting IT contracts than ever before. As a result, the company that I worked for sent me off to develop new clients, which I was more than happy to do. I practically lived in hotels and at airports across Europe and India, going from client to client.

All in all, work was going well. Of course, there were challenges. Most of these were to do with company politics, for which I used the guidance of my Inner Diamond to handle or avoid becoming entangled. Somehow, life was much easier now. With so many of the loose ends in my prime relationships tied up, so much deep healing having taken place, I felt lighter and freer than ever before. It left me able to take on much bigger opportunities at work and create relationships anew in my personal life.

Over the last ten years, I had gradually spent more and more of my spare time, and eventually all of it, to becoming an avid student of personal development. I went to workshops and programmes, which I later learnt to lead myself. These were about thinking positively, but more than that, they were about learning how to take responsibility for your own actions, understanding your own emotional reactions to people, learning how to see things from their perspective, and making choices that were right for you. These training programmes focused on turning life's challenges into golden opportunities for personal growth. They were about what it meant to be 'human' and 'winning' effectively at the game of life. The underlying premise that all these programmes had in common was that, once you had cleaned the slate of your past, you were free to have a fresh future, one that was of your own creation, a future that was not coloured by the conditioning of your past experiences.

"How time flies. Seems like only yesterday since we spoke," Gina said as she greeted me in the buzz of the newly opened café bar, in a square just off London's Carnaby Street, behind Liberty. Though we had stayed in touch over the phone, I had caught up with Gina only once after coming back from Hawaii some months back. She took a seat by the window. A waitress came over to take our orders and went away to get us cappuccinos and their most decadent chocolate cake for our four o'clock sweet fix. Gina and I talked for a while about how life was going for her, now that she had been back in London for quite some time. She told me about how happy she was in her relationship with her wonderful husband, Matthew.

"So sorry about your grandmother passing away, Smeets," Gina condoled warmly. "You've talked about her so many times, I almost feel like I knew her. How are you doing now? I know how much she meant to you."

"It's like a big hole in our family," I replied. "With the way my work has been over the years, I wasn't able to go and see her as much as I would have liked to, or should have. She had such a huge presence. For me, she was the glue that bound all of us together, through all our ups and downs. While Motima was around, there was a reason to get together and celebrate the good things about our family." My eyes moistened as I relived our great loss and the impact on our family of Motima no longer being with us.

"Hmm, having lost my own mamma some years ago, I know just how difficult it is to lose your mother," Gina said. "And I know she was like a mother to you for a long time." She reached across the table and held my hand in both of hers.

I nodded slowly, trying to smile to acknowledge that I appreciated Gina's affection. "I miss her. It was a difficult moment when she passed away but I feel relieved and liberated that she and I were able to connect in a meaningful way in her important final hours. It was so moving," I said, tearful, remembering those moments as if I was with Grandma Motima all over again.

"Oh, I'm so pleased, Smeets. I'm so pleased that you had those hours with her and both of you were able to meet in that genuine, heartfelt place. I know how important that was for you."

"It was a real privilege to be there with her, especially that night before she passed away. I'm so grateful to both our higher Selves, hers and mine, for that opportunity."

"I'm sure that experience will stay with you." My friend gave my hand a quick squeeze.

The waitress returned with our coffees and chocolate cake, wreaking havoc as she accidentally dropped some cutlery and one of the saucers that came with our coffee cups, sending them crashing to the floor. Thankfully, she didn't drop the coffee cups as well. Profusely apologising, she cleared everything up and brought us fresh cutlery and saucers.

After the waitress had gone, Gina turned her attention to one of the topics that we had regularly talked about. She asked, "You know, you've come such a long way from the first time we met, all those years ago. You've had a couple of serious relationships, yes? So what are your thoughts on Mr Right, now? Got any plans for him? How long have you been single?"

"Six years, nearly seven, that's how long I've been single. I remember that conversation we had all those years back about me feeling like a cardboard cut-out," I said, with a laugh. "I couldn't feel more different now. Did I ever tell you about that glimpse I had of the future, just before I left home when I was twenty-one?"

"Remind me," Gina said.

"Well, I had a vision of what it felt like to be a person who was free inside," I said.

"Ah, yes, I do remember now. Wasn't that when you had a flash of who you could become?"

"Yes, that's it. Looking back, it feels like then, my Diamond had planted a seed of who I could be."

"But that's how you are now. Look at you!" Gina smiled broadly. "See just how far you've come. You're actually living it, that inner freedom."

"Can you see it? I mean, is it so obvious?" I asked, curious to get an objective view. "What do you see that's different?"

"Well, for one thing, you're so much more, how to put it, *comfortable* in your skin. You look grounded and secure in yourself. It's like you know who you are now, like in a way that no one can take that away from you again," she said with a warm smile.

I nodded, smiling, appreciative that Gina and I were still in tune with each other. "You know, the world outside goes on as ever, but the way I experience it is that I've come *home*. You know what I mean? I'm *at* home within myself, connected to something that feels more real, richer somehow, than just my personality."

"That must feel incredible," Gina said. "What do you put this down to? All those trips to India, learning about spiritual philosophies? Or is it the meditation?" she asked.

"I'm not sure. It feels like everything has somehow helped to chip away at the things that were in the way," I replied.

"Didn't you do a lot of personal development programmes for a few years in London as well?" she asked.

"Yep, and you came to one of the ones that I myself was leading, remember?"

"I do, I do. It was a big group too." She looked a little sheepish as she recalled that she'd actually been to one of my groups.

"Three hundred and two people," I said.

"I saw you in action, teaching them how to look at issues and at themselves from a very different perspective. You coached several people in front of the group, too. You were amazing, spot on with your insights," Gina said, generous as usual with her praise.

"Ah, you remember that too. To answer your question, I'm not sure that I can put my growth down to any one thing," I replied. "All those things have helped to move me forward, not to mention the insights from that Inner Diamond. To be honest, everything that I've learnt from work to yoga to doing crazy things like bungee jumping and even scuba diving—all these things have done wonders for shifting the way I see things."

"I can imagine. They must've helped to overcome fear."

"Oh, definitely. I'm able to be more of myself, regardless of who I'm with. Even at work. Who I am now, it feels to me like a coming together of all the different things that I've done to find who I really am," I said. "Does that make sense?"

"It's amazing how if you bring your awareness to it, everything, even work, *especially* work, can help you to know yourself better."

"It's so true. Awareness. That's the key ingredient. By bringing self-awareness to it, everything you do can become an opportunity to set you more and more free."

"Yeah, and it helps if you can add a dose of being honest with yourself, too," Gina said. "It's all a bit like looking for a needle in the haystack of your persona, don't you think?" She took a forkful of the rich, dark cake, then added, "Hmmmm, this chocolate cake is devilish. Absolutely heavenly!"

"You know, you work and work towards something, chipping away at it but along the way, you forget why you were interested in doing those things in the first place." I helped myself to the sweet dessert. "Then, wham! You're in! Things suddenly come together when you least expect."

Gina agreed. "Usually, just when you've let go of wanting to be this way or that is right when it happens. And you're there, right there, being and feeling in a way that at one time you could not even imagine was possible."

"That's it. It's exactly like that." I nodded.

"So, when was it that you started to feel differently about yourself? About life?" Gina asked. "Did you notice if there was a specific moment, as such?"

"Good question." I sipped some more of my coffee, thinking. For me, so many breakthroughs had taken place, one after the other, that they had become a way of life by now. "You know, mostly, things sort of happened over time, sometimes a drip, drip of change over here and at other times, a wave that would shift something over there."

I paused to take a sip of my cappuccino and suddenly remembered a specific event. "That said, there was this one specific moment when something altered quite dramatically. I was on a flight back from Mumbai, having taken a bunch of my clients for meetings at our offices in India. I was really tired but not enough to fall asleep, so I was reading this book about the teachings of this great Indian sage called Ramana Maharshi. I still remember this one specific quote. It said, *'You are awareness. Awareness is another name for you. Since you are Awareness there is no need to attain or cultivate it. All that you have to do is to give up being aware of other things, that is of not-self. If one gives up being aware of them then pure awareness alone remains, and that is the Self.'*

"That's beautiful," Gina said. "He makes it sound so simple. I mean, it's easy enough to understand conceptually, but to get it in a way that it alters you forever, that's something else altogether."

"Well, that's the thing. That's exactly how it was for me. I understood it intellectually for a long time, but on this day, these words landed in my head like a string of glistening crystals. They blew my mind."

"Hmm, I can imagine," Gina replied, thoughtful.

"I had to stop and take a deep breath or two to let those powerful words sink in," I said. "I stared out of my window, and right there was this unbelievable, astonishing vista. There was a huge, warm orange-golden globe outside. I swear I could've touched it if only I could open the airplane window. A stunning sunset was taking place in the vast empty space that stretched out into infinity. The sky was simply soaked, streaked with an exquisite glow of golds, oranges, reds, pinks, purples, and peaches as the sun was setting. Above the colours was a pitch black sky that opened up into the cosmos, with early stars already twinkling."

"Oh my God. That must have been heavenly."

"Right in that moment, I kid you not, Genes, I lost myself." I paused to have a sip of my coffee, relishing and reliving the memory of those special life-altering moments.

"I can imagine." Gina gave a sigh. "Aw, that sounds divine, Smeets. Can you take me with you the next time you fly somewhere? The best that happens to me on a plane is I fall asleep and start snoring. The last time we flew, my husband had to wake me up because the person in the next seat complained of the noise! And that's just me. I haven't even started telling you about Matthew's snoring."

I laughed at the thought of Gina's sonic snoring.

Gina giggled, then said, "Sorry, I interrupted what you were saying. Carry on."

"Well, as I looked out into that gorgeous emptiness— empty but for the setting sun and all those breathtaking hues—right in that moment, something clicked into place, a vivid new realisation. Call it a breakthrough. Call it an awakening. It was as if everything that I had ever done in my life to discover who I was suddenly merged, like the awe-inspiring hues outside blending one into the other. Everything came together in one single point, like lines of energy striking into a spark," I said.

"Wow," Gina said, fascinated. "So, what was the realisation?"

"What I got, clear as crystal, was that my life was filled up with certain things, like being successful in my career, wanting to be in a relationship and happily married, having to achieve a certain status or reputation in life, having to be treated a certain way by other people, and so on. These were things that on the one hand I knew, intellectually, weren't that important and yet I was driven towards them anyway."

"Like a fish on a hook," Gina said, then chuckled.

"Pretty much."

"In those moments, you fully *got* just how much you were defined by them," she said, right there with me.

She, too, had had these same realisations during the course of her life.

"Right," I said. "My ego defined me through these things, but that's not what life's about, is it? And yet, even when you know that, you just get carried along, don't you? I mean, we just let ourselves, don't you think?"

Gina said again, "Like a fish on a hook."

"Exactly. Like a fish, I'd been dragged through the water on that fishing hook of yours, and I didn't even know it," I said, speaking excitedly. "But after that incredible realisation, it was like a waking up to a brand new reality. Almost all at once, I was freed from being dragged along by that hook, at least from my version of the hook."

"And relieved, too, I bet," Gina said.

"Absolutely. I'd been shackled without knowing it. Having to achieve this and accomplish that—be this way and not that. All that stuff that I'd grown up with or picked up along the way, stuff from the past, suddenly no longer bothered me because I got what that amazing sage, Ramana Maharshi, meant. I got that I *am* Awareness. We all are. That's it. Free, unbounded, pure awareness. I *felt* myself in that state. I mean, I *knew* myself that way. I actually experienced it, Gina." I felt so alive as I recounted that exceptional experience.

Not being able to contain my enthusiasm, I said, "My ego, in that moment, took a back seat and the Inner Diamond came to fore and took charge. It was truly humbling, like getting a blessing, sort of a grace, from the higher Self."

"It must have been something like that. You switched drivers, Smeet. The ego let go of controlling your decisions and the Inner Diamond took the driver's seat."

"Yes. I switched drivers." I felt fired up. "All that enquiring, looking within, letting go, taking responsibility, forgiving, everything, it all just converged there and then, and I felt the shackles of my past fall off me, all at once, or so it seemed."

"That's amazing. People give up their worldly goods to have that kind of experience." Then, not being able to resist having a joke on me, she said, giggling, "You didn't suddenly feel the urge to go and live in a cave, did you?" She pushed back my arm playfully with her fist.

"Haha! Yes, okay," I replied, contorting my face into a show of begrudging amusement. "You can have that one."

"So, how did you feel then, when that mystical lightening bolt hit you?" she asked.

"For a long few moments, I felt myself steeped and soaked in that Awareness that Ramana Maharshi was referring to. As if I had absolutely no boundaries whatsoever, I was boundless and yet so alive, fully awake. I actually experienced myself that way—expansive, full and empty all at once, in the innate state that we all are. After I came back to 'normal', I mean to my physical self, I felt like a right twat!"

"Why?" she asked. "I would give up my babies for experiencing something like that."

"Haha," I laughed and said in a Cockney London accent, "It's just as well you don't have any then, innit?"

"No, really," she said. "Jesting aside, when you have that profound an experience, it must absolutely alter your outlook forever. These things, all said and done, are priceless. Who wouldn't love to have that? But why would you feel ridiculous afterwards?"

"Well, for all that striving and effort and hard work to realise my 'inner being', it was there all along. I was free all along." I threw my hands up in disbelief. "Of course, now it's all as obvious as the nose on my face. I just had to create the conditions for the Inner Diamond to be able to have more space in my life."

"That's amazing. Pretty damn profound," Gina said in sincere tones. "Has that state of inner freedom continued, or did it come and disappear after you landed back on earth?"

"No, it's still there. It's as if someone switched my hard drive and installed a brand new operating system and software. It's upgraded my entire outlook. I might look the same, but how I feel and think about the exact same things that have been around for years, how I respond to them, has shifted massively."

"Uh huh, that's seriously amazing. People would give up everything to have that kind of a shift. So tell me more about how you felt then?"

"In a word, liberated."

20

Mr Right

Gina studied me for a short while, then said, "That's so inspiring, Smita. How does that effect the way you think about relationships now? Do you still want to be in one, or don't you feel the need for it?"

"That's such a good question. You know, I do and I don't. I mean, I don't feel the way I used to about myself. It's like, there's nothing missing in my life anymore, in my own self. Before, I used to crave to be in a relationship, to be loved and all that. That's not there now."

"I think what you're saying is that you don't really *need* a relationship now," Gina said.

"That's it." I nodded. "I mean, don't get me wrong, it would be an amazing adventure to be with someone who's also somehow 'whole—"

Gina interrupted, teasing me. "You mean, as opposed to someone who's an asshole." We both burst out laughing.

"Oh, you're so irreverent." I giggled. "You've no sense of the sacred whatsoever, woman!"

"Carry on," she said, gesturing by sweeping her hands towards me.

"That could be really amazing, being with someone who's worked on himself, you know, dealt with his demons. For once and for all, I've had enough of being with blokes who, instead of being utterly turned on by a ballsy woman, they feel *threatened* by her. What is it with men? I want someone who'll be absolutely thrilled to be with me. I'm not going to be put in some box and forced to play small, just because he's too insecure to be with a woman who shines," I said, passion oozing.

"Quite! *He* needs to have balls. No pun intended." We both burst out laughing again. "No, but really. Insecure men can't be with audacious, empowered women. We want someone for you who knows who he is, someone who is secure in himself. Someone who himself excels in his own life and who can give you the space to do the same. We want someone for you who finds your 'bodacious' nature an utter joy to be around."

"Right. See, with someone like that, you're not walking on eggshells, worrying about denting their delicate ego with the slightest sneeze, or mothering him, or paying his bills. When you meet on a platform of equality, and I don't mean physically, but more psychologically, emotionally, and spiritually, then you're talking. *Then* you have a place from which you can create a vision for your lives together," I said. "And be of service to others in some way, too."

"Hmmm ... you know you're talking about soul mates ..."

"Maybe, though that term does make me cringe a bit." I grimaced as if I'd had a dose of sour lemon juice. I asked, "Did I ever tell you about this incredible epiphany I had? Must have been some seven years back,"

"No, I don't think so," she replied. "What was it?"

"Well, I was on a Vipassana meditation retreat. It was sixteen days and nights straight of not talking to a single soul, not even communicating with anyone using signs or anything. I mean, you couldn't even look in anyone's direction."

"I looked at that once. You're right, it seemed properly torturous," she said. "I decided to give it a miss."

"Well, I can tell you, it wasn't for the faint-hearted, silence for sixteen days and nights, especially for me. But towards the end, when my ego had realised that resistance was futile and my mind had stopped fighting the process that we were being taught to follow, something truly remarkable happened. In one of my meditations, as if I was watching a movie, I saw something that so captivated my attention, and inspired me so much, I could never go back to seeing things the same way again," I said.

"Like an epiphany, you mean?" Gina asked.

"I suppose so. It was one of those things that touched me so deeply, that I couldn't pretend or ignore it," I replied. Gina nodded, listening intently.

"I saw a man and woman holding each other, entwined, in the most tender and intimate embrace." I shrugged, feeling my way forward. "Though they were in a deep embrace, there was so much spaciousness in-between and around them. I sensed freedom in the energy between them. It was so beautiful to watch. They were so into each other, but it wasn't merely lust or need. It went far beyond that. The pull between them was obvious, but the attraction went soul-deep, like they could see the beauty in each other's core being. That's what drew them to each other." I paused to gauge Gina's reaction, relieved to see that she was engrossed, listening intently.

"Their dynamic created a field of energy around them, a bubble, that was unusual. They were so connected to each other and the way they reached out to others was very different to anything that I knew. It was kind of special, you know? They were two people but there was an easy oneness between them. At the same time, they were able to stand on their own, on the strength of their own merit, individually whole and complete," I said, remembering as if I had seen it only yesterday. "I doubt that she would have to go around picking up his dirty socks and undies after him."

Gina laughed. "Oh dear God, give me *that* guy." She sighed. "I bet he could make his own Chilli Paneer and everything!" We laughed.

"But seriously, don't we all want a *man*, someone all grown up, and someone who doesn't fall apart when you're away for just two days? I certainly do," I admitted. "Those two, the ones I saw in my third eye movie, they could remain in that beautiful embrace, *connected*, even when they were apart. I was struck by the way they held each other, like they were each other's most precious treasures. It was all very sensual but there was also real trust and acceptance of the other."

"Be careful, now. You're dangerously close to being responsible for me dumping Matthew." Gina gave another sigh.

"Oh, leave off! You've just spent half an hour telling me how wonderful he is. Say what you will, but for me, given my track record, that I could even dream of something like this being remotely possible, was a revelation," I said.

"A sacred union," Gina said.

"Haha! Are you trying to prove that you *do* have a sense of the sacred, after all?" I chuckled, jumping to life in my seat. "And you're spot on. That's precisely what it was. It touched me so deeply. What I saw was so powerful that it completely altered how I thought about relationships. Now that I had an inkling of what was possible in a relationship between a man and a woman, I made up my mind there and then. That's what I wanted for myself, too."

"It's true that most of the time, we stumble into relationships. Very few relationships are created from any sort of inspiration," Gina said.

"That includes me. I made a stand that either I would have a partnership in which we had authentic connectedness or I would rather remain single for the rest of my life and bear the consequences. I know you'll probably say that I'm being unrealistic, that I'm aiming too high, but for me, settling for anything less just isn't interesting anymore." With a laugh, I added, "And there you have your explanation for why I've been single ever since—seven years, to be precise."

"True, but look at how hard you've been working on developing yourself. That's not normal, and not everyone can be bothered. It's hard work, owning up to stuff about yourself that doesn't work, that keeps you miserable, stuff that keeps you from succeeding and being fulfilled in life," Gina said. "I know, because I'm constantly uncovering these things for myself, too."

"You're the one who inspired me, Gina, all those years ago," I said, grateful. "You said something about how important language and communication are. As a young woman starting out, that really motivated me and I was hooked. Like you, I wanted to become masterful in the art of listening and communication. Especially being in sales, the better I could be at these things, the easier it was to build relationships and do better at work. So thank you, you inspiring woman!" I raised my almost empty cup of coffee, saluting a toast to Gina.

"Aw, that's very sweet of you to say, but you're the one who's been busy at work," Gina said, humble as ever. "So, tell me more about that epiphany. How has it shaped what you want? I mean, what kind of a guy do you see yourself with?"

"Well, it's someone who's on the same wavelength, someone who's ... well ... intelligent, and in more ways than one," I answered. With anyone else, I would have felt awkward talking so frankly about something so private, but Gina was an exception. "I mean, emotionally and spiritually intelligent. And damn it, why not financially, too? I think I've done pretty well on my own, and so ought he to have done. At least, he's capable of making money and preferably, he's inclined towards helping others in some way, too," I said frankly. "I used to think that the physical equation wasn't that important, but I've changed my mind about that. It isn't just about looks or lust but about who he *is*. It's the whole package. If you're not in tune with each other sexually, that's likely to impact intimacy in other areas as well." I hesitated, then asked, "Am I sounding pernickety and unrealistic now?"

"No, not at all. Look, you've put time and energy into getting really clear about who's right for you. That's smart, that is. Frankly, it's essential because it gives you the option to choose your partner consciously.

Otherwise, we float from one relationship to the next, eyes closed, hoping for the best." As always, she was honest. "Part of the reason why people just sleepwalk into relationships is because they haven't done the work to get the clarity they need, to know who they are and, therefore, who would be right for them, much less what kind of relationship would inspire them." She looked at me earnestly and said, "No, for you, it's clear. Two people meeting on the same platform, having a vision of why they're together and being stimulated by each other to become better human beings, to achieve more of their potential. When you really 'get' each other, together, you can be so much more."

"I think it's even more scary to bury your head in the sand, ending up in a relationship where we say 'yes' to each other, knowing that things are far from right. Hoping and praying that things will work themselves out over time. Spending the rest of our lives being utterly frustrated with each other, because they only go from bad to worse. In sufferance, years go by. You have kids and it's too late to do anything about it," I said.

Gina laughed. "Then there's that misguided notion of two people coming together to complete each other. What you're saying is, rather, two wholes are more than the sum of their parts." Gina had just captured the essence in a single phrase.

"Yeah, then there's that old chestnut," I said. "I don't need someone to validate me. I don't *need* someone else to make me feel good about myself anymore, or even to give meaning to my life. It's all about pure choice now. If the right guy shows up, then we'll see. If not, there are plenty of interesting things to be getting on with. It would be great to be with someone who wants me to get on in life as much as I want that. At the very least, someone who doesn't want to chop off my wings the minute he sees that I have some potential. I've seen that happen all too often," I said, trembling at the thought, and memories of old times flooding back. "Never again!"

"With all that awareness, though, comes a different dilemma," Gina said, perceptive as ever. "So now, you're more discerning and that's going to limit your choice of men, don't you think?"

"Yes, but if there's one out there who's right for me, then I'm absolutely certain that we'll come across each other somehow, somewhere. To me, it feels inevitable. There's one thing I firmly believe: what's for you won't go past you."

"Hmmm, I like that. *What's for you won't go past you.* I like that a lot." She looked deep in thought and added, "A bit bold and optimistic, perhaps, but why not try it on, eh?"

"My Grandma Motima used to say that a lot. She used to say that no one could take from you what's in your *naseeb* or destiny. She also used to say that when Lakshmi, the Goddess of good fortune, smiled on you, you had to first recognise her and then know how to receive her. You had to have the humility to respect and honour her so that she would stay around."

"It's true. Your grandmother was a wise old owl. It sounds simple, obvious even, but it's not so easy to do. If you're not open to receiving the good that comes your way, to take it in your stride and enjoy it, then it'll pass on by, diminish, and wither away," she said.

"What I do is keep holding the vision that I had and at the same time, keep being vigilant to remaining unattached to it happening," I told her. "Like it's none of my business when or where or how it will happen. That I have to leave it to my brilliant Inner Diamond."

"Hmm, that's beautiful. That must make you very peaceful. I like that. I'm going to use that myself, in the different areas where I'm working to make something happen."

"The thing is, Gina, it's not that you don't take action towards what you want to make happen." I felt a need to clarify. "You do, but the context is so different to when you're coming from scarcity or insecurity or from fear of any kind."

"I know exactly what you mean," Gina said. "Like when you want something so much, and almost everyone else seems to easily to be able to get it, say a boyfriend or husband or that special job, and it makes you all the more desperate."

"Exactly! Desperation is nothing if not a sense of scarcity. But most of the time, you don't *know*, you have no clue that you are coming from lack, like there's not enough good men out there. It's mostly subconscious."

"That's a good point. You don't go around thinking, 'I'm so special' or the opposite, 'I'm not good enough'. For most of us, we're just not aware of how deep our insecurities run, so that lack of self-awareness itself gets in the way," Gina said.

"Or we don't want to acknowledge these things," I added.

"And denial sucks up so much precious energy," Gina said.

"I mean, we've all been there, at one point or another. Whether it's in personal relationships or issues around money or professional goals. These issues are often so subtle that, like clever rats, they elude you. Some of these patterns are also persistent and sticky. You do need someone else, someone who's trained in being able to help you to see what's in your psychological blind spot, don't you think?"

"Right! I do. Lack of self-awareness or denial just nail your feet to the floor but that's often what stops you from fulfilling your heart's desire." Gina understood such issues only too well from her study of people.

"Don't get me wrong," I said. "It's not that my eyes aren't open to guys. It's just that desperation or neediness have evaporated. I don't crave to be loved or accepted, like I used to. All that disappeared over the years, and whatever was left of it, flew out of that window when I had that realisation on the airplane."

"Hmm, I can see that."

"I'll keep open to the possibility of a relationship," I said.

"I'm sure he'll show up. Someone with whom you can be yourself. And your Self."

"I know it's a big ask, but hey ho! That's just how it is."

"Hmmm, what if he doesn't show up?" Gina asked, turning into the devil's advocate. "What then?"

"Right, and he might not. Then, I'm prepared to face the consequences. I might have to be single for the rest of my life. It takes way too much energy to 'settle' for someone who'll frustrate you to hell and back for the rest of your days, and not before he's strangled the life out you," I said, certain in how I felt.

Gina smiled. She fully well understood the dilemma. "It's so ironic," she said smiling. "See, it's amazing that you've taken down all those barriers that hid your vulnerability and kept you from being with the right guy. Now, though, you do realise the kind of man you're looking for, don't you?"

"Tell me," I said, knowing that she was about to burst my bubble anyway.

"An enlightened man, that's who you've just described. Now *he* is not going to be easy to find," she said, my best friend as ever. "Honey, you've set the bar so high that you've made it that much more difficult to find him. Good going, girl! Always full of paradoxes, you are. That said, challenging as it seems, I know you'll pull it off. I can feel it in my waters." She rubbed her hands on her belly, as if she was about to give birth. "It's written all over you."

"Ah, sure it's a challenge." I leant back in my chair. "But that doesn't bother me. I'm not going to be the one who 'finds' him. *And* it will happen. Do you know why I say that with such conviction? Because my relationship with my Inner Diamond is that much stronger now. I'm way more connected to it than before. I've got complete faith in its ability to deliver. After all, why show me that vision? What did you call it? Sacred union? Yes, that. Why knock my socks off with it and then not fulfil it?"

"That Inner Diamond of yours."

"And yours! I'm not so special that I'm the only one on the planet who's got one. We all have it. You just need to switch yourself on to it, that's all." Gina had a big grin on her face. She knew I was right.

She conceded, "Yes, that's true. It's time I stopped resisting doing something about it. I tell you what, I'll start with ten minutes of meditation a day. How about that?"

I winked at her and indicated a thumbs-up, saying, "I'll hold you to it."

I took a sip of my now nearly cold coffee. "Now, don't get me wrong, Genes. I'm not saying that the kind of guy that's right for me is right for every woman. I'm not saying that at all. We're all different and it's important to honour our own unique design. But I do think there are a few things that are common to us all when we're looking for a partner, male or female. The first thing is ..." I made a fist with my left hand and pulled at my left thumb. "... you must become conscious of why you want to be in a relationship. Is it 'cos you feel you're missing something in yourself? Is it 'cos you believe that being with that man or woman will somehow 'complete' you? You do need to know if that's going on for you."

"Granted." Gina nodded.

I plucked my left index finger with my right hand, and said, "Don't look too hard. Don't force outcomes. At the same time, be open. Trust in your inner Self, what I call the Inner Diamond. Listen to its cues. Then, as if by magic, things will begin to flow in the right direction."

"Also true. Listening to that voice within will set you on the right track," Gina said.

"The third thing ..." I pulled at my longest finger, "... is to take the time to get clear about what qualities are important to you in a partner and why. In answering that question, you get to learn so much about yourself as well, which is maybe most important."

Gina nodded her head in agreement, saying, "All very true."

"Then, finally, be prepared that the one who's right for you might not come in the package that you think he should," I concluded, pulling at my ring finger. "He or she might look different to how you thought they might. He or she might not be the same race as you. He might not even live in the same country as you. But when it's right, it's just right. Trust that you will be able to work things out with mutual satisfaction to create a fantastic life together." I paused to pick up the last few crumbs of the cake with my fork. "So don't look too hard, but be switched on to recognise him when he shows up."

"Hmmm ... you know, I think you're right. Those were all the things that I'd considered before I met Matthew, though I hadn't articulated them in the way you just did. I went through a period of soul searching. Anyone who's looking for a life companion could get a lot of value by looking at things in that way, I'll say."

A mobile rang and both Gina and I looked at each of ours. It was one of my colleagues with a short query.

"Goodness, is that the time?" Gina said, startled. "We've been sitting here gassing for the last three hours! It was lovely to catch up, Smeets, but I have to shoot off to pick up Matthew now. He's coming in at St. Pancras, by the Eurostar from Paris in less than half an hour."

We gave each other a warm hug and promised to not leave it so long to meet up the next time.

21

Tractor Man

Several months after that conversation with Gina in the café bar behind Liberty of London, I had the misfortune, or so I thought, of being shuttled off for a work assignment to dreary, cold, rainy old Germany. What could there possibly be for me in Germany?

I'd notched up hundreds of thousands of air miles travelling for work over the last few years, and would have been much happier focusing on the banks in the City of London for a change. Reluctantly, I found myself in the basement of a globally known bank in Frankfurt. I say reluctantly because this opportunity seemed like one that would suck up a whole lot of time and energy and give back little, if anything at all.

In my work, I would often be asked by large companies to give detailed solutions for how my company would solve specific computing related problems for them. Typically, they wanted the response yesterday. This meant weeks of working day and night, and weekends, with up to twenty or so experts based in the UK and at our offices in India. It was my responsibility to manage the team and ensure that everybody did what they had to do. Even though my colleagues, some of the best in their field, had strong and differing opinions about what should be done, I would have to ensure that everything came together seamlessly in the end. Even though we had to give it our best every single time, we knew full well that, more often that not, we would not win the work. That was just how things went in our industry, but we had to play the game anyway, if we wanted any chance of being able to win maybe just one of the next contracts.

This assignment smacked of being that kind of a wild goose chase, and I had other ideas of where I could better fulfil my multimillion dollar annual business target.

So, here was I in this by-invitation-only gathering, in the windowless basement of this big bank in Frankfurt. Dark when we arrived in the morning, it would already be dark when we would leave in the evening. My lack of enthusiasm plummeted even lower as I looked around the room. As usual, I was among just three, possibly four, token women. A sea of podgy, middle-aged men, around fifty of them, surrounded us—mostly from Western Europe and all dressed in cautious grey or depressingly dark suits.

This was far from my idea of a good time. A sense of loathing overwhelmed me as I realised that I had little choice but to be cloistered among this seemingly boring bunch of blokes for three whole days. Possibly even evenings, depending on what conversations the client needed us to have with each other about their requirements. Something about the gathering felt as forced and awkward as it did surreal. It was as if things, and these people, could never quite gel, being competitors at each other's throats. And yet, at the same time, I had a strong feeling that there was also a sense of destiny pervading our space.

My lack of enthusiasm remained unchanged as I walked around the room, going from business suit to business suit, shaking hands, and introducing myself and my company. The customary formality at such events greeted me, and being one of the few young women in a room full of dreary men, the odd—usually clumsy—flirtatious remark camouflaged as friendliness was to be expected.

In the large auditorium, also in the basement, we sat in semi-circular rows of ascending seats, just like in a cinema. Only we were not watching an exciting movie with a hunky lead actor, but listening to unending hours of people droning on and on. First, the client's team, over three or so hours, explained why we had all been summoned there, what their problems were, what they wanted to do about it and how we, the 'service providers', could help. They left us more confused than when we had arrived. Then, each of the twenty-five companies, who had been specifically chosen to be invited to these sessions, had to do a presentation in front of everyone else, saying who we were, why we were the best ever in the history of computing, and why the client should work with us.

I listened to the presenters attentively, pen poised on note paper to jot down any significant points that might be useful to discuss later but my note paper remained blank. That is, apart from writing down the name, an oddly long European one, of one particular man. He seemed to give the impression of being someone with a quiet temperament, yet he had a commanding air about him that made me want to pay attention. It wasn't so much that his presentation was perhaps the most crisp, sharp, and relevant so far, but more because something intrigued me about him. Something told me that there was more, much more to him, than met the eye. There was something about him that made me want to like him immediately.

In our type of business circles, however, if there was one thing that I had learnt again and again, it was this: you could not trust anyone. I had a lot of experience of guys who gave the impression of being friendly, or even of being a friend but with almost every one of them, something happened which had me regret my trusting them. The friendly, likeable ones were the worst, snakes pretending to be delicate caterpillars or sharks pretending to be dolphins, and in this gathering, which dangled the promise of a massive contract, there were likely to be many such snakes slithering and sharks circling.

I had to be careful of how to go about conducting myself among this bunch, especially with this guy. He wore a tailor-made, checked, autumn-palette wool-silk blazer, sporting the latest trend in oval leather elbow patches, worn with perfectly creased, dark brown trousers. All very trendy in the shires of Europe, I felt sure, yet it made me think of an upmarket farmer with a tractor. I started thinking of him as Tractor Man. I decided that I should be careful of Tractor Man. He gave the impression of being a calm, friendly, clever, what-you-see-is-what-you-get type, but I would bet anything he was one of the snakes in the grass here that I had to watch.

Coffee break followed Tractor Man's presentation. Almost everyone rushed out of the auditorium to get their caffeine fix in the large room just outside, while the few others fled upstairs and out of the building desperate for a smoke. I wanted to get some fresh air, but needed caffeine and a sweet more.

Just as I was walking out of the auditorium and over to the buffet tables that held fresh pastries and hot drinks, a man with a German accent strutted over cockily and asked, "You must be from one of zoze Indian IT companies, *ja*?" I told him I was and he asked, "Did you come all ze way over from Bangalore for zis meetings?"

"No," I replied. "I'm from London."

"Oh, you changed flights at London Heathrow?" he asked, puzzling me as to why this was so important to him. "Zaz muss have been a very long journey vor you."

"Oh no, it was very short. I'm *from* London," I said. "As in, I've lived in London most of my life." I'd noticed that people outside of the UK didn't seem to make any distinction between Indians from India, British Indians, Indians born and bred in America, and so on. We were all just Indians, riding around on camels and elephants, living in shacks and begging at street corners and now, we were also doing IT work and taking away local people's jobs to call centres, also housed in roadside shacks, in Bangalore. I almost felt like saying that I had parked my elephant at Terminal 5's long-term car park and wondered if he would get the joke.

"My naam ist Wolfgang," he said, arrogant as a crocodile. He gave me some long, important-sounding title and told me the name of the company he worked for. "*Ja*, okay. Wiz hotel are you staying at? Perhapz we can discuzz the possibility of working zoegetter, over dinner, *ja*?" He gave me a cheesy broad smile which told me that the last thing he wanted to do was discuss business.

"Thank you," I said, "that's a great idea." Then, turning around to find my colleague, I called out to him, "Suraj, can you please come over?" When Suraj joined us, I said, "This is Wolfgang," and I told Suraj where this guy was from. "Wolfgang has very kindly extended an invitation to us to discuss the possibility of partnering with his company on this project. I've already committed to being at another meeting. Why don't you two have a chat over dinner this evening?" Wolfgang's face turned red with rage as he mumbled some excuse that he had to rush off to make a call and would catch up with us later.

"Blimey," Suraj said, "like a little lamb to slaughter. You did that pretty deftly."

"Oh, yes," I replied, amused at the arrogance of some men. "I've had many a year to hone that craft."

Suraj joked, "There shall be no love in this basement, then." I threw him a sharp sideways glance, making daggers of my eyes.

After I'd picked up a light-as-a-feather, hot Brussels waffle with a fine dusting of vanilla sugar, I poured myself some coffee. Just then, a blond, muscular Dutch man in a dark grey suit, and almost twice my height, came up to me. "Hello, er ..." He bent over—almost doubling towards me as I turned to face him—and tried to read my name badge, "Er, Sameetaa. That was a wonderful presentation you did earlier this morning. I thoroughly enjoyed it. You're such a good presenter."

I looked at his name badge and, being as diplomatic as I knew how and trying not to laugh, I said, "I'm glad you liked it, Kees." Tractor Man, who was standing just behind Kees, overheard Kees' compliment to me, turned around, and looked at me with an expression of laughing bewilderment. He made a face at me that expressed the question, "What presentation?", because it was my colleague Suraj, and not I, who had presented for both of us.

Not being able to help myself, I looked at Kees with a straight face and said, "What did you like about it, Kees, more specifically?"

"Oh, you're just very good. You came across very beautiful, I mean, beautifully," Kees replied in an Amsterdam accent.

And there you have it. Snake disguised as caterpillar, number two already, and just five minutes into the first break, I laughed to myself. And two and a half more days to go. I managed to dismiss Kees eventually, after a few more minutes of useless, inauthentic banter. Tractor Man came over. "Well, that *was* a wonderful presentation you did, Smita." He laughed. "When do we get to see you in action again?"

"Haha," I said. "I really enjoyed it, too. Next time, when I *actually* get to do one, perhaps it will be just as memorable."

"You must get guys hitting on you all the time at these events." The cup he was filling with hot tea kept sliding out of his hand as he looked at me. He was clearly nervous as he spoke. I noticed that I found his nervousness sort of endearing, but then rejected it out of mind and did my best not to let him see it either.

Yeah, yeah, whatever ... and you're no different. I wrote him off, like I did all the others, usually with good reason. Being one of the few women working among largely alpha males, I had come to be disdainful about how often men underestimated women in business, even in these modern times, still relating to them as a sex object first. In my yonder years, I used to lash out infuriated when encountering sexual inequality or harassment at work. Then, I learnt to hide my fury and instead seethe with frustration in private. Now, after some twenty years of realising how the minds of men worked and having become more secure in my self, grounded in a deeper confidence, I tackled these things very differently. You could say, with less force and more power.

"Hmmm ... I haven't noticed," I replied dismissively, thinking that he was dangerously close to trying to chat me up himself.

Tractor Man and I bantered a bit about the client, then I asked, "So, are you any the wiser about what they want? I thought I had a good understanding when I arrived, having read the thick pile of documents they sent us, but now I'm really confused."

"You and me both. Though I think it's a good idea to start looking around for companies to partner with. This programme is way too big for any one company to handle. You watch, before the day's out they'll be telling us to group up with a few other companies to do the work jointly," the tall Tractor Man said in perfect

English, spoken with a soft accent that wasn't obvious enough to place.

"By the way, I'm James," he said, flashing a charming smile. He gave me a friendly look. I didn't buy his friendly act one bit. Meanwhile, I tried not to look self-conscious about the fact that, for some bewildering reason, his was the only name that I had written down during those uninformative and boring presentations.

We talked about the client's programme, exchanging bits of information, and he shared with me some interesting snippets about the client's background since he had been working with them for some months. I was rather surprised to find that Tractor Man was starting to show himself much differently to the other men I had met in these business environments.

Sure enough, in the closing session of the first day, our client laid out just how large their requirements were, concluding that no one company could possibly deliver the whole programme alone. Just as Tractor Man had said, they instructed the companies to join forces with each other. This meant that I had to start looking for other companies with whom we could work and decide which one it would make the most sense to go with.

It was now clear to us why they had invited all the large companies in the IT industry to this seminar.

For the next two days, my colleague Suraj and I spoke to all the major players at this conference to decide which ones we might be able to partner with. There were all kinds of things to consider to see how well our companies, who usually competed with each other to death for the same contracts, might work together. In the final wash, there were really only a couple with whom it made sense to work. Even then, we had experience of working successfully in the past with only one of these two. Collaborating in this way was highly unusual in our competitive industry, and it would be difficult to persuade my senior colleagues at our head office in India to agree to partnering like this. Our client, however, was adamant that if we wanted to be in the game, we had to play it their way. It would be better to recommend joining forces with the devil we knew.

There was only one company that we could realistically work with. This was because there were only three or so of the largest companies in the world who could lead such a huge piece of work like this and have a real chance of winning the contract. With two of those, we did not get along. As it turned out, that one company happened to be the one for which Tractor Man worked.

Within the coming weeks, I convinced the board of my company that our two businesses should join forces to pitch for this huge programme.

Our client had thrown us all into a set of unusual circumstances. We all got busy in the next months in coming up with the solutions that our client had asked us to give them. This meant countless meetings with the client and our partners. Three more companies had now joined our group, with Tractor Man leading our 'consortium' in working together on this one contract.

Over the coming ten months, or so, our teams worked closely together to drive the discussions forward, and since I was the lead on behalf of my company, James and I came into regular contact.

James had an unusual brightness—a brilliance—about him, both intellectually and energetically. Professionally, we got on with each other like a house on fire. He stood head and shoulders above most guys in our industry, and if ever there was good reason for someone being arrogant, it was James. Yet, he was down to earth and humble, unassuming, oblivious even, of his brilliance and intelligence. The programme we were bidding for was extremely complex and, by now, large teams of different experts, fifty to a hundred per company, were involved from all five partners. The client had as many people from their side, and more than a thousand pages of questions that we needed to answer. Regardless, he surprised me again and again at the calm manner, ease, and exceptional ability with which he rallied everyone around to take things in the right direction. It was easy to see that he commanded respect from client and partners alike.

Though we often had reason to work closely together, I found him always honest and respectful, kind and professional, and far from the shark I had written him off to be when I first saw him. Rather, he showed up more as a dolphin than a shark. Of all the people that I had worked with, he was turning out to be one of the easiest people to get on with. He would start a sentence and I would finish it, or vice versa. Unlike most other business meetings that were often boring to death, our meetings were actually enjoyable and we seemed to be on the same wavelength. The fact we shared a sense of humour helped. I had reason to believe that we could actually succeed in being awarded this programme.

He was a long way from the type of man I would typically have found attractive. A long way. For one thing, he had hardly any hair. And yet, there was something enigmatic about him that I could not help noticing. Almost like a crew cut, his short, shaven, receding head of hair sported a balding, but cute, round head that gave prominence to his bright sea-blue eyes. The self-assured, cultivated manner in which he conducted himself told me he must have been older than he looked. Though not classically handsome, he was undoubtedly charismatic. Something in the twinkle of his blue eyes said this guy had hidden depths. I sensed something mystical with him, too. He was lovely. And smart. Whereas I had got used to meeting, again and again, sales men or so-called company executives who would say or do anything to get the business, or the girl, I could not help feeling that there was something honest and genuine about Tractor Man. I could not help *liking* him, and was a bit annoyed with myself for it.

Still, I had to be careful. In the months we had worked together, though women were charmed by him, I saw no evidence of him chatting any of them up, or showing disrespect towards them in general. Still, I didn't 'know' him well, nor had I known him long enough. In the past, I had been stung several times by my own naïvety, not realising that with just a friendly smile or in sharing a harmless laugh and a joke with a male colleague, it could be construed that I was flirting. To my seething fury, I would later hear through the company grapevine that he had been going around boasting to all and sundry that I was 'interested' in him. As a woman in a male dominated environment, I had learnt to perpetually walk a tightrope—being professional yet approachable, but not so uptight that I ended up with my head up my own backside and ended up being unable to be quick and agile. I had to be able to respond intelligently to any situation. On the other hand, I also wanted to be free to be myself, which included being a woman, on the ball but at ease, warm and friendly but not mistaken for being a dizzy flake head or 'easy'.

I had begun feeling more and more at ease with him and we were able to talk about difficult work issues that, normally, we may not have trusted anyone else with at work. That said, I was at work and I made it a rule not to let my feelings run away with me. Our industry was a small world. Everyone knew everyone else, or knew someone who knew someone you knew and, as a woman, I had to make sure my reputation was squeaky clean. Besides, some while back, I had staunchly determined that in future the one that I would be with, if that was ever going to happen, had to be a British Indian man.

But why on earth was I having these ridiculous thoughts at all? It had been ages since I even went on a date and certainly not with anyone from work. Besides, in the seven years I had been single, at some point I gave up even dating after a series of odd and very awkward occurrences. After a few years of attempting to go on dates, most of which never went beyond the first evening, I had developed a sharp sensitivity to men's energies and I noticed this time and again. Every time I attempted to go out with a guy, no matter how nice or gentlemanly, I found that within moments of sitting down in front of him, I would find myself feeling nauseous. To make matters worse, within minutes, I would be throwing up, *actually* throwing up.

It got to a stage where I would not go on a date without stashing a pile of plastic carrier bags in my handbag, because it was inevitable that I would throw up at some point. And not just once or twice, but several times within minutes of being with my date. It was really bizarre.

On one occasion, a really lovely guy, who happened to be British Indian, had asked me out. He was so excited when I said yes to meeting him that he went to a whole lot of trouble to make sure the date would go perfectly. He drove all the way over to my house from the opposite side of London in his impeccable, top-of-the-range, freshly polished, convertible Mercedes. He had even reserved tables for us at not one but two of London's top restaurants. "Just in case you don't like one, we can always go to the other one," he had said so sweetly.

There he was at my doorstep, frankly reeking from an overdose of one of my favourite scents 'til then, Issey Miyake for Men. Dressed in a dark blue denim shirt and matching jeans, it was all a bit too stiffly ironed for something that was supposed to be casual, a look that was intended to state, *I'm not trying too hard, honest!*

At the time, I thought it was sweet.

For some unfathomable reason, no sooner had I answered the door to him, I began to feel nauseous. Thinking that it was probably just the hot summer weather making me feel queasy, I took a few plastic carrier bags with me, praying that I wouldn't need them. As we were driving along the A40 toward central London, I had already asked him to stop the car four times so I could get out and throw up in one of my carrier bags. After the fourth time, I was already out of bags and my vomiting showed no signs of relenting. So, I asked him to stop off at the nearest petrol station to pick up a few more. By the time we got to the restaurant, sure enough, I had been sick a few more times. The chances were, if I attempted eating anything at all, not only would I be throwing up while we were at the restaurant, but all the way back home as well.

Poor guy—I felt so sorry for him. The fault lay with me, not him. Unbeknownst to me, my antenna had become so fine-tuned for sensing men's energies melding with my own, that I could no longer even pretend to be having a good time on a harmless date.

The thought that he made me sick, literally, was embarrassing for both me and for my date. I asked my Inner Diamond what on earth these shenanigans were about and it replied simply, *"Enjoy the wait. For the one who is for you will not make you sick. Not only will you not feel sick when you are with him, but you will relish being by his side, always."*

Great. Not only did I have to be single forever but now I couldn't even go on dates without throwing up. Thanks, Diamond!

I caught myself wondering if Tractor Man could pass the vomiting test, and was shocked at the thought.

Where on earth had that come from? And why on earth I was thinking about this now, here, at a meeting that could eventually result in one of the biggest deals of my career and possibly make me a star in my company? Just because we had clicked professionally did not mean anything else. No, these were merely the pathetic flutterings of a single girl's idle mind. In any case, if I was going to be with someone, it had to be a British Indian, not some European, and certainly not a balding one. Besides, I knew nothing of his personal life. Not a thing. Occasionally, something about the things we were each interested in outside work crept into the conversation during our business meetings, but we hardly knew much about the other. Apart from work, what could I possibly have in common with this guy, this nondescript Belgian, anyway? Our worlds were bound to be planets apart and even if they weren't, I was sure to find a way of making them so.

I castigated myself—who was being a dizzy flake head now? Why would he be of interest to me? No, no, I wasn't interested in him. Definitely not.

I had now, with intense day and night focus, been working with my teams and that of our partners on coming up with the proposal for this one massive opportunity, and it was time for a well-deserved holiday. The magic of my previous trip to Hawaii and Kauai still reverberated within my soul. I could once again hear the call of those beautiful dolphins off the coast of Hawaii. The magnetic pull of the mystical Shiva temple in Kauai seemed to be tugging at me, too. Though it would be for the second year in a row, I made up my mind to go back to these two islands to replenish my energy and reinvigorate my spirit.

I booked my flights to coincide with the summer break period of my key clients. While I packed up for my well-deserved holiday, I sifted through the thick pile of business cards that had accumulated in my handbag over these busy months and dumped them all in my office drawer. In any case, by now I had all the important phone numbers and emails in the contacts folder of my mobile phone.

Just as I was leaving the office, I went back to my office drawer and unlocked it. Something niggled at me. I looked through the pile of business cards that I'd just decluttered from my handbag and shuffled through the pile once more, not quite knowing why. Just then, one of the cards fell out of the pile and landed on the floor, upside down. I bent down to pick it up and as I did so, sudden ripples of gladness involuntarily surged through my belly. Just for a moment, as I held the card in my hand, I felt a strong sense of the person to whom it belonged. A warm and delightfully mysterious energy leapt up, as if coming from the card itself, and wrapped itself around my being. I turned the card over. It bore Tractor Man's details.

I placed it in my handbag. It was the only business card I took with me on my holiday.

" ... the mind is
the most powerful tool
we have.

You can step out of
a mindset of suffering
into that of
harmony and ease."

22

Bound by Snow

L ife has a way of catching us unawares. Just when I thought my life had returned to the usual mundane, the weather—of all things—put me on a whole other track.

The programme for which we were pitching had turned out to be bigger and more complex than any of us could have imagined, and getting our responses together, with five companies involved, had proven to be a mammoth task. After coming back from holiday, I continued to work on putting together our proposal for several more months. Just under twelve months after we had started on this large initiative, the deadline to submit our proposal had, at long last, arrived. We unveiled our proposition to the client by giving them a big, rip-roaring presentation. Given how big each proposal that the client had received from the various supplier groups was, ours alone being about five thousand pages, they asked for at least three months to read and compare them. During that time, they would call us back in stages to answer any big questions they might have.

A whole year of my life had gone into developing work with this one client. Contrary to my negative preconception about coming to dreary, boring Frankfurt, it had already proven successful for me. While working to develop the large proposal, I had also managed to win a number of smaller, interesting computing projects for the same client, which helped to keep me in the good books of the people that mattered in my company.

With the significant proposal handed in as well as winning new business, turning this household bank into a good client, I breathed several deep sighs of satisfaction. I was now much more free to pick up on other opportunities that I had simmering in the background. Usually, when I worked on setting up several potential opportunities for business, one or two, if I was really lucky, might come alive. But no sooner had I submitted that major proposal, than every one of my opportunities, like lights turning on one after the other at dusk in a big city, began to come alive. This had me not only working out of London, but travelling weekly to not just Frankfurt, but Munich, Paris, Milan, and Oslo. This didn't include the frequent trips, as many as twelve in one year, to our offices across India.

One morning, out of the blue, my mobile rang at six in the morning, waking me up from deep sleep.

"Hello, Smita," I answered in a sleepy voice. Who on earth was calling me at this ridiculous hour? I felt annoyed to be woken up so early on one of the rare days that I could work from home. Normally, my colleagues in India were careful not to call before eight o'clock in the morning, even for urgent matters. "Hello? Who's calling? Anybody there?"

"Hello?" a shocked but soft, whispering male voice answered, as if he was speaking into his phone from a distance. "Hello? Who's this?"

"Who's that?" I asked, though full well recognising the voice and, of course, now that I looked at the screen on my mobile phone, I could see the name of the caller. I heard leather-shoed footsteps plodding on a wooden floor.

"It's James," he replied, sounding extremely apologetic. And embarrassed. "Who's that?"

"It's Smita," I replied.

"Smita, I think I have a bug in my Bluetooth headset. It seems to call random numbers all by itself."

I laughed, thinking, *Yeah, yeah! Of course it does! What a pathetic opening line!* I laughed again and said, "Oh, don't worry. No problem. I was waking up anyway." Then, trying to diffuse his embarrassment, I asked, "How are you? Have you heard anymore from the client?"

"Oh, I'm really well, thank you. I had a meeting with them yesterday as they had a lot of technical questions. How about you?" he asked.

"Yes, I had a call from them recently to get some clarifications as well, but I couldn't get any more information out of them about whether we stand to win or not," I answered.

"No, it's still early days, I think," he said, and then I could feel an awkward silence about to arise.

"Great, well give me a shout if you hear anything more," I said.

As we closed the call, I smiled to myself. Was that an ingenious excuse to call me or was that really a faulty Bluetooth calling out randomly? And if so, what were the odds that it would pick out my number, out of the hundreds that must be on his phone, and not someone else's? I couldn't help feeling that the Inner Diamond was up to something.

A few days later, exactly the same thing happened again, and around almost the same time. I had begun to secretly look forward to being woken up in this way. There was something about the quality of his voice that made me want to carry on listening to it. It was soft, yet decisive and strong, with a dulcet velvet quality to it. When the faulty Bluetooth randomly called me yet again, to my amusement, for a third time the following week, I could tell James was as baffled as he was embarrassed. From what I had seen of his character so far, he was not a man given to pursuing women, and certainly not with subterfuge or pretence.

How could I be so sure? In the last year, I had got to know how he had handled and operated in one of the trickiest and most difficult work environments in which I had worked during my twenty-year career. In a cut-throat industry, we were working with some of the shrewdest business people, who wouldn't think twice about selling their mother-in-law to the devil, hungry for success and status, and who would do whatever it took to win. We were all in competition with each other, even as we were forging a reluctant partnership to serve our client's needs. Though a competitor, I found Tractor Man to be a trustworthy ally in difficult business situations. He was a perceptive, straight talker who had a strong sense of fairness. Time and again, he had proven to be a man of his word, something rare in the duplicitous world of the hardcore corporate. I quietly observed his unusual quality of being sensitively intelligent even in the most challenging social and emotional situations. This had me sit up and take notice of him. You had to grant a man like that respect, did you not?

So, was he calling me under the pretence of a randomly randy Bluetooth or was the universe playing tricks on us both? I knew from our conversations in the past that he had qualified as an engineer and had a PhD in a subject that made him think like a scientist. This gave me good reason to doubt if he indulged in thinking of occurrences like these being 'mystical' or the work of the Inner Diamond, or anything else that could not feasibly be explained away by logic and rationale. And yet, here we were, with my phone being randomly dialled by his, not once, not twice, but many times. In any case, I had to smile to myself, enjoying these mysterious shenanigans, more amusing than spooky. What a novel way to creep into the heart of a woman.

Over the coming weeks, our paths continued to cross at work. We talked mostly about work with the odd jovial moment here and there that did nothing to disprove that Tractor Man was anything but thoroughly likeable. With every interaction, though, I got to see a bit more of his character and the real person within, the person beneath the business suit, so to speak. Still, I had no clue as to Tractor Man's personal background. How old was he? Was he single? Where did he come from? Who was he, *really?* And perhaps that question that troubled me the most, *why did I care?*

One late February Thursday evening, I was in Frankfurt Airport rushing to the gate to catch my flight home to London. A horrendous snowstorm brought traffic in the streets of Frankfurt almost to a grinding halt, making my taxi take an hour longer than usual to get me to the airport. "You'll only make it now if you run to the gate," the lady at British Airways' check-in desk had told me in brisk and no-nonsense tones. I ran up the escalators and on to the gate. As I ran, breaking into a sweat, my briefcase flung out of my hand just as I reached the gate, and fell open as it went crashing to the floor. Reams of paper with my handwritten notes went flying out of my case and covered the floor around the entrance of the crowded gate. I bent down, flustered, to pick up my papers and bag. I wondered why the gate was still crowded. Shouldn't these people all have boarded by now, since I was late getting there?

"Always causing trouble, eh?" I heard a familiar voice say, cheery as a sunbeam. I looked up, irritated, to see who this joker was, only to find Tractor Man bending down too, helping me to pick up my things.

"Very funny," I snapped like a terrier with an irritable bowel, still flustered but now suffering more from embarrassment. The last thing I needed was for one of my important work colleagues to catch me in my clumsy spell, being a Bambi on an ice pond for the first time. "Where did you come from?" I asked a bit more jovially, suddenly snapping out of my skittish mood and feeling delighted to see Tractor Man, here of all places. "First all those randomly dialled phone calls and now at my flight gate. You're not stalking me, are you?" I chuckled, then immediately worried that my sarcastic British humour might get lost in translation and throw me in the doghouse.

"Haha," he laughed warmly, putting me at ease. "No, no stalking here! I'm on my way to London Heathrow, too. I have an early morning meeting in the City and so I'm going there this evening."

"Great! What a coincidence to be on the same flight. Great minds, and all that," I said.

Just then, a loud announcement came over the tannoy speakers informing us that our flight had been cancelled. The tinny voice informed us that the snowstorm sweeping across Europe had disrupted flight schedules from many other airports and, as a result, all flights out of Frankfurt Airport would be grounded for the evening.

"Great. I can't believe this!" I ranted. "So we're stranded here."

We both went over to the airline agents who manned the gate and asked when we could expect to get to London.

"Not before the morning," they confirmed, as they handed out vouchers of paltry sums with which we could buy some refreshments. "Please come back in the morning."

"Oh well, I guess we're stuck here, then," James said, looking less than disappointed.

"I guess so." Outside, the relentless snowstorm pounded the windows. As more and more airlines announced cancelled flights, the noise of angry passengers demanding clarity of information bellowed through the departure lounge. I looked around at the mounting chaos of people scurrying to leave the airport or head towards the bars and restaurants or to the airline lounges.

I suggested, "Let's go and find a hotel before everybody else does."

"Yes," Tractor Man said. "But the roads were all blocked with snow on the way here. It'll take hours before we ever get to a hotel, and don't forget that this is rush hour." We both looked around as we walked away from the gate.

He thought for a moment, then said, "Look, I don't know about you, but I'm really exhausted after an early start this morning. I'd like to get something to eat and drink. How about we have dinner here at one of the restaurants, and then hopefully the traffic will have died down a bit later. Let's look into getting a hotel then."

Smart thinking, Tractor Man. "Sounds good!"

We found a restaurant-bar and I asked if I could look at the menu before we went in.

"Finding vegetarian food in these parts is like foraging for rare garlic truffles in London's Hyde Park or New York's Central Park. When I ask for vegetarian options, they usually offer to take the meat out and give me just the leftover vegetables. Or they offer things with fish. How can eating fish be considered vegetarian? I mean, it has eyes and everything." I chortled. "Where I was born, eating even eggs is a carnal sin."

"Oh, are you vegetarian? How interesting. I've been eating less and less meat in the last few years and have been thinking about giving it up altogether, too," James said, as we went inside the restaurant and waited in a queue to be seated—the line grew behind us by the second. "So tell me, why are you a vegetarian?"

"Well, I was born in deep Gujarat, where most people, even today, are by default vegetarian. The diet I grew up on is based on the ancient principles of Ayurveda and it suits me very well," I said. The waiter seated us at one of the few remaining tables in the corner at the very back.

James hung the jacket of his suit on the back of his chair. "Very interesting. Tell me, what are those principles?"

"Well, one of those principles is that the mind and body are supremely connected, and the other is that the mind is the most powerful tool we have. Just as it can create sickness, so you can use it to heal you. So it makes sense to keep the mind as well as the body healthy. And eating dead animals is not considered conducive to overall health," I said, passionate about my stand. "Frankly, in my younger years, when I tried eating meat, not only did I not like it but I had nightmares about the poor beasts being hurt and slaughtered just so that

I could have the luxury of eating their flesh. And that really disturbed my peace of mind."

"Hmm ... I don't eat much meat either, the occasional bit of bacon and maybe some salmon, here or there," James said thoughtfully. "You've really got me thinking about this. But tell me about the foods you actually eat."

"Okay, let me just put it this way. If you gave me a bag of potatoes, I would be able to cook it for you twenty different ways and not one of those dishes would taste the same. See, vegetarian Indian cuisine is so vast, rich, and balanced that meat becomes irrelevant." I felt concerned that I might be sounding evangelical.

"Wow, yes. I can believe that. You're in danger of converting me," James said with a smile. "But, do you mind if I ask you something personal? And please don't answer if it's too personal." He looked at me to see whether he could go ahead.

"Sure." I offered him a slight nod.

"Do you remember that time, just after that three-day conference with our client, we had lunch with a couple of your colleagues in London?" he asked.

"You mean that time when we went to that Indian restaurant in Mayfair, last year? Just before I went on holiday?" I asked. "When I was trying to get my colleagues to buy into partnering with your company?"

"Yes, that's it. Well, I had this really strange thought when I looked at you, and though you looked gorgeous, as usual ..." He turned his eyes down for a moment, as if he felt suddenly shy. "There was something about your mouth, not that there was anything wrong with your mouth, mind. It sounds really weird now that I'm talking to you about it." He hesitated, searching my expression to carry on. "It's just that I had the strongest sense that you were really ill. I mean, really quite sick, like you might only have a few more months to live and you needed an operation in your belly soon. Does that sound bonkers? I mean, was that just a crazy notion or were you actually sick? And please, you don't have to tell me." James looked really concerned.

"Really? Goodness. That's extraordinary. How could you possibly have known? I mean, no one knew. I deliberately kept it all quiet because you know how people are in our line of work. Any excuse to steal your hard work and parade it as their own. No, you're quite right, I was really sick." I was immeasurably impressed to find that Tractor Man wasn't just switched on, but that he had a sensitive perception as well.

"Oh! So it wasn't just a figment of my imagination, then?" he asked, and his shoulders sagged in relief.

"No, no, not at all," I replied. "You remember there was a period when I wasn't on the scene for a few weeks, when I told you I'd be taking care of some other urgent matters?"

"Yes, yes, I remember." He leant forward in his chair, and studied me intently.

"Well, that was because I had to have surgery, one of four, to tackle an illness that had been creeping up on me very silently," I said. "Then, as soon as I was given the green light to be able to fly, I went away to recuperate. My doctors said that it was absolutely essential, if I was going to heal myself thoroughly, to avoid anyone and anything stressful, and to take a proper rest."

"I see." James wore a look of thoughtful concern. "But, how are you now?"

"Oh, I'm so much better. Really well now, though I did go through a bit of a harrowing period," I replied.

"So it wasn't just a regular surgery, was it? I mean, what I sensed was that you were really sick. As in, you could *die*," he said with a sound as though the words choked in his throat.

I explained to him about my illness. Even though I would normally not have shared so much of my private life within someone whom I associated with work, there was something about James that had me be increasingly comfortable to trust him.

"You've really gone through the mill, haven't you? But you look amazing. I mean, no one would know that you've had to deal with such a life-threatening scenario," he said softly. "I mean, at work, even though you had so much going on, you were always so sharp. There was I admiring how dynamic you are! You did a great job with getting the client's confidence in working with you," he said with an earnest gleam in his eyes. "You managed very well in overcoming all the negativity from the other competitors."

The waiter came back with the food we had ordered.

"You don't have to eat vegetarian, you know, just because I do," I said.

"No, no," he replied, cutting pieces of his tomato and mozzarella salad. "This is one of my favourite things, and besides, like I said, I'm not big on meat either. I mean, I can see myself being a vegetarian, easily."

His openness made me smile.

James then said, "There's something else I want to ask you."

"Something else? What is this? Twenty questions? Oh, go on then." I chuckled.

"Well, one time when I was speaking to you on the phone, I saw the strangest thing. It was a room with a deep purple wall, like the purple of an aubergine. Then, in the corner of the room, I saw these big crystals, really big." He expanded his arms, as if holding a massive child. "One of the crystals was orange, more like a burnt orange, and the other one was again purple, but a different shade to the wall. I also saw these glass crystals dangling in the window, reflecting the sun, throwing little rainbows onto the walls."

I listened, rapt.

James continued, "And you were sitting right in front of the aubergine coloured wall, on a big cushion or something. You had your eyes closed, like you were meditating. Is that another crazy notion? I mean, why would I see that? Do you ever meditate?"

My eyes really did feel like they might just hop out of my skull any moment and run away with themselves. How could this guy know? How could he possibly know?

"Are you sure you haven't been stalking me?" I attempted to hide my consternation with a joke. "You've just described the room in my house that I meditate in." I looked at James, realising that my own intuition about him, that there was much more to him than just a smart business suit, was proving true. He, too, was mystically intelligent.

"Really? Can that be true?"

"Oh, yes," I said. "I've often spoken to you on the phone sitting in my meditation room."

A phone rang. Both of us had the same ringtone and we both reached out to look at our smartphones.

"Hello, James," he answered and then listened patiently for at least a minute or two. The person at the other end seemed to be giving him a long explanation about something or other. But then I heard James burst into an exclamation. "We've won! Are you saying that we've actually won? What, the whole deal?"

I looked at him, smiling, thinking it must be one of his other clients calling to tell him that he'd been successful with one bid or another. He carried on listening for a bit longer and then again asked, "So, you're saying that you're awarding us the entire deal?"

It seemed the person at the other end of the phone answered in the affirmative. James completed the call, looked at me, and said, beaming ear to ear, "We've done it, Smita! We've cracked it! We have won! The entire bloody deal!"

As soon as I realised that the call he had just received was from our client, breaking the news to James, as the lead of our consortium, I yelled, "No way! Oh my God! No! What, the whole shebang? The whole billion dollars?"

"Yep, yep, yep!" He grinned with delight. I cupped the sides of my head with my palms, my eyes popping in astonishment.

"Amazing! We did it. Honestly, I thought it would go on and on and on forever and then just fizzle out. I just didn't think they would keep their word and actually go ahead with this monster of a programme." I looked at James, amazed. "Well done, you, for steering us through to the finale."

"And to you, for the brilliant work you and your colleagues put in. But let's not jump the gun. That was just a phone call. Anything can happen between now and the day we finally sign. The real work will begin now. From here on in, we really need to get to work on agreeing terms, and dotting the i's and crossing the t's," he said.

"That's true. But we've won!" I chuckled.

We ordered a bottle of champagne and celebrated for the rest of the night, stuck at Frankfurt Airport. The programme we had just won was a landmark deal, the largest and first of its kind. What we could not have known about each other in the space of a year of working together, we made up for in the space of a few hours as we waited overnight for our flight to London. I told him some more about what I had done in Hawaii, about swimming with dolphins, and about the special temple in Kauai. He told me some stories that gave me a window into his life and I found out that he was newly single.

We chatted about all kinds of things and completely lost track of time. One of the biggest airports in the world, Frankfurt Airport rarely ever shut completely. At some point during the night, we were the only ones left in the restaurant-bar, when the cleaners came and cleaned around us, hanging the chairs upside down on the tables, still we carried on chatting. In the early morning, the airport filled up with people. One of the waiters from the morning shift came and asked us if we wanted breakfast.

"Yes, let's both have a full English breakfast, but without the bacon, sausages, and black pudding," James said with a big grin.

"Black? You mean oozing blood pudding?" I laughed.

When we finally reached London the next morning, I realised we'd been chattering and laughing non-stop the whole night through and for the entire flight home.

After that, we got busy with the contract negotiations, with each company in our group having to negotiate their own part of the deal. This meant we saw each other for work more frequently in Frankfurt. We had unexpectedly and suddenly connected on a personal level and it was fair to say that we'd become good friends. From then on, it wasn't James' randomly dialling Bluetooth that called me first thing in the mornings but, instead, he called me himself.

Only now, the calls were in the evenings, long after work.

23

The Date

A few weeks after we had begun our evening phone chats, James asked, "So, how about you make me a few of your many vegetarian potato dishes? ... You know, the ones you were bragging about while we sat around at the airport that night."

"I know this news flash hasn't yet reached the neck of the woods that you hail from, but there's more to vegetarian food than just potatoes, you know." I sniggered. Jesting, I said, "And anyway, I won't be cooking for you anytime soon. Now, if you were to put to me a more original offer that might get me to see you outside of work, then I may consider it."

He laughed. "Okay, then let me take you out. What would mademoiselle prefer, breakfast, lunch, or dinner?"

"Well, I'm not big on breakfast. Lunch, don't have time for it and anyway, if it's going to be at that all-day breakfast place at Frankfurt Airport, you can forget it!"

"Oh, I see. So, not that lovely restaurant at Frankfurt Airport, and not breakfast or lunch. Dinner in a proper, posh restaurant, then?" he said.

"Hmm ... depends. Wait. Are you actually asking me out on a date?" I asked.

"Yes, I am," he replied in a tone that gave away a smile at the other end of the phone. Then, in the most charming way to which you could not possibly say no, he asked, "Would you go out with me, Smita?"

"I see ... Let me think about it," I replied, enjoying not making it easy for him. I fell silent for a few moments, and then said, "Okay, I've thought about it."

"And?" he asked.

"It depends." I couldn't keep the amusement from my voice.

"On?" He sounded a bit anxious.

I laughed. "On where and when."

"Oh! Okay. Let me look at my diary," he replied.

I chuckled as I heard him get busy, clicking away on his computer, looking at his schedule. Being Belgian, he took what I said literally, rather than as me pulling his leg with my cheeky British humour just to make him sweat a bit before accepting.

"Oh? You're laughing? What's funny?"

"Nothing," I said, smiling, finding his eagerness endearing.

"Hmm. ... Where do you want to meet? London? I'm in London on Thursday next week," he said.

"Nope, I'm in Oslo. How about Tuesday after that?"

"No, that's no good. I'm in Johannesburg," he said. "How about ... ?"

And so the conversation went on for a while until we found a time and a place during which we were both in the same city, which turned out to be Paris. Not a bad place for a first date.

It had been many years since I'd gone on an actual date and I was nervous, but very excited. I prayed and hoped that, having developed a high regard as well as affection for James, I wouldn't discover that he, like so many before him, was a prize jerk. Likewise, I didn't want to disappoint either. In the past, if I really liked a guy, I would have made allowances for his shortcomings or overlooked something that my instincts told me needed my attention, only to later discover that it was those very things that turned into major issues, a source of pain and suffering, and in the end, they became a showstopper for our relationship. Now that I was a bit more seasoned, and hopefully the wiser for it, I had learnt to not railroad my intuition, but to take heed of the little niggles that tried to communicate to me when something was off, a mismatch.

After my near-death surgery, I had made a commitment to myself to make choices that fostered happiness, satisfaction and freedom, both within myself and in the external circumstances of my life. This meant being brutally honest with myself about my thoughts and behaviour, and when things weren't working out.

The days went by slowly as I waited for the evening to arrive when we were to meet. I made sure my meetings in Paris were planned in such a way that I could, taking into account the mad traffic of Paris, be at my hotel in good time to freshen up and look my best for the date. I had even bought a new dress and a few fresh items of make-up for this, hopefully, auspicious occasion.

At seven o'clock sharp, the phone in my hotel room rang. It was the concierge. "Mademoiselle, your visitor, Monsieur James, has arrived and he is waiting for you in the bar of the hotel." I put the final touches of black mascara to my eyelashes—referred to my friends as 'spider's webs' because of their voluminous presence—then I grabbed my cross-body clutch bag, rushed off towards the lift, and pressed the 'call' button. I was staying in this old Parisian hotel that must once have been used by the rich and famous of Europe visiting the city of lights, la Ville Lumière, for a good time, but now it operated as a business hotel. It had been beautifully restored and combined its classic art nouveau style with modern functionality. The elevator, however, must have been there since its early days.

The moments that it took for the lift to arrive protracted into eternity, giving way too much time for my mind and belly to play gymnastics with each other. I became more nervous by the minute, which made me realise just how much I was looking forward to seeing James in this new context. After all, my Inner Diamond had it be that his was the only business card I had taken with me on my trip to Hawaii. Why? Was it possible that something about his energy or deeper being, despite the distance, had been working away on me in the inner realms? Something in me had recognised something exceptional in him, and it wasn't his looks. As though an unseen force was at work, drawing us together, it felt beautiful and right. Though I had kept his card with me on that holiday, hand on heart, never in a million years did I think that we would ever come to this, *a date*, and a *romantic* one at that.

I stepped into the elevator and closed its antique interior door, made of dark metal bars, and only then did the machine decide it was safe to make its way down.

As I stood in the elevator and saw the lights of the floors pass me by on the agonisingly slow descent to the lobby, my mind kept wandering away. How did we even end up in a situation where we were on an actual date? I couldn't recall any of us taking conscious steps to go after the other, with both of us living in different backgrounds, living different lives, from different countries. Yet, somehow, the universe must have conspired to bring us together. It seemed perfectly natural and as if it had to be. Were we in the flow?

So now, I hoped—no, prayed—that I wouldn't come back to my hotel room shrouded in disappointment yet again.

The lift finally stopped with a shudder and clunk. One of the lobby boys rushed to the elevator and wrestled open the sliding door so I could step out gracefully. I looked around the busy lobby and soon located the large open doors to the lounge. The place was packed with lots of people standing in small groups with glasses of beer or wine in their hands, chatting away in all kinds of languages.

He sat at the bar, positioned so he could see me approach. "Hello!" he said, springing off the bar stool as soon as he saw me. He walked over to give me a kiss on the cheek, or rather, three, because that was the Belgian way. His sea-blue eyes twinkled, and he looked me up and down admiringly with the maturity of a grown-up man and the unadulterated, refreshing zeal of a teenager and said, "Wow! You look beautiful."

"Oh, you charmer you. There must be some French blood in you," I said, tongue-in-cheek.

"Indeed, there is. *Bonne Maman*, my grandmother, was French," he replied.

"There, I knew it. Keep tapping into that and we shall get along famously."

He had reserved a table at a well-known restaurant, not too far from the Champs-Elysées. He hailed a taxi queued up at the stand of my hotel and told the taxi driver in fluent French where to take us.

"It's a fabulous restaurant and they've assured me that they're accustomed to vegetarian requests. I must say I remain sceptical. In French cuisine there are a lot of wonderful vegetarian dishes, but they don't even recognise that their own dishes are vegetarian. If you ask, they look at you like you're asking in Japanese for cheese on toast with tomato ketchup in a Michelin starred restaurant," he said.

"I'm sure it'll be wonderful," I said, touched by his thoughtfulness. The restaurant, although contemporary, had charm and buzzed with an upbeat ambience. The waiter guided us to a small table by a window on the first floor. From where we sat, we could see the busy, never-ending traffic in the street, the flow of the people walking quickly by, and the klaxoning scooters trying to slalom their way in between the jammed cars. The street lights reflected on the metal surfaces and windows of the vehicles, like so many moving mirrors. Over the roofs of the houses on the other side of the street, the white beam of light from the top of the Eiffel Tower swept by every few minutes, like a gigantic lighthouse in the middle of the city.

With so much in common at work, it was no surprise that we began by talking about our day on the job and our various challenges. The client we had in common gave us countless anecdotes to share and talk about. Then, we began chatting like two long-lost friends who had just rediscovered each other and could not catch up quickly enough with what the other had been up to in life.

A while later a waiter came up to us and introduced himself. *"Bonsoir mademoiselle et monsieur, comment allez-vous? Je m'appelle Gaston et je suis votre garçon pour ce soir."* Then he added in broken English, as he handed us the menus, "Zall I start by bringing you *une bouteille d'eau pétillante?* Ze special of ze day is *homard*, how I say, lobsteer in champagne sauce. Excellent!"

"Not for us", James said. "We will eat veggie. You know, no fish, no meat".

"Très bien monsieur, in zat case, I can recommend you ze *faisant,"* he answered.

We both chuckled. "No pheasant for us, please. In fact, nothing that can walk or that has eyes," I said.

"Neither oysters nor other *fruits de mer.* I heard somewhere that you have a vegetarian version of your degustation menu?" James asked.

"Certainement monsieur," he replied. "I will inform ze chef. Will you care to choose the accompanying wine,

perhaps?" The waiter handed James a big leather-bound book, the size of an encyclopaedia.

It never ceased to amaze me how much you could learn about a person just by watching them go through the process of choosing and ordering food and drink in a restaurant. James looked down the wine list and asked me if I preferred red or white. "Definitely red, especially with dinner," I replied. "Though what I know about wines, you could scribble on a grain of rice."

It turned out he knew a lot about wines, their regions, the different types of grapes, the differences of soil that gave different tastes and scents, and the way in which different types of wine were made to age and mature. His passionate manner of talking about these things immediately had me hooked on learning more about wines, and in one evening alone I picked up all the basics. It set the foundation for my learning more in time to come.

The fascinating thing was, it wasn't the wine that was of interest to me. It was his energy. He was full of verve and had an irrepressible zest for life, passionate about and fascinated by so much—wine, food, work, what was going on in the world. Like me, he too had travelled across many parts of the world, and I mean *travelled*, not just visited. Like me, he had learned just how important it was to have a cultural appreciation of people from different parts of the world. He had an insightful knowledge about cultures and the importance of understanding how countries with similar backgrounds had distinct yet subtle differences, and that if you did not know how to address them, it could cost you a big contract or take away what could have been a fulfilling personal experience. Like me, he had spent many years learning about the nature of people. He, too, understood just how valuable it was to make the effort to understand ourselves as well as the nature of others so that you could relate to people with more ease.

"There's something I've never told you. I didn't want to be presumptuous and, also because we have been working together, it wasn't appropriate," James said.

"Have you chosen the wine, sir?" Gaston interrupted.

"Yes, we will have a St. Estephe Le Crock, 1998," James replied.

"An excellent choice and a fine year, if I may say, Monsieur." Gaston then left for the wine chamber in the back of the restaurant.

"So, what is so important that you need to tell me? Please, God, don't let this be the moment he grows balls to come out and tell the world. Don't tell me that you're really a woman in drag!" I laughed. We both giggled like silly teenagers.

"No, no. Don't worry. They're fully grown and well and truly in their element," he jested, making a fist of his hand and punching the air with it. "So, what I've been wanting to share with you for a while is this. The very first time I saw you in the basement of that bank in Frankfurt, I saw just your back, and that too from the other side of the hall, outside the conference room. I didn't know who you were but something about you caught the corner of my eye and I turned around to face in your direction, wondering, *What is that? What did I just see flashing and shimmering?*"

"You hadn't been on the sauce the night before, had you?" I chuckled.

"Haha! No, I only drink wine and that, too, only with a meal," he replied, taking what I said literally, again.

I must teach him about the sarcastic cheekiness of British humour. I chuckled to myself.

"As I was saying," he continued, "What stood out, in a sea of grey, blue, and black suits was you, even though you yourself were wearing a navy-blue suit. I hadn't seen your face, and yet, I saw these vibrant colours radiating from you, dancing around you. It wasn't just a visual perception, but actually I felt them within me, as if somehow they were extending out and were a part of me. Honestly, I'd never seen or felt anything like that before. I was mesmerised and, at the same time, mystified, but I put all that to the back of my mind. I mean, after all it was a peculiar thing, and all the more strange in a work environment."

I felt touched and humbled. For the first time in my life, I was with someone who had the capacity to see a person, to see me, beyond just the physical. I did not immediately know what to answer, except an abashed whispered, "Oh!"

The waiter brought us two large tulip glasses, poured wine into James' as if it was evident that he was the one to have to try and taste it according to the customs of the restaurant. James turned the wine around in the glass, sniffed at it, and had a quick sip. "Excellent, well aged," he said.

"*Merci beaucoup, Monsieur*, we do our very best to bring the best out of our wines," Gaston said proudly, as he poured the two glasses.

James raised his glass. He looked deep into my eyes as our glasses gently touched with a faint but clear crystalline note. Involuntarily our gazes locked for what seemed like infinity. It was as if he saw and recognised all of me. "To a very special evening," he said softly.

"There's something else, something a bit more worldly I suppose, that I find remarkable about you," he continued as he put down his glass. "Whenever you have to present or explain something to an audience, the way you're able to carry the room with you is amazing. I've noticed how people sit up and listen. Your ability to communicate in general, written or when you speak, there's such clarity about it. It's just beautiful to watch you," he said and smiled at me, dismantling my defences, layer by layer, with his generous acknowledgements.

I took a deep breath, a sigh of relief and gratitude for this amazing man sitting in front of me. Who was he? How come he was so generous with his acknowledgement of me? What was it that made it possible for him to recognise me? "You're very kind," I replied, smiling, or more accurately, trying to squeeze my beam into a smile so as not to betray too much of my enthusiasm. The years of disappointment in relationships had trained me to go cautiously and take my time. "Are you sure you're not on a stealth mission to sweet-talk me into giving away my company's top secrets?" I chuckled.

So far, he'd been trustworthy in our dealings at work, but could he be trusted with my heart and soul? I quickly asked my Inner Diamond, *I want to trust him. The food hasn't arrived yet, so it's still too early to call, but will he pass The Vomiting Test?*

"Ah, damn, you've rumbled me. Or maybe, you are the Mata Hari?" he kidded, then, looking earnest again, he continued, "It seems to me that the professional in you is just the tip of the iceberg. I mean, you're very good at what you do, no doubt, exceptional even, one of the best I've worked with. I can't help feeling though, that the real you, beyond work, is so much more—creative, mystical, and passionate about life."

"Aw, there you go with that French charm again," I joked, abashed. "But, please, don't let me stop you. Flattery will get you everywhere."

He chuckled and said, "No, really. I've noticed that you have this amazing ability to read a situation that's uncanny. I've seen you disarm the most aggressive of guys in a charming and compassionate way, but strictly professional, of course. I mean, you're really empathic in how you're able to understand people. It's not often that you see those qualities in a person. I've been admiring that about you. What brilliance and intelligence." As he spoke, his eyes smiled and danced. I could see that he wasn't just flattering me to get into my knickers. I was utterly humbled to see that he was genuinely taken with me.

Gaston brought us a first dish of vegetable terrine with cress sauce. *"Bon appetite, Madame et Monsieur,"* he said. *Diamond, here we go,* I said in my mind, but somehow I already felt I knew how things were going to go.

"There's something else, too, that I've been really struck by." James picked up his knife and fork. "You have this mystical quality to you. Maybe it has something to do with that light I saw around you." He looked at me, searching for clues on my face. "Now, I've read a lot of books about philosophy, psychology, the nature of mankind, and so on, and I'm sure you've done similar things. It just shows, but with you, it's even more so. It seems to me that, rather than just reading about it, you've actually looked inside of yourself, battled with your demons and come away vanquishing them," he said, matter-of-fact, as if it was something he was reading off a menu. I looked at him, stunned, as his perceptiveness punctured more of my cynicism, more of my layers of past disappointments and despair of not being 'gotten'. I merely looked at him, my lips stuck together in a soft smile, soft but dry, despite my heart thawing. I wanted to say something, to dance with him in the conversation, but was too touched and moved by his acknowledgement and by his recognition of the being beneath my persona.

He continued, "You know, Smita, it strikes me that you have the ability to look into the eye of the tiger and talk to it, and if it attacks you, you're not afraid to take it right on and fight it. But rather than shutting down, you've become stronger, more sensitive, more compassionate and your strength has become your sweetness, your ability to be honest and vulnerable." He looked at me, searching for more words to match his feelings. "What I'm trying to say is that you have a depth to you. *Have* you been doing a lot of work on yourself that gives you this kind of substance?"

I was the one impressed now, that he had the sight to perceive all this, that he had seen it all along when I thought I was the one hiding my feelings for him. I held myself together, as if with a single thread of silk, to keep myself from bursting into tears of joy for, finally, being with someone exceptional.

"Well, I haven't had any plastic surgery on my boobs, if that's what you mean by 'work on yourself' and 'substance'." I tried to camouflage my shyness with humour, as well as to diffuse the intensity of warmth for him that surged within me.

He burst into hysterics, saying, "You know that's not what I mean. You are more than perfect the way you are." He gesticulated with his arms, pretending to be upset and then laughing, clearly happy he was able to slot in a small compliment.

The waiter came over with our second course, gushing as he explained, "*Madame, Monsieur*, especially for you, the chef has sent this, a very special boiled quail's egg, *organique* and fresh from our own farm, together with a salad of our finest lettuce, tomatoes and other fresh produce." The couple at the table next to us turned around to see what the furore was all about. Then, thinking it was farcical that our second starter was just a small egg, however organic, they cracked up, chortling. James and I looked at each other and tried not to laugh at the waiter's well-meaning offer.

"At least he didn't bring us roast chicken, insisting that it was vegetarian because it had been fed on organic corn," James said as the waiter left, then fell about in fits of laughter at the woeful efforts to meet my vegetarian demands.

"Or a slice of that poor pheasant," I added, laughing myself.

"So now, there's something I have to confess to, and I can only do this if you can laugh at yourself, I mean," I said. I knew I was about to take a risk, but I really could not be with someone who was pompous about himself, who took himself so seriously that he could not laugh at himself.

"Oh? Try me," he replied, curiosity aroused.

"Well, you know the first time I saw you, you were dressed dapper in impeccably tailored business clothes, but I had the image of a well-healed landowner or farmer or something pop into my mind." I looked at him, trying not to burst out laughing as I said, "I started to think of you as 'Tractor Man'!" Now I could not contain myself and fell about laughing.

He laughed, saying, "Really? How on earth could you have known? As it happens, I actually own not one but two tractors!"

"No kidding! Why on earth would you own a tractor at all?" I asked in disbelief.

He explained that some years ago, he had bought a dilapidated old property in the countryside. It came with some land that took quite some maintenance and the tractors came in handy for this. "Have you really been calling me 'Tractor Man' all this time? You didn't just make that up because you heard me at some point talking about my tractors?"

"No, really. You were 'Tractor Man' even before we'd formally met," I said. "Knowing what I know now, I don't have to feel wicked for thinking of you that way."

"That's astonishing," he said, baffled, deep in thought.

Gaston was back this time with the *'plat de resistance'*, a main course made up of roasted artichoke hearts, stuffed with some delectable mini vegetables and a special sauce.

Just as we had our first bite of the course, we heard some sounds from the street. We looked outside and saw what looked like a group of Chinese pilots and air hostesses arrive at the hotel across the street, making an almighty din, clearly stressed.

"Don't you ever get tired of this lifestyle of travelling all the time?" I asked.

James paused for a second, then answered, "Actually, I don't mind."

"But, don't you get stressed by all the hassle? Nothing glamorous about standing in airport security queues every day."

"It's true that I used to get stressed," he answered, "wondering whether I would arrive on time. But then about ten years ago, by coincidence I saw this Indian *guru* on television. He was talking about the flow of time and about the concept of being 'already always there'. He was saying that when we truly live in the moment, it also means that in every instant we are always somewhere. In a sense, we only travel in the gaps between these moments of consciousness. We get stressed because in our mind, instead of being at peace with where we are in the moment, we already want to be somewhere else and we get impatient. This was a bright light bulb moment. It had quite an impact on me. Once I got this simple sounding but really quite profound truth, I stopped being stressed about a lot of things, including my frequent travels."

"Wow! You got that? That's quite something," I said with delight. "That's only one of the most important awakenings a human being could ever have. I mean, I can't think of a single one of India's ancient texts that doesn't try to teach that key tenet."

"You know, Smita, changing subjects a little bit, I have no clue how old you are, and it would be very impertinent to ask. But it's pretty puzzling. On the one hand, you have this beautiful freshness about you. You look like you're twenty-something, but on the other, you conduct yourself with real maturity. It's as if there's an ancientness wrapped up in that young body, as if you are full of all these ancient teachings."

"Are you saying I'm an antiquated mummy or a dried prune?" I chuckled, trying not to show just how much I was melting inside by this man's sensitivity and keen perception. When he looked at me, it was as if he was gazing directly into the ocean of my soul, deeper every time he looked into the very core of who I was, and I felt received and held, even though he hadn't touched me. In the smile on his face, I saw the intensity of a loving presence that I had not known before, though it felt strangely familiar.

He took hold of my hand and held it in his. I was startled by the velvet sensation of his touch, causing a sudden flow of plush warmth to race up my arm and into my heart, encouraging it to open. With an absolute absence of awkwardness between us, a graceful yet bubbly flow of thoughts, ideas, and humour had filled the evening, having time fly swiftly and yet, become audaciously elastic so that our few hours together seemed like we had been with each other the whole day.

Time flew as we continued to talk over a divine dessert of *chocolat moelleux* and French cheese, the intense conversation making us spin as if it was just the two of us in this city, inside a little bubble of our own. The rest of the buzzing restaurant, Gaston, the crowded street, everything faded to the background and into one big, cocooning haze.

James insisted on paying the bill and left Gaston a generous tip on the table as we walked out of the restaurant. We stepped into the fresh but wonderful evening air, and discussed whether to walk or take a taxi back. "If it's not too late for you, how about we take a walk? There's the Champs-Élysées, or the River Seine is close by, too—just a couple of blocks from around the corner," James said.

"My already-full heart fluttered
with even more joyfulness
and deep gratitude
as I acknowledged
the divine grace
that rippled through our lives."

24

The Kiss

I looked up at the dark but clear late-Spring evening sky. The stars twinkled in delight with Venus particularly bright tonight, and the disc of the large full moon reflected its shimmering light to bathe Paris, the City of Lights, in a silvery glow. Time had flown in a bizarre way that evening. It seemed the dinner was over in an instant, yet it felt like we had spent eternity together. Both of us seemed not to want the special feeling of that evening to stop yet.

"Let's walk along the Seine," I said.

We walked through the city streets down to the river. Once outside of the busy main streets, we were on our own. The city lights shone gently and coloured the old and imposing sandstoned buildings with their orange glow. This was Paris at its most beautiful.

The riverside was as romantic as it was serene. The moon cast its sensual silver beams on the Seine's glassy surface, which reflected the light. A bit further, behind us, on the other side of the river, stood the Eiffel Tower in its full glory, an imposing statuesque representation of Parisian pride. A revolving lantern, its bright, brilliant beacon pierced through the night sky. As we walked on the wide pavement along the waterfront with the lights from the Eiffel Tower guiding us along, chattering incessantly, I became aware of feeling so content, my heart so full, that there was nowhere else in the world I would rather have been. I so enjoyed this extraordinary man's company, attraction apart, and had never come across a man whom I had *liked* quite as genuinely as I did James.

We had now passed several bridges along our riverside walk and were approaching yet another one, a medieval looking bridge, when James said, "Let's go onto that bridge. You'll get a superb view of the river in the direction of Notre Dame." He led me toward the arched middle from where we would get a better view of the beautiful river carving its way through the centre of Paris. Just as we stepped onto the almost empty bridge, from the corner of my eye, something caught my attention. We carried on walking but I turned back to look and saw a white plaque with large blue antiquated letters with the name of the bridge we were on: *Pont Saint-Michel*. My face broke into smile as I had a flashback of mystical encounters in my meditation with the angel-bird Michael, just after my surgery and again on the islands of Hawaii and at the temple in Kauai. My already-full heart fluttered with even more joyfulness and deep gratitude as I acknowledged the divine grace that rippled through our lives.

As we approached the end of the first arch of the old bridge, the lights of the lanterns that illuminated the bridge flickered. These lanterns had modern light bulbs that had been cleverly designed to mimic the looks of the first gaslights that had given Paris its nickname, *La Ville Lumière*. Their sudden flickering now seemed to also mimic how it must have been when the bridge was lit by candles, centuries ago.

"Strange, I didn't notice these lights flickering as we walked up to the bridge," James said. "Now the whole place looks like a flickering Christmas tree." The further we walked, the more irregular the lights behaved, some of them going on and off like blinkers.

We stopped over the arch. Beneath Pont Saint-Michel, a rowdy *bateau mouche* passed by, an open excursion boat that gave visitors a view of the city from along the River Seine. We watched it go under the bridge right beneath us. I breathed in the crisp fresh air, cherishing every moment of this exquisite evening as I looked up at the sky again, having my hands on the stone balustrade. As he stood behind me, James came closer. His breath ruffled my hair. He took my right hand, edging a little closer still. I was taken by surprise to find myself breaking into tingles as his palm, pressing into mine, activated electricity to shoot up the nerves of my arm. Mouth beside my ear, he said softly, "You know, Smita, it is as if I've always known you, as if you were round the corner all my life, and now, when the time is right for both of us, we finally get to meet once again."

But for the twinkling of the bright stars and the softly lit riverside, I was grateful for the darkness that hid the details of my face, trying to contain blissful delight. But then, impulsively, I turned around and faced him. He took my other hand, and said. "You're an enigma, you know. A beautiful and brilliant one at that." He whispered with such a warm tenderness that I found him hard to resist.

"You have the most beautiful expressive eyes. When I look into them, I feel as if I am falling, as if diving into deep dark pools of mystery. But then, sometimes, those eyes of yours can suddenly turn into daggers when you become very passionate about something or when you're defending yourself against the aggression of some nasty old character. I just *love* that bewitching, dazzling fire inside of you," he said.

He came even closer towards me, then leant over to kiss me. Though I could feel my legs turning to jelly, with so many years of practice my instant reflex was to keep holding myself firmly together. "Oh no you don't, you cheeky bugger!" I said, playfully but firm. I was surprised that he was being so amorous so soon, while I was not quite ready, still in a spin of my own, not willing to lose control but swaying in my resolve all the same. I pulled back gently, smiling but exercising my prerogative in being absolutely clear that this kiss he would be denied. Just as I pulled myself back from his lips, which were almost touching mine, the lights of the old lantern that lit the bridge just beside us popped with a small dry bang and went out for good.

Another *bateau mouche*, shining its big spotlights on the ancient and historic buildings close to Notre Dame, was just passing underneath us and suddenly turned pitch black at exactly the same moment as our lantern did. We both burst into laughter.

"Must be a sign from the universe, turning Paris into the city of flickering lights", James said.

Was my Inner Diamond trying to tell me something?

James took my hand and walked me down the bridge to the taxi stand on the corner. We jumped into the back of the first taxi of the row. James told the taxi driver where to take me and also told him that once we arrived at my hotel, he would have to wait there a while before driving James to his hotel.

The driver put the name of the street of my hotel into his GPS satellite navigation system, only to erupt in a typical Parisian rant. *"Merde, nom de dieu!"* he exclaimed. We were holding hands and had eyes only for each other. We both turned to look at the driver in the front to see what was going on, wondering if we had somehow upset him. He banged his fist a few times against the screen of his GPS, continuing to shout in his not very flattering French. *"Il y a t'il un probleme?"* James asked the taxi driver if there was a problem.

"Mon GPS soudainement ne marche plus," he exclaimed in frustration. *"Semble être problème d'electricité."*

"His satnav suddenly has electricity problems and doesn't want to work anymore," James said to me.

"More static in the air?" I chuckled. "But you don't need to translate, you know. My French is more than good enough."

"Surely you know the way without needing a satnav?" James said to the driver.

"Oui mais je dois calculer le montant á payer," the driver said, still frustrated, as he wouldn't know how much to charge for the ride without the satnav showing the distance.

"Don't worry," James said, "I'll pay whatever seems fair to you."

With that, the taxi driver got under way, leading us through the streets of Paris, creatively taking us from street to street, meandering through the city in order to avoid the never-ending traffic jams. We just sat in the back, happily holding hands, quiet, watching the city lights and lit windows of shops pass us by, sometimes turning to each other, smiling and looking into each other's eyes. Though we were in the dark in the back of the car, it seemed we could see deep into each other, nevertheless. Was it a twinkling sparkle we saw inside of the other or a mere reflection of the city lights? While we drove through the softly lit streets, he held my hand and I wondered if he, too, felt the heat of the electricity that ignited from the touch.

When we arrived at my hotel, the driver stopped in front of the stairs to the majestic doors of the old palace. A bellboy in a spotless uniform came up to the car and held the door open. We got out and walked up the steps. Just as we reached the entrance, a crowd of people in suits and cocktail dresses poured out the main hotel doors, forcing us to the side corner of the entrance. I looked at James and said, "Well, thank you for a wonderful evening, for turning me into a wine boffin, for showing me the gorgeous River Seine, and for your fabulous company." What I was really thinking was, to my surprise, how incredibly attracted I was to him, more than I could have ever thought possible, and how much I didn't want this evening to end.

"Not at all. The pleasure is all mine. I had so much fun," he said, again reaching for my hands and interlacing my fingers with his. "You're just so exceptional. I have no words for it."

The bubble of companionship in which we had been cocooned all evening, as if there was no one else around but just us, now bound us tighter in a unity, like we'd always belonged together. Once again, he leant towards me, then said tenderly, "Sweet Smita, may I kiss you now?" My mind, my ego, wanted to resist, play the game a bit longer and say no again but my heart, swirling with delight, joy, pleasure, contentment and just plain simple happiness, took me over, and all I could do was to smile at him with my eyes. He wrapped his arms around me in an embrace and I sensed the barrier of our personas dissolving into a fusion, electricity intensifying, sending sparks shooting through my entire body.

My nervous system came alive all at once, like the branches of a banyan tree ignited by a bolt of divine lightning. Just as our lips were close enough to try and touch into a kiss again, our second attempt after the bridge, the alarm of a nearby car started shrieking, startling us out of our embrace. We turned around to look at what was going on and, right then, the hotel's fire alarm went off too, immediately creating a deafening rumpus, sending guests rushing, frantic to get out of the building, and employees all over the place trying to control the situation.

We both looked at each other and burst into peals of laughter. "What on earth is going on here?" I exclaimed. "First, the lights going on the blink on Pont Saint-Michel. Then the *bateau mouche* suddenly blacking out. The poor taxi driver's satnav developed an electrical fault out of the blue, and now the car alarm and the hotel's fire alarm have gone ballistic!"

"I tell you, it's your mystical magic. Must be that special *prana* you always talk about showering around you, like you're some cosmic fountain," he said, smiling and holding me once again in his arms. "I love you, sweet angel. How long I've been wanting to say that to you." For once at a loss for words, defenceless, I just melted.

After things had settled down and we were allowed back into the hotel, we finally parted and I went upstairs to my room.

"So, he did pass The Vomiting Test, didn't he?" My Inner Diamond whispered.

With flying colours! More than that, my dear Diamond, much more, I answered.

For weeks to come, I walked around with eyes sparkling like champagne diamonds and an unerasable smile etched on my face.

25

Love Food

Our short break together was over all too quickly, but we did keep in touch via the phone. Lots of phone calls, in fact.

"This time I'm not going to let you off the hook so easily," James said. "We've now been to a couple of Indian restaurants since we messed up the street lights in Paris. Every time, you tell me that your mum's cooking is so much better than these posh Indian places. You've even been bragging about how your own cooking's a lot better than the restaurants, and that you learned the trade from your mother and grandmother."

"It's true. It's all true," I said with a chuckle.

"Great! Well, given how much I love Indian food, it's about time you showed me what you can do." The challenge was clear.

I teased, "You're just looking for an excuse to come over to my house."

"No, I mean, yes, I'd like that too. But I'd love to try some authentic, home-cooked Indian food, you know, the real stuff," James said earnestly. I chuckled, finding his honest straightforwardness endearing.

"All right, all right. This time, I'll let you into my house and cook for you." I was happy that at least someone was eager to taste my cooking and, besides, we had dated long enough for him to at last come over to mine.

With work and travel, the earliest we could meet wasn't the next weekend but a Wednesday, in the middle of the working week. To make it work, James was going to fly in to London but would have to take the last flight out the same evening. Hopefully, his plane wouldn't turn into a pumpkin when Big Ben struck midnight.

I had to be abroad myself until Tuesday, and on Wednesday I had business meetings in London, so I was somewhat stressed about how I would get everything done. By sparring ferociously with James about the superiority of vegetarian Indian food versus French cuisine, I had raised James' expectations sky-high and made my job much harder. Now, there was no choice but to deliver. Happily, I managed to re-arrange my late Wednesday client meeting, and was able to drive back to my home in the West London suburbs via Wembley's

Ealing Road. You would be forgiven for thinking, as you entered this street, that you'd taken the wrong turning and landed in India, in a typical street in some Gujarati town. The street teemed with Indian fabric and *sari* shops, jewellers, and grocery merchants. Almost anything you could find in India, you could find here. The greengrocers were laden with the freshest eclectic Indian produce, making it hard to narrow down what I would put on the menu for the date.

Without overthinking it, I picked up the lesser-known variety of vegetables, that on first glance may not have looked appropriate for a romantic date, and yet, if they were cooked to excellence, they could really impress. Fresh baby aubergines; small new potatoes; *tindora*, finger-sized gherkin-like stripy green vegetables from the watermelon family; *karela*, another bitter melon variety with a green, knobbly, waxy exterior; some freshly ground cumin; coriander; red chillies; turmeric; fresh bunches of green coriander; and also some *methi* or fenugreek leaves. I realised that I was probably going way over the top and was going to stuff the poor guy, but as per my grandmother's training, it was always better to err on the side of more rather than less. Oh, and did I mention that I also wanted to show off my skills? It had been ages, longer than I could remember, since I had cooked for a man and, surprisingly, it made me feel rather wonderful.

Back at home, I dived into my kitchen and got stuck into preparing the food. On the menu were four curries and one *daal*, made of yellow lentils, a curry of tiny aubergines and baby potatoes stuffed with a fragrant mix of spices in gram flour and chopped coriander, embellished with lemon juice and sugar, and a curry of chipped *tindora* cooked to perfection in yet another concoction of spices, and dry, sautéed *karela* delicately spiced and balanced with *gor* (sweet jaggery). James was a big cheese fan, so even though it was all going to be way too much, I also made a spice-tempered, buttery tomato sauce for a *paneer* (Indian cottage cheese). To bring balance to these textures, I pressure-cooked some lentils and blended them into a puree, then flavoured them with the crushed ginger and a couple of mild green chillies, cumin-coriander and turmeric powder, and some *garam masala* powder that included ground cinnamon and cloves. To finish, I added just a tiny amount of tamarind, and the Gujarati *daal*, soup-style, simmered away. Finally, it was time to knead the dough for the *methi trikon parathas* and leave it to rest for at least thirty minutes, until it was time to roll out these flatbreads.

There was a lot to be done but, once I started, I was a whirlwind. My poor mum once told me that she found it terrifying to be around me when I was whizzing about preparing and cooking food, in my flow, routines becoming semi-automatic. My kitchen was now a melange of fragrances from the fresh roasting of cumin and mustard seeds, all popping in spoonfuls of hot olive oil as I made the *vaghaar* or *tadka* base for the different curries.

As the cooking of the curries and *daal* got underway, I juggled all the cooking pots on the stove at the same time, while finely chopping the fresh green fenugreek leaves, just enough to knead into the dough for the *methi trikon parathas*—flatbreads that I would later roll out into perfect triangles. A few drops of olive oil spread in a special technique of rolling out the *paratha* would, when shallow fried, give soft but crispy layered flatbread to die for. After the dough was elastic with vigorous kneading, I prepared a chutney of shredded, fresh coconut and yogurt, tempered with cinnamon sticks, mustard and sesame seeds, all popped in a half tablespoon of hot oil, flavoured with puréed fresh tomato.

At six-thirty, two-and-a-half hours after I started, all that remained was to roll out and shallow-fry the triangular flatbreads. This left me with just enough time to freshen up and change into a decent dress before James would arrive at seven o'clock.

Beads of sweat poured off my forehead as I went around frantically tidying up the kitchen and other parts of the house, so as to give the impression that not only was I a fantastic cook, but an all-round veritable goddess in the kitchen and home.

Just as I was rushing, panting up the stairs to freshen up, I received a text from him. "So sorry! Will be 45min late. Plane delayed. Just landed. Love, James."

Thank you, Diamond! Thank you, Universe! Thank you for holding him back a bit, but bring him home safely.

I'd just put the last finishing touches to my mascara when I heard a car stop in front. A door slammed and a few seconds later the doorbell rang. I rushed downstairs, heart pounding. I opened the door and there he stood, a lovely bouquet of flowers in his hand. "Oh, you shouldn't have!" I said, thinking *yes, yes, you should have indeed.* "Where did you manage to get these from?"

"I told the taxi to stop in the high street on the way here," he said with a grin, clearly happy to see me. "My God, you look more beautiful every time I see you." We instinctively reached out to each other to give a kiss and then laughed as we both had the same reflex of giving a furtive, quick kiss on the mouth rather than lingering. "Don't want to send the neighbourhood into a frenzy with your alarms going off," he said, laughing softly.

"No, please, it would be a shame if the neighbourhood watch would prevent you from coming back," I laughed.

"I take it as a good sign then that you intend to let me come back in the future," he said. "I'll do my best to behave then."

Oh, please don't! The wicked thought flashed through my mind and made me blush. All I said though, was, "You'd better, or I will have to tell Passport Control to not let you in again." I let him in, taking the flowers from him. "You must be starving. If you like, you can freshen up quickly in the bathroom here and join me in the kitchen downstairs after that?"

This little manoeuvre gave me time to put the flowers in a vase and to check that there had been no catastrophes on the stove while I was upstairs. He came to the lower floor, where the lounge and kitchen were, just as I lit the candles. The stereo on my small kitchen table was playing one of my favourite CDs, *Positivity*. "Ah, that's Incognito," James said. "One of my favourite bands from the eighties and nineties. Brings back memories of working through long nights until early morning on my research in the lab while listening to all these funky bands."

"Maybe we were listening to the same music at the same time," I said. "The flowers are gorgeous. Thank you, darling. Taking your advice, I bought a bottle of Italian wine, a Rosso di Montalcino. I hope you'll like it. Can you open it?" I said all of it in one breath.

"Mmm, that was a good year," he answered, while he looked the bottle up and down and placed it on the table. "It's so nice to be here. The whole house emanates this vibe of yours." He then came back to the stove, looking over my shoulder, curious to see what was in the pots. "Smells divine," he said.

He put his arms around me and gave me a kiss on the neck. It surprised neither of us that exactly at that moment, the CD got stuck and started giving us repeated metallic clicks. I turned round quickly to stop it. James sighed. "If it wasn't for the fact that it feels so right to be together, you'd think that the universe was playing cat and mouse with us. First, there's this powerful flow that pulled us inexorably together, almost having us bump into each other, and then, when we try to get close, there's all sorts of dissonance that keeps us apart."

"I know, darling, but I have a really good feeling about this. I think the universe is rather trying to tell us to align our energies because the alchemy is so potent."

"Hmm, I hope you're right. And I think you are. But somehow it seems to me there's another important message in there, as if it is trying to give a hint there is something important we need to do. I wish I knew what that was," he said. I smiled to myself, realising that he thought a lot like I did, sensitive and finely-tuned with the energetic flow.

"What an artistic kettle you have here, Beauty!" he said, indicating my electric kettle that had just switched off. To my surprise, it radiated the colours of the rainbow as it cooled down. "Wow! It's a proper LED light show. I'd like one of those in my home, too."

"Oh, when did it start doing that?" I felt dumbfounded. "I didn't know it could do that. Must have switched itself on spontaneously this evening." We looked at each other and started laughing again. "A romantically intelligent kettle!" James said. "What's next, your toaster serenading a love song? The oven cooking us up some divine poetry?"

"Silly! Why don't you sit down at the table so I can serve you piping hot *methi parathas* as we go? That way, you'll get to sample how authentic Gujarati Indian food is meant to be eaten." James said down, eager with anticipation to sample the food. I served the plate with taster portions of the stuffed baby aubergines and potatoes and the other curries and a small side-bowl of *daal*, and a piping-hot-off-the-griddle *methi paratha* triangle. Then I joined him.

"Bon appétit!" he said, tucking in.

"Hmm. This food is heavenly, Beauty," James exclaimed. "You really should have invited me before. What a treat. Where did you learn all this? These preparations seem so much more complex than the French cooking my grandmother taught me, and I thought that was already complicated."

"Well, glad you like it." I smiled, raising the glass of red wine to him. "I learned it all from my mum, my grandmother, and the women in our family. They're all great cooks. We take great pride in our cooking traditions."

"So I see. Truly amazing—I'm going to eat until I drop. This is so good, I won't be able to stop," he said while noshing up a second portion of everything I had served him. "You definitely didn't learn it from a book, then!" he said, mimicking the Spanish accent of Manuel, the waiter in *Fawlty Towers*. We both laughed as we recollected the well-known punchline from the hysterical, classic British comedy television series that we had grown up watching.

"Let me make you another hot *paratha*," I said, as I got busy with rolling out a few more triangles from the dough and then placing them on the hot *tava* griddle to shallow-fry them.

"Pfff, I am so full already." He sighed. "But okay, why not? Your cooking is just as impossible to resist as you are."

I laughed. "Aw, you keep feeding me with compliments and I'll keep stuffing you with *chapattis* and *parathas*."

"Sweetie, I wonder, it cannot be easy for women like you in the workplace," James said, while turning around the wine in his glass.

"What do you mean? I don't need your pity," I said, slightly reactive.

"Sorry, I said that a bit clumsily," he added hastily. "I mean, beautiful attractive women, that are competent, well, any competent woman for that matter, you must be like a real threat to insecure men, no? You probably get hit on all the time and when you don't respond and then, on top, do a good job and dominate meetings and all, a lot of men must get pissed off and resentful?"

"Yep, story of my life." I sighed while I turned over the triangular pancake-like *paratha* to roast the other side.

"Still a glass ceiling, isn't there? Or at the very least, a lot of invisible resistance," he said. "It's almost as if you have two jobs, the one men do and then the one on top where you constantly have to look your best and defend yourself at the same time. I really admire how you pull it all off." I found his compassion touching.

"I'll drink to that," I said, sipping the wine, not wanting tonight to get into a serious conversation about the gender politics of the workplace.

Then, while I put the rolled out triangle on the hot *tava* pan and then poured a few considered drops of olive oil around its edges, setting the oil sizzling, he said, "Coming back to how it must be difficult sometimes for smart, independent women, I had this sudden thought yesterday. A beautiful woman like you, dare I say, a sexy attractive woman, so smart, intelligent, energetic and full of confidence, mystical—your dark, mysterious eyes, one moment seductive and sweet, the next, flying daggers—in the old days you would have been a high priestess of the temple of knowledge, attending the oracle, surely what they called a witch in mediaeval times in the days when alchemy and science were still one. Gosh, you would have ended up burning at the stake, or hanged or something."

Shocked with surprise at hearing his insightful words, I dropped the plate with the freshly fried *paratha* that I was just bringing to the table. The plate fell on the floor but I was able to grab the *parathas* before they wasted. The glass plate, however, went crashing, and shattered on contact with the floor. For just a moment, I froze in the middle of my swirl from the stove to the table. How could he know? My past life of being sentenced to hanging for being ignorantly branded a witch, though I was merely then a ten-year-old, came rushing back to the surface of my mind.

"Are you okay?" he said, rushing up from his chair and coming over to help me regain my balance.

"It's all right," I said. "I'm okay, don't worry." I tried to dry my forehead which had broken into an instantaneous sweat and wiped my palms, which had turned clammy, onto my dress. I managed to flash a smile, feeling silly for overreacting. After all, how could he have known? He probably didn't. This was all just a coincidence. Or maybe not? Maybe we were becoming more in tune with each other that we could pick up on the unsaid that hung in the air around us.

"I'm sorry, that was so tactless and clumsy." He took a tissue and delicately tried to wipe my forehead.

"Thank you," I said and took the tissue from him so I could wipe the smears of black mascara that I could feel under my eyes. "You couldn't possibly have known this would upset me."

"What was so upsetting about what I said? What landmine did I step into?" he asked as he took hold of both my hands.

"Let's leave that conversation for another day," I said. "I want us to enjoy our precious evening together."

After that, I served him some more food while he protested loudly that he was full, but he still managed to finish everything, clearly enjoying it. "I could eat this every day," he said. "This really is my kind of food. I knew there was cuisine that was just right for me, and without realising it, I've been looking for it, all across the world and never quite found what I was looking for, until tonight. As good a French cook that my mum and grandma were, I always felt the real food that would satisfy me was something else. As if my taste buds had a memory of something else."

"Well, there you go. But hey, dude, don't you go expecting me to cook for your everyday." I caressed his hand from across the table. "Let me quickly clear everything away," I said, unable to think, still in a mess.

"Let me give you a hand," he said.

Hmm, a man who helps in the kitchen. This I like very much!

We stood up and started doing the dishes. It may sound silly, but I observed that we were automatically in sync on who did what in terms of clearing the table and pots, washing, drying, and so on, as if we had long fallen into a habit. He struggled a bit finding which pot, pan, and plate had to go in which cupboard, but got most of it instinctively right.

"You've organised your kitchen more or less the way I would do it," he said.

I joked, "Great minds think alike. You know what, let's leave the rest of the cleaning up for now. I'll do it after you've left."

"Are you sure?" he asked. "I don't mind. Feels good to be with you, whatever we do."

"Don't worry about it. Time flies and our evening is short," I said while I took off my gloves and led him out of the kitchen and into the lounge.

We sat down beside each other on the couch. I turned on the digital set-top box and the TV to watch the news, keeping the volume low. We only had eyes for each other as we faced one another and held hands. I looked into the bright blue discs of his eyes.

With his right hand, he gently pushed a strand of my hair to the side and tucked it behind my ear. He leaned over to kiss me so I closed my eyes, waiting for his lips to touch mine. We locked in a kiss that grew more passionate as we went on. He drew me closer to him by my waist and I put my arms around his shoulders. For an instant, we forgot everything around us.

That is, until the instant the television suddenly grew deafeningly loud and the screen started dancing and then flickering wildly, so that I could even see it with my eyes closed. We unlocked from our kiss as I scrambled to find the remote to quieten the screaming television. Right then, at the same moment, the doorbell rang.

"I'm afraid that's my cab," James said in a disappointed tone. "I wish this evening would never end."

"I know, my darling," I said. "There's nothing better than to be together."

"At least I got a kiss from your magical lips," he said with a huge grin. "The universe can never take that away from me."

We held each other in a tight embrace for as long as we could, until another impatient knock at the front door reminded us that he needed to rush to the airport. "I will see you soon, my lovely goddess," he said, as I threw him a last kiss while he walked to the cab. "See you soon, Beauty!"

"It takes courage to
trust the Self,
that part of you
that you can't see."

26

Sorrento

"I absolutely loved your cooking the other day. I can live happily ever after on that sort of food. You must invite me round again soon to sample some more of your culinary delights," James said to me the next evening when we spoke on the phone.

I caught myself wondering if he was being sarcastic, but what would you know? His sweet, tender tone conveyed that he actually meant it.

"I'd like to reciprocate by doing something quite special with you. How about you join me for a weekend away? I'm thinking Sorrento, on the Amalfi Coast in Southern Italy?" He paused for a moment and then, chuckling, said, "Maybe next time I try and kiss you, we can spare the electronics of your television, radio and kettle from going haywire."

"We can certainly try, but the chances are, the sprinkler system will spontaneously burst and drown us both." I enjoyed jesting with him. "Sorrento, huh?"

"Hmm ... Amalfi Coast," he said. "Paris is romantic, but the Italian coast below Naples is to die for."

"Sounds like a plan," I said. "But how did you know I've been looking at going to the Amalfi Coast? I was just about to book a weekend there with a girlfriend."

"Ah. But the travel angels came and whispered it in my ear." He chuckled. "Great. Can't wait."

A couple of Fridays later, we flew from London Heathrow to Naples, where a car would be waiting to take us to a beautiful hotel in the picturesque city of Sorrento. I couldn't wait to get a view of the Bay of Naples, which our hotel overlooked. The hotel's brochure had said that from the hotel's terraces, you could see in the distance the outline of the volcano Vesuvius, and the Roman ruins of the old city of Pompeii.

On the flight to Naples, I gazed goggle-eyed out of the window, bewitched by the glorious views. We soared across a crisp, clear blue sky that was the most perfect backdrop for the stunning sun to show off the jaw-dropping masterpiece of the Alps below. Carved out by giant, ancient, icy glaciers, its breathtaking valleys were the playground for rivers gushing forth from different directions to meet and merge. For miles and miles around, snow-capped mountains, bleached brilliant by the blinding afternoon sun, boasted pinpoint peaks and razor-sharp precipices. Now and then, patchwork villages surrounded by crystal clear blue lakes and framed by Alpine forests came into view, punctuating the pristine beauty of these frozen sierras.

As I sat next to this wonderful man, with whom I lost the sense of my self, my thoughts wandered away. I realised that we had been in preparation all our lives, and perhaps for several lifetimes, for meeting each other and for the relationship that we were now embarking upon. Some years ago, I would not have been able to recognise James even if he had bumped right into me with a big bunch of red roses and my favourite Belgian chocolates.

With so much noise from my past experiences and drama filling my head, so many preconceived notions about how 'he' should look, where he should come from, what his circumstances in life should be, what my family might think about him and so on and so on, I would not have been able to see him. Thank God that this was now not so. I had my Inner Diamond to thank for this transformation, for it had woken me up, little by little, to the limitations of my ego. It had taught me the humility that was required to become capable of recognising the essence, usually hidden deep within, of a person.

Now that we had recognised each other as being the one that our souls had long been seeking, without being consciously aware of it, and now that we were 'together', things moved at an alarmingly swift pace. My days began with James sending me beautiful texts that opened my heart a little more to him. Though we didn't see each other every day or even every week in the beginning, we stayed in touch with short, sweet texts and long phone calls. The physical distance and separation, rather than impair our relationship, drew us closer together, fuelling an intense yearning to know the other ever deeper.

Like two individually complete pieces of a whole that had somehow found their way to each other again, we were becoming finely attuned to each other. Even when apart, we remained intimately connected. Just when I was thinking about calling him, for example, or would pick up the phone to ring his number, the phone would ring and it would be him calling. Or we would start talking about exactly the same thing at the same time. Or, just when I was feeling down or anguished or in pain about something, he would call me right at that moment and describe to me the very thing that I had been feeling. Even when in different countries, it felt as though we were close together, almost feeling each other's touch.

All my life I'd carried a niggling sense of not quite 'fitting in' anywhere, and now I was amazed at the effortless affinity, intimacy and companionship that we shared. Underpinning the relationship was an openness, spaciousness, and freedom just to 'be', with nothing to prove. Within just a few short weeks of being together, I already felt utterly at home, in a way I had never felt with another person, not even with my parents. Like two peas in a pod, it became clear that we belonged together. Yet, if you were to ask me what it was about James that I found mesmerising, I could not tell you. There wasn't any one thing in particular and, then again, it was everything. We had an unfolding admiration of each other and yet, I couldn't explain why we gravitated towards each other the way we did.

For the first time in my life, even during the silent moments of being together, or when we were apart, I felt fully heard and 'gotten'. Like rubbing two dry branches of wood together, communicating with each other sparked an exchange that was energising and enlivening. It went beyond just spoken words, nourishing each other's deeper being. In the mutuality of understanding, our energies were beginning to be well-blended, just like that moment of an emerging dawn, when the night moon holds hands in harmony with the rising sun. In this ease of rapport, we could listen to each other's perspectives with genuine interest, and no forcing of viewpoints. Being heard and received in this way, experiencing such a quality was nothing short of a gift of healing.

Our vision for life was similar and we shared a sense of purpose. When differences did arise, this helped us to resolve things without falling out with each other. Though we were very much individuals with unique personalities and had our own separate contributions to make, our destinies, having now collided, were converging. The paradox was that though we were getting closer and closer, rather than losing our distinctiveness, basking in the recognition of the other, we were now able to be more of our individual selves. With him, I could be more of myself, not having to hide anything. I could continue to expand and grow into being more of who I was and far from making him insecure, he revelled in this. For me, this was something so special that it felt sacred.

On the flight, we held hands, happy as teenagers in love for the first time. "I'm not a big shopper, but I'm looking forward to spending Saturday strolling around the little Italian boutiques. I'd love to get a feel of the atmosphere in those quaint little streets and alleys of Sorrento," I said.

"Sure, and maybe we can take a walk along the Bay of Naples." He nodded. "Luckily, the weather promises to be superb, not too hot for June, with clear blue skies and definitely no rain."

That evening we sat down for dinner in the restaurant of our hotel which overlooked the curvaceous bay and had a magnificent view of the coastline. This promised to be a memorable evening, what with the hotel's restaurant boasting a celebrated Italian chef and a dining room that was ambient with candlelight and soft lighting. The flames of the candles danced with the gentle warm draft coming from the open terrace door, projecting soft flickering shadows on the walls, undulating to the tune of the South Italian music that played softly in the background. The dining room was otherwise quiet, only half-full, a couple at each table, men smartly dressed, Italian style, the ladies in the latest Roman and Milanese elegance, holding hands and whispering intimately to each other.

The waiters moved around almost invisible, discreet but efficient. One came to our table and introduced himself. "*Benvenuti* in our restaurant. My name is Massimo and I will take care of you tonight." He poured olive oil on our side plates and placed a bowl of small black olives on the table, along with three types of *tapenades*.

"Extra virgin oil from our own olive yard, mixed with juice of our home-grown lemons. The olives come from the same orchard as the oil and have been left to ripen before being marinated in our cellars during the winter. The crushed salt and pepper and the sun-dried tomatoes are all local produce." His pride for the heritage and tradition of this fancy estate for which he worked was obvious.

"I have heard from the Maestro, our *maître d'hôte*, that you are vegetarian," he said, handing us each a menu. "You will see, Signore and Signora, that our menu is full of excellent South Italian dishes that are so succulent they do not need any fish or meat. But, if there is nothing to your liking, please let me know and the chef will make it his pleasure to cook whatever you want. *Uno aperitivo*, perhaps?"

"Two glasses of Champagne, please," James said, "or rather, your best Prosecco."

"Very well, Signore." Massimo bowed and moved away, walking ceremoniously backwards then turning and clicking his heels as he headed for the kitchen.

James and I looked at each other and could not help giggling just a little at the sweet, pompous pride of our waiter, and instinctively reached out across the table until our hands touched. "You look stunning," he said. "More beautiful than I've ever seen you. And I love that perfume of yours. What is it?"

"I am not wearing any." I smiled to myself, thinking of all those times when I would have gotten nauseous from the aftershave or scent of guys with whom I had gone on dates.

"Oh? But how can that be? That scent is so strong," he said. "And I smell it around you all the time."

"No, I assure you. I stopped wearing perfume some time ago. An allergy, so to speak," I said, looking for a diplomatic explanation to avoid talking about my nausea to certain scents, especially those worn by men not meant for me.

"Are you sure you're not pulling my leg?" he asked. "Even your house is permeated by that fragrant scent, it is almost overwhelming when I come in."

I chortled. "Are you trying to tell me that I have a hygiene problem?"

"No, no, quite to the contrary." He laughed. "If it's true that you really don't wear perfume, it must be that your skin naturally gives a sweet scent. You seem to be oozing the stuff. I always smell it around you and it's a blend of violets, jasmine, roses, lilac, bluebells, and a hint of sweet mango and honey."

"Wow! You can pick up all that? You must have been a sniffer dog in your previous incarnation!" I gave an embarrassed, abashed smile, regressing to feeling once again like a seventeen-year-old on her first grown-up date, who hadn't quite learned how to receive a genuine compliment. With this very special man, it seemed that I was losing all sense of who I was. Like a snake shedding its skin, the identity I knew myself to be was slithering off in the trust and ease of being with someone who knew me more than I knew myself.

Before I could say anything, Massimo came back with two tall flutes of Prosecco.

James raised his glass and looked into my eyes. "To a beautiful goddess!"

I smiled, melting. After all, what woman did not love to be acknowledged? I raised my glass to click with his, only to be instantly distracted by something twinkling and flashing at the bottom of my flute as it caught the candlelight. I looked into the flute from the side, and then peered into it from the top and saw that, sure as the sun was bright outside, there was indeed something at the bottom of my glass.

"But wait!" I exclaimed. "There's something in my glass! And we cannot drink bubbles without looking each other deep in the eyes, you know what the consequences are otherwise."

James chuckled. "I know, seven years of bad sex."

"Exactly." I tried to put my fingers into the tall, narrow flute, to take the sparkling object out. It was too deep for my fingers to reach the bottom so instead, I took the fork laid out for the appetisers and tried to pierce the sparkling thing out from the bottom.

It was a ring! A beautiful diamond ring. I guessed it was set in white gold. Could it be an engagement ring?

Small, perfectly cut diamonds encrusted its shank and shoulders. Its crown held up a large, glistening solitaire supported by dainty and elegant prongs. Even I—whose knowledge about technicalities of diamonds could fit on the back of the fork with which I had just rescued this treasure—could see that it had to be of fabulous quality. The stone was translucent, utterly white and seemingly flawless. No sooner did I hold this ring between my fingers, than the candlelight christened it with its beams. Light poured through the delicate jewel, which became like a precious prism, casting its brilliant rainbow radiance in all directions. The central prominent gem that sat atop, crowning the ring, shone unapologetically all around us, as if it were sparkling with indescribable joy, waiting for this very moment for its glory of recognition and belonging.

"Wow. How on earth did this get in here?" I asked, at first perplexed and then dumbfounded. "Is this a mistake? I think this glass must be meant for someone else." I carried on staring with meerkat eyes at the mesmerising exquisiteness of the diamonds. "These diamonds are simply stunning." I stared at this work of art a little longer, caught by the surprise of it all. "But," I said, "is this what I think it is?"

"Well, if it is what I think that you think it is, then yes, in that case, that's what it is," James said with an ironic twinkle in his eyes, enjoying the enigma.

"Surely not?" I asked, even more perplexed, now feeling that my eyes were sparkling, just like the brilliant solitaire. "Is that true? Are you proposing to me?" I made a futile attempt to compose myself, but my voice gave away that I was full of emotion when it broke off at the end of my sentence.

"Yes, my beautiful Smita, darling, will you marry me?" James asked tenderly, as he held my hand and looked deep into my eyes.

"Er, yes, er, NO, NO, er, maybe, I mean, how can you know so soon? How can you be sure?" I spluttered inelegantly. "I mean, I don't know! I don't know what to think! Let me think." I spewed out some more unexpected awkwardness. I was touched by James' charm and I could even see he was being authentic. So when I started to get cold and hot at the same time, feeling flushed all over my body, sensing the air get suddenly sticky, I felt more confused than ever. It was all happening so quickly. "I, I can't breathe," I managed to say. "I'm so sorry!"

With that, I got up and rushed to the door leading to the terrace and ran outside onto the large platform—a classic Roman patio. In those moments, I was oblivious to the erudite Roman male and Venusian statues all over the patio, and the large terracotta flower ornaments.

Once alone on the terrace, I leant on the sea-facing, stone-carved, opulent Renaissance balustrade and caught my breath, wheezing in large gulps of fresh sea air and looked around. I could hear the music wafting out of the restaurant and the faint sounds of clinking cutlery coming through the open doors. The bay drifted calmly into the open sea that was preparing to embrace the dusk sun, a saturated, shimmering orange orb, fast plummeting to dive into the horizon.

Beneath me, below the cliff on which the hotel stood, lights were being lit one after the other in the terraced restaurants and bars of Sorrento. The town brimmed with couples and families, as they finished shopping in the Italian fashion boutiques or went to dinner.

"So this is it," I said to my Inner Diamond. "What do I do now?" It felt as if the Diamond was listening quietly for me to finish my thoughts.

"In these years I've been alone, I've only ever considered being with the right partner, but hardly a thought have I given to *marriage*. In fact, come to think of it, the very idea of marriage makes me feel suffocated. It seems to me that marriage is about everything that I am not. I am about freedom and liberation from all things that constrain. I hadn't expected him to *propose*. I thought we were just getting started on a romance, a long, slow romance to enjoy the incredible affinity we have. Oh, why oh why is he talking about marriage, and why so soon? I just want to run away at the thought of it. Part of me just wants to run as fast as I can and jealously guard the independence I've worked so hard for all these years. Another part of me, though, and this is what's confusing me, wants to marry him on the spot and spend the rest of my life with him."

The terrace soon became dark. I paused in my thoughts as I stared into the plunging dark orange disc, painting the sky with a palette of oranges and reds, willingly submerging itself into the bountiful blue sea in front of me. "I'm so scared, terrified. It feels to me like James is asking me to leap into the deep, vast ocean, the unknown ocean of marriage and it terrifies me. I've got so used to being on my own, to managing very well without a man in my life, thank you very much. What if I don't like it? What if all that permanent closeness ends up feeling more like suffocation? What if it all goes pear-shaped at a later date? And at the same time, a part of me feels the rightness of it. A part of me knows if I can make it work with anyone at all, he's the one, and I'm so thrilled that I could shout with abandonment from these very rooftops. I'm so flippin' confused. Oh, whatever should I do?" In the twilight of dusk, any remaining clarity slipped away from my mind, leaving clouds of turmoil.

"*The confusion you are feeling, is simply your ego being afraid. Or put another way, your personality, how you know yourself to be, is afraid of disappearing,*" the Inner Diamond said. "*Clenching on to your independence, to your notion of freedom, is mere ego speak. True independence is the power not to hang on to the past, but to choose freely to step forward and offer yourself as a confident partner for the relationship. In a genuine partnership, you should be able to blossom, be more of yourself. Don't be afraid to take the step. When it feels right, when there is mutual respect, you will be able to be truly self-sufficient while being part of something bigger. Don't let the anxiety of your ego trick you from seeing what the right choice is.*"

I listened and remembered how smart a rat the ego can be. It could trick you into going down a path of what seemed like perfect logic or emotion so intense that it felt absolutely real. And yet, the ego is all about self-preservation. It rarely allows bold or original thought, let alone positive personal growth.

"For years, you have been working towards creating a new future for yourself, one that is not in the shadow of your past. Trust in your Self. After all, I have never let you down so far, have I? It takes courage to trust the Self, that part of you that you can't see. Fear can never let you make a powerful choice, and especially in this case, fear is inappropriate. Put your personality now in the back seat and let your inner Self take the driver's seat."

Immediately, I regained control of my senses. Of course I was scared and terrified of losing my identity, of how I knew myself to be. Though I hadn't known James for years, I *knew* him. I knew him well, as well as he knew me, and that was better than I knew myself. If ever there was the 'right' partner for me, he was the one. Besides, I was cuckoo over him.

"Remember, when you are whole and complete, at one with the Self, you are nothing if not 'independent' or svatantra. It is not an independence that separates but one that connects and unites. Nothing can disturb that, so long as you remember that you are not your fearful identity, but your complete Self."

These words of my Inner Diamond and its beautiful *bhava*, its authentic loving power, penetrated my heart and mind, melting my resistance but still, clouds of confusion lingered. "But then, why do I need him? Or anyone else? Shouldn't I be able to love life on my own altogether and be fulfilled?" I spoke mentally to my Diamond, panic subsiding but still there. "I've worked so hard to establish and nurture this relationship with you, my higher Self, my Diamond within, and it's so precious to me. That's what gives me courage and *real* independence. Now, I don't want to go and jeopardise that."

"Once connected, you cannot break this bond," the wise Diamond said. *"The relationship with the deeper Self is not born of scarcity. It is prosperous in every way and lives on infinitely. It will always be there. It cannot and shall not disappoint you. Standing on the foundation of this relationship, go and live, truly live, the rest of your life. So choose. Choose freely and joyfully. Choose to build a beautiful life, liberated from the limitations of the stories of your lives that have strangled your potential. Feel your 'Sat Chit Ananda': genuine conscious joy."*

As my higher Self's sterling counsel cleared my muddled mind, my heart suddenly felt full, bursting with its love. Tears welled up behind my eyes. I remembered once again that James was not a coincidence in my life. Somehow, my beautiful Inner Diamond had guided my every step towards him, had me even learn the languages at school that he would speak. With my heart open once more, I felt the power held in the symbol of the ring with which he had proposed, declaring his love for me.

In the next instant, I accepted it all: just how much I had fallen for him, how I could not help loving him, and how abundant he had shown his love to be for me.

Quite honestly, I had never known anything quite like this relationship before.

"Okay," I replied to my higher Self, "Okay, now I feel like a right numpty for having run out like that."

I took a deep breath, swept my hair back with my hand, turned around and walked back inside.

I smiled at James as I went to sit down at the table. Massimo rushed forward and held my chair as he helped me to sit. He gave me a fresh napkin and disappeared again. My hands dampened, and I wiped them on my thighs, as if to straighten out the creases on my cocktail dress, composing myself and taking another deep, calm breath.

I flashed a smile again at James, and he said, "Smita, sweet darling, falling in love with you has been like nothing I've ever known. It feels like we have known each other for so long, like I have ancient memories of you. I wish I could explain the feeling. I have never been able to love anyone the way I love you and never will. It just seems completely obvious to me that I want to be with you for the rest of my life, and beyond. Getting married is the proper thing to do, the only thing to do. It is a symbol, a celebration of our very special love, and at the same time it is—"

"Yes!" I erupted.

"Yes? Yes what?" he said, looking at me quizzically, a proper Belgian, taking what I said literally.

"Marry you, for goodness sake," I answered, a little short but smiling. We both laughed. He took my hands from across the table as we looked into each other's eyes.

"Is it not a bit too quick?" I said, still taken aback and raw from the emotion of it all. "I mean, we haven't known each other that long. How can you be so sure so soon?"

"Sweet angel," James answered. "I just know. And though in linear time we may not have been together for long, it has been very intense and more than that, it feels like I've been waiting for you my whole life, as if you were just round the corner so many times. Being with you, it's like a lock and a key coming together, it just clicks. It feels to me like you've just unlocked a brilliant future for us both. I am sure you feel it, too."

"It's true. I do feel it, but part of me is more cautious. I don't want to lose my independence and certainly don't want to be hurt again. More so, I want to continue to build on what we have both worked on so far. I want us, both of us, to thrive and flourish, not shrink into the oblivion of marriage."

"I want to see you growing from strength to strength. I'll be the one cheering you on from the sidelines, seeing you excel, your proudest fan," James said, melting my heart all over again. "Nothing will give me more pleasure. Now, what kind of a wedding do you want? A big Indian wedding, I hope, the full works, the whole enchilada?"

"Well, I've never thought about the details, except that I'd like our family and friends beside us."

"You can have anything you want, my sweet darling," he said. As we talked some more about making a life together, he removed each and every one of my objections and concerns gracefully, and with a commitment that I had rarely seen in a man. We smiled at each other and at the same time, let go of each other's hands to take our napkin to dry the tears of joy that had welled up in our eyes.

James stood up and said, "Let me put that ring on your finger." He looked across the table, only to discover the ring was nowhere to be found. "Uh, where is it? Have you seen the ring, darling?" I looked around and frantically tried to think of what I had done with it as I had rushed off to the terrace. Panic surged in my belly and my cheeks flushed as I thought of how valuable this ring was. Oh God, don't let me have lost this beautiful diamond ring. Definitely not on the night of his proposal, even before I have ever worn it. Then I realised that I must have left it somewhere on the terrace.

"Wait here," I said. "Don't go anywhere."

In a whirlwind, I got up to rush off to the terrace again. Meanwhile, thinking we had finished our romantic tête-à-tête and that he could finally safely approach us, Massimo had discreetly crept up behind me with two huge plates in his hands with our appetisers, compliments of the chef. Frantically trying not to collide into me, he leapt backward, juggling the plates in his hands so as not to drop them, trying to avoid the food sliding off the plates. I ran onto the terrace as fast as my tight dress allowed, trying to stay elegant and composed. Luckily, the terrace was still empty, apart from one couple enjoying the view at the other end.

I looked around in the dim light of the outdoor darkness and tried to remember where I had stood before. Then I saw something glisten on the balustrade. Lit by the moonlight, the diamond called me. "Over here! Come and get me," it seemed to say. I let out a massive sigh of relief, rushed to the balustrade, and grabbed the ring. *I am not letting you go, ever again.* I planted a little kiss on it.

Relieved, I dashed back inside, gave James the ring, and sat down. Once again, Massimo, in his infinite patience, was there to help seat me.

"We'll order in a minute," James said. "But first, there is something I must do."

Massimo bowed and walked away.

James stood up again and came to my side of the table. He kneeled, took my hand, looked into my eyes and said, "I love you so much, my goddess. Let's create a beautiful life together." Then, he slid the ring gently onto my third finger. How he had known what size the ring had to be, I still don't know, but it fitted me perfectly. I looked at the ring on my finger from all sides and beamed.

"I love you, too, darling. I feel so blessed." I wanted to say his name but, somehow, found myself from then on addressing him only in one form of endearment or another.

27

Rapture

After dinner, we walked back onto the terrace where I had stood alone two hours earlier, talking to my Diamond, wondering whether to say yes. Now, as we walked to the balustrade, hand in hand, that first moment I had run out to the terrace already seemed like an eternity away. I experienced a sense of freedom and elation for having moved through the sticky resistance that my ego had thrown up. To have made a clear, empowered choice to accept James' invitation to make a life with him felt right and even obvious. How could I have needed time to think about it? At the same time, I realised that my relationship to the Diamond within had become such that I did nothing important now without ensuring that I was aligned with its 'knowing', or without its grace and blessings. Being 'strong' or 'independent' had brought me this far, but I had now learnt that it was being 'Self-sufficient' that brought me into the flow of synchronicity, harmony, and peace.

We looked out over the Bay of Naples, and over the night-time hubbub of the charming town of Sorrento, its small streets now in full swing, frantically driven little cars and buzzing Vespa scooters whizzing around its narrow alleys and roads. Terraces fast filled up with Italian families, chatting away animatedly, laughing. Singing from the locals floated onto our hotel terrace, all beautifully blending to give a typical Southern Italian soundscape. In the distance, on the other side of the bay, flickering lights brought into focus another city, Naples, just as active late into the night. The sun that I had seen setting while pondering over James' life-altering question had long gone to sleep over the horizon, giving way to a moon, now boasting its full glory. Its silver rays reflected resplendent onto thousands of tiny waves and ripples on the Mediterranean Sea. Against a few white clouds highlighted by the moon, we could make out the dark contours of Mount Vesuvius, standing solid, majestic, and unperturbed by centuries past, a sleeping giant concealing its smouldering fire.

I smiled as it brought memories of that other volcano flooding back—Mount Kilauea on the Big Island of Hawaii, where Archangel Michael had shown himself to me and where I had received exquisite epiphanies and breakthroughs. What a distance I had come. Never had I been more ready for the commitment of a deep relationship as now. Never had I felt more eager to take on the world. Thank you, Angel Michael, thank you, Goddesses for your gracious hand in guiding me to this place, to be with this amazing man.

James stood behind me and wrapped me in his arms as we gazed at the silver glistening sea beneath. I felt nurtured, cherished and excited, all at once. On this terrace, high on the side of the hill above this Italian town, I felt at home in his arms. Wherever I was, with this man, I was in heaven. My partner, my husband, had come home to me. This was it. There was nowhere else to go. Nowhere else to be. It felt as if we had, somehow, always belonged together, had been together. Long-lost lovers who had parted because of circumstances unknown, centuries ago. Soul companions that had been thrown in different directions, pushed further and further apart over hundreds of years, over many lifetimes, scattered across the earth, connected only by an invisible fine golden thread of our souls' shared memory, until eventually, purely by intuition and divine guidance, we had sought each other out again. Now, the time was right and that time was now. Faint, distant memories of what it had felt like to be together in times past arose in my awareness, explaining why it felt so reminiscent and familiar to be in his arms. It felt strangely proper and right, the way it had always been. Had there been such a lifetime long ago when we were indeed together? It surely seemed that way.

"You know, Smita," James whispered in my ear. "A few days ago, I had this vivid dream. It felt so real and I saw it in full Technicolor, in HD, so to speak."

"Tell me. What was it?" I asked, enjoying just listening to the sound of his voice on this warm, balmy evening.

"I was walking through some temple complex, in some city in the middle of India. It wasn't in our time but many, many centuries ago. I was a visitor there, travelling from far away, from what we now know to be Europe. My party and I were guests of the local *maharaja* of a tiger and diamond region."

"Huh huh ..." I said, listening intently.

"The walls of all these temples were packed with row upon row of extraordinary stone carvings and statues. Statues of men, and especially of women, most of them were beautiful goddesses in all kinds of dance or yoga postures. I was surprised to see that some of the scenes depicted were surprisingly explicit," he said.

"Mmm, sounds like the ancient city of Khajuraho," I said. "Built around 1000AD, by the Chandella Dynasty. It was a masterpiece of Indian culture of the day, heaving with art."

"Well, so was this place. As I was walking alone, along a quieter side of one of the main temples, I felt a gaze boring into the back of my head. You know, like when you feel someone is watching you. I turned and looked around, not just once but several times, but there was no one there. Then, I noticed this beautiful, very life-like statue of what must have been a goddess, dressed in opulent finery. Well, that is, she wasn't wearing many clothes but was garmented instead in lots of jewellery, draped around her ankles, wrists, neck, waist, belly, ears, hair, and so on."

I teased him. "Huh, you do have an eye for the ladies, don't you?"

Half-ignoring my comment, he continued, "I swear that, as I walked on by, her eyes were following me, even though she was only made of stone. Somehow, and don't ask me why, I sensed this in my dream, it felt as if she were alive, as if in one quick instant, she had been captured and frozen in stone, so life-like was the statue. I turned back to take a closer look at her and it seemed as if she was ignoring me, a bit like a girl would do if she does not want to show that she's interested in you."

I teased him again. "You seem to know everything about girl psychology."

"Probably not at all, but then, still in my dream, I realised that she looked exactly like you," he continued. "Only in those days, I hadn't met you yet, but I was somehow aware of your existence, maybe I'd dreamt of you and forgotten the dream, I can't be sure. But I remember thinking in the dream that, somehow, I recognised the goddess in the statue."

"Ahh, so you've been trying to meet me in your dreams, you naughty boy!"

"Anyway ..." He kissed the top of my head. "That evening, after the obligatory ceremonies and dinner, I asked the *maharaj*, the high priest, about this peculiar statue. He told me that the woman in the statue had once been a high priestess. She had been so beautiful and sensual, even more so than the Goddess of Love, to whom the temple was dedicated. This Goddess of Love, on hearing countless men praising the beauty of her high priestess, became so enraged with bitter jealousy that she cursed her, by freezing the stunning high priestess into a cold, stone statue."

"Aw, what a beautiful dream," I remarked, feeling the plight of the poor priestess. "And how utterly tragic."

"'How can the spell be broken?' I asked the high priest after dinner that night," James continued. "'Legend has it,' the priest replied, that on a full moon night like tonight, at the precise moment when the moon shines fully on the statue, and this can only happen a few days in a year, a chosen stranger can help thaw the frozen high priestess.' So, that night I waited for the moon to rise high enough, and then went back on my own to the dark temple complex. By now, it was empty except for a few guards at the gates and a few priestesses that kept tending the sacred *homa* fires of the shrines. I found the statue again, *your* statue, there in the dark, standing stock still. I lit it with the flame from my torch as I waited for the moon to move through the midnight blue sky, until it was able to light up your statue. It could only do so if it was shining straight through the top windows of the tall temple, to the south of where your statue stood." He stopped to look up at the sky above Sorrento where the silvery full moon glistened, embedded amongst a star-studded canopy.

"What happened next?" I asked, absorbed.

"When the moon's beams finally illumined the statue of the stunning high priestess, I dropped my torch and rushed forward, towards the carving. Not sure what to do, I stood still in front of you, freeze-framed, and looked at you. It seemed as if your dark, beautiful eyes, though carved in stone, were staring right back at me. Instinctively, I touched your waist and then moved my hands upward, along your sides, gently brushing past your breasts, passing by your cheeks and caressing your hair." While he talked, the hairs on my arms stood erect on goose pimples.

"Holding your face, I then kissed your lips," he said, and I no longer felt sure which was the dream and which the reality. "I felt a bit silly doing all this but, instinctively, I knew it was time. It was the right thing to do. A flash of a second later, I was actually kissing the real you, the high priestess, dressed like the statue, but now you were flesh and blood once more. Sure as the legend had it, the statue, *your* statue, had come alive, just as the high priest had said. You took me by the hand, whispered a grateful 'thank you' in my ear, and before I could realise what was going on, you ran nimbly away, round the corner of the temple. I ran behind you, shouting for you to wait, but you were gone." He paused, gathering himself from this captivating reverie. "What a dream. I can still feel it all as if it happened in real life."

"That's *so* beautiful. So sweet," I said. "It feels like it really did happen, when you explain it like that."

Moved by his sensitive nature, I let myself relax a little more. I became more receptive to his gentle touch as he pressed his face into my hair, stroking my cheek with the back of his fingers and planting soft kisses on the back of my head. My heart blossomed with pleasure and joy with his every touch. Closing my eyes, I cherished these delicious moments with him. I'm not sure how long we stood this way—it could have been forever. Then, lowering his face to mine, he gently kissed me on the neck and behind my left ear, sending my spine tingling. As his lips ever so slightly touched the lobe of my ear, I got shivers and goosebumps all over, aglow within the bounds of my skin.

Still wrapped in his arms, I turned around and let out a soft sigh as our faces touched. His lips sought mine and, for the first time in weeks, they touched without sending the external electricity haywire. Not that this time we would have noticed anyway, as it felt like together we were blissfully alone in the world. We held each other, locked in the sweetest embrace as we kissed, finally able to express our passion for each other without having to hold back, without disturbances. Though the electricity on the outside may have remained intact, it was a different story where we each were concerned, as tiny electrical currents rapturously raced up and down our bodies ignited by the other's passionate touch.

As our lips slowly parted, I lowered my face, brushing it ever so lightly against his cheek, chin, and neck, caressing his skin. Then I laid my head to rest on his chest. His heart, as if it were leaping up and down to kiss my ear, beat in tandem with my own, pulsing in unison. Had, somehow, the declaration we had just made to the universe of our eternal commitment to each other brought harmony and peace to our electromagnetic fields, and therefore to our surroundings? Had our energies harmonised? Were they flowing, at last, in tune with the other's? Or, dare I say, were we in tune 'once again', resynchronised after what seemed like aeons? No need for exploding light bulbs, no electrical calamities, was this just pure synchronisation of *shakti* energy?

I put these questions aside, and sank some more onto his chest, attuning to the pulsation of his body, receiving the vibes of love surging up from him. No longer able to hold back the irresistible passion for him that now cascaded in waves within me, I finally surrendered and reciprocated to his charm and strength. Again, we embraced passionately, our lips brushing against the other's. Locked in a deep kiss, our heads whirling like spinning tops, we were oblivious to everything around us.

S ome time later, we lay on the bed, naked, his body on top of mine, his warm hands caressing my torso and breasts, gliding his fingers slowly up and down the side of my waist, just as he had done in his dream. With every touch of his hands arousing my flesh, my nipples sprang up alert, as if they were going to pop out and walk away. With the heat of love coursing through my body, pleasure pulsated through me to the point that, tonight, I felt I might just explode with delight. An involuntary surge of emotion flooded through me—a cautious wariness, anxiety, anticipation, excitement, curiosity, and just sheer sexual passion. In the moment of becoming aware of this melee of feelings, I made a conscious choice to let them go and trusted myself. It was time, I realised, to let go of my remaining defences and at long last, give myself, heart and soul, to this man. Or rather to our love, to this very special coming together which seemed to have manifested a persona of its own.

Only when I had a moment to think, did I realise that we were upstairs in our room and not on the terrace. Quite how we got there, or even when, I still cannot remember. My cheeks reddened, hoping that we had not made a spectacle of ourselves while making our way upstairs.

As James' face came close to mine again, moving up from kissing me on my shoulder and neck, I caressed his head and whispered with a small chuckle, "I don't remember how we got back to the room, I hope we didn't make idiots of ourselves."

"Not sure myself," he said. "But I am sure that in Italy, in a place such as this, dating back to the rampant Roman days, a bit of romance won't rock anyone's apple cart."

We kissed again and I noticed what a novel sensation of liberation it was to let myself, at long last, dive in and surrender in complete trust and openness to the man I had so deeply fallen for. His body covered mine from top to toe, his warm glow making me tremor inside, sparking a sensation of tiny little butterflies flying up and down, palpating my spine into a rod of light. Ancient memories surged forth a familiarity of being this close, our bodies intimately entwined, fitting perfectly together. The rhythm of our movements wasted no time in synchronising effortlessly, as if it were the most natural thing in the world. No clumsiness of a first love night. It was rather like two lovers picking up where we had once left off, just days ago. His hands caressed the contours of my body in the dark, as if he knew exactly where to go—where every shape, every curve, every little hill and valley of my body were. As if he already knew perfectly how and where to stroke me, please me, and excite me more and more.

As the slow and seductive, fiery tender strokes and caresses brought our wanderings into a flow of lucidity, neither of us were sure where my skin ended and his began. The physical boundaries between us seemed to dissolve and disappear. So in tune with him, so close were we, I could vividly sense his subtler presence, his essential energy, and I was able to touch it with my own. It then seemed that I could hold that subtle essence of us both in my being and blend it together until we harmonised, vibrant, as one. Two complementary souls, two complete beings, somehow pulled as under aeons ago by some great wave in the universe, now rediscovered in the infinite circle of time, fitting together perfectly, remembering their original, greater wholeness.

Was this even lovemaking? It was much more a merging of two beings, minds and hearts, of energies, my softness and his ruggedness melting into union. As intense as our physical embrace felt, simultaneously, we also seemed to be meeting in love on some other plane, floating in the hum of a deep, blue, boundless void, acutely aware of our pulsing, throbbing bodies below.

At the same time, the energetic or ethereal aspect of us was very clear, and I wondered if this is what the Satguru Sivaya Subramuniyaswami of the Kauai Temple called *anandamayakosha* (body of light). I had never felt anything like this. The giant *rishi* Sri

Aurobindo, my father's *guru*, said that this was the inner or true divine Self. For me, *anandamaya kosha* felt like the Self expressing itself, through the human body, with unadulterated delight, and so I liked to think of it as our body of delight. Somehow, the intensity of this lovemaking did not feel like sex at all. It was something much more. Beautiful, natural language beyond words that, through the medium of our bodies, recognised and united our two souls into an intimate and sacred dance.

Completely losing my control, light, sound, taste, and form dissolved into a tingling apex of sensuousness, exploding throughout my body into an exquisite, sensory feast of fireworks at the festival of *Diwali*. The tips of my toes, my fingers, teeth, all of them prickling with the sweet pain triggered by a rapid succession of countless needles nicking my every cell with intense pleasure and joy. Every tiny hair on my body, every long, dark hair on my head seemed to have a will of its own, arousing with goosebumps and tremors. At the same time, it felt like our intertwined souls, cocooned in their own ecstatic embrace, exploded together like a thousand luminous stars in the night sky. I heard him finally let go with an exhilarated sigh, gleefully tortured by similar sensations.

Exhausted, we fell back on the bed, steaming hot, wet perspiration soaking our heads and hair. We were completely overtaken by the ferocious exquisiteness of what we had just experienced, our hearts still racing a thousand beats per minute, our breaths heavy and deep with the fulfilment of pure pleasure. The echo of the powerful climaxes continued to ripple on and on through our bodies, leaving us hardly any time to recover. We lay on the bed, still in each other's arms, totally absorbed in a shared euphoric rapture like never before. Words became unnecessary, having just experienced, through the vehicle of our physical and ethereal bodies, a profound coming together of our subtle being. Wrapped contentedly in his arms, I rested my head on his chest and dived into a deep sleep of delight.

"You are a precious drop in a
vast ocean of consciousness,
and of 'Shakti' energy.

Don't be afraid to
explore that ocean.
That's where the deep happiness
you are feeling today
comes from.

Keep opening your heart.
It is your connection to that
ocean."

28

Blissful Beginnings

The next morning, I awoke to the bright light piercing through the open slit between the curtains. The sun sprayed its rays, as if refracting through a sparkling diamond hung mid-air. I felt the comfortable, warm touch of his arms around me. Still asleep, he purred with his gentle snore like a contented lion.

Slowly, I slid away with my right arm, carefully removing it from under his so as not to wake him. I lifted my hand to shield my face from the bright sunlight. But then I adjusted my hand, lifting my ring finger until the sunlight pouring between the curtains shone its rays straight onto the finest point of the diamond at the very top of my ring. The rays of sun met with the crystalline jewel and the beams shot off into hundreds of tiny laser-sharp rainbows that projected all around, and onto the white walls of the room. I turned the ring slowly. As I moved, so did the spectrums of light projected on the walls. I couldn't help beaming with sheer pleasure at seeing these dancing rainbows of light. In awe, I realised that they all emanated from one teeny, tiny point of a single, delicate diamond that sat on my finger.

"How far have I come, my precious Diamond?" I wondered, thinking again of my higher Self. "I remember that ominous night in the park, when I was down and out, redundant, about to lose my house, utterly alone and abandoned with nowhere to go. Then too, a ray of sunlight woke me on that bench. You, my sweet Inner Diamond, were there as always, in my hardest of times to guide me along. Thank you. Thank you so much for always being there, for being my inspiration, my guide, my absolute everything. I am so grateful that I had the good fortune to carry on and follow your advice. Here I am now, here WE are now, you, my Inner Diamond, and me and my newly found, or rediscovered, soul partner. Where do we go from here?"

I listened intently in the still quietness, the only sound his soft snoring, to see if I would hear a response. A minute or two seemed to pass as I concentrated, attempting to hear the familiar whisper impressing its words through my intuition. Then a lucid stream of awareness came flooding in.

My Dear Smita

After so much hard work, sacrifice and perseverance, you have now reached a stage where you caught a glimpse of how the natural state of your soul looks and feels, 'sukh', 'santosh' and 'anand': intrinsic happiness, contentment and joy.

You may have discovered a lot about yourself already, but know that this is only the beginning. You are a precious drop in a vast ocean of consciousness, and of 'Shakti' energy. Don't be afraid to explore that ocean. That's where the deep happiness you are feeling today comes from. Keep opening your heart. It is your connection to that ocean.

And so, where do we go from here? Share your experience with others and serve. After all, what else could be greater to do in this universe? Help others to connect with their inner Self. Help them with the best of your talents and abilities. Do good for good. 'Nishkama karma' and 'seva', selfless service will be your next stage of fulfilment. And while you should not expect anything in return, know that everything you give, you will receive manifold.

Create clear intentions for what's important to you in your life. Make sure that they are intentions that elevate your aliveness and vibrancy. Follow them up with concrete actions so that they become reality. Intentions without right action are like branches of a bare tree that bear no fruit.

The secret is to co-create your intentions together with your higher Self. When you do this, you will be in full alignment with your inner being and in the flow that makes life effortless, that increases the 'rasa' of life, that sweet juiciness which makes you feel that life is worth living. Make every minute count. Enjoy but remain purposeful.

At the same time, never forget to keep working on yourself. Know that bitterness makes you unhealthy and ages you. To stay young, keep letting go of resentments. Watch out for unpleasant or nasty thoughts creeping up every day through the little things in life. Accept the whole of what you are. Acceptance means making peace with the way things are and the way they are not, without negating or trying to change them. Once you are at peace with the way things are, then you can make the choice to let go of those thoughts, beliefs, behaviours and decisions that do not serve you to be your gorgeous Self and that prevent you from being there for others.

Above all, let go of your addiction to drama and struggle. Live liberated from the stories of your life.

Live life to the fullest. Enjoy the fruits of your 'karma' but avoid becoming a slave to superficial enjoyment or to anything else that traps you in wanting endlessly more. While your desires can often lead you to enjoyment, worldly desires are often mere 'maya', illusions that cloud your judgement and lead you astray from what is authentic within.

All of this, you will see, is what will give you 'jivanmukti', your 'moksha now' as it were, fulfilment in your own lifetime, finally free of sticky, crazy 'karma'.

As you become more light and liberated within yourself, you'll naturally radiate the beauty and brilliance that is your Inner Diamond.

Be free and fulfilled, my angel.

"As you become more light
and liberated within yourself,
you'll naturally radiate
the beauty and brilliance that is
your Inner Diamond."

About the Author

Born in the port town of Porbandar in Gujarat, India, my parents and I moved to London when I was ten. I studied in England, undertaking English, French and Politics at college. In a career spanning 25 years, I took on increasingly challenging responsibilities in the corporate world. One of my main roles was selling multimillion-dollar contracts into well-known global companies. Through the business I was in, I'm proud to have been one of the pioneers bringing India's Information Technology services into the heart of British and European companies.

Alongside my corporate career, I became a life coach and led personal transformation programmes to groups of hundreds at a time. As a freelance TV presenter, I interview *gurus*, entrepreneurs and politicians. A devoted practitioner, I'm also a certified *yoga* instructor.

I'm married and live in London.

Behind the Author

My birth town of Porbandar, a buzzing port along North West India's Arabian Sea coastline, is better known as the home of Mahatma Gandhi. I was brought up in a traditional Indian home with values rooted in ancient Vedic culture. We lived for most of my childhood close by the sea and some of my years were spent in a beautiful sea-facing house of my grandad's, a well-respected lawyer. As with many children in India, I was fortunate to have the influence of a grandmother who imbued in me the values of the age-old culture into which I was born. She encouraged me to read daily the *Bhagavad Gita* in Gujarati and to recite various Sanskrit *mantras* before I'd turned seven. This gave me a solid foundation on which to later build as I strived to heal the traumas of my past, and bring balance to a hectic life while working as a business executive with large global companies.

I loved my life in London and its flourishing entrepreneurial culture. Like a duck to water, I thrived on working internationally in hardcore business environments, selling leading-edge technology contracts to multi-national corporations. I am proud to have been one of the pioneers to convince large Western companies to start working with the Indian IT industry, which was growing in those days from its infancy into one of the largest parts of the Indian economy.

But at the same time, while working in the cut-throat world of business, I was fascinated by who we are deeper within. It was not long before I felt compelled to balance my professional corporate existence with, at the same time, finding a way to nourish my soul.

I yearned to experience more of the soulful, radiant inner being that I had seen glimpses of at various times in my life. During my holidays and sabbaticals, I travelled across India with *yogis* and *gurus* to see what more I could discover about the Self within. I pored over the *Vedas, Bhagavad Gita*, Shiva Sutras, the Puranas and Upanishads, soaking up whatever I could and went about applying some of these teachings to improve my quality of life, including in my work. Later in my quest, I travelled to many other places, including New Mexico, Hawaii and Kauai to seek out special people, places and answers to unresolved questions that throttled the possibility that life offered.

As my self-awareness grew, so did my desire to serve others. Alongside of my business life, when not travelling for work or meeting deadlines, I dedicated my weekends, holidays and any spare time over a number of years to become a life coach. I first followed a few years of hard training on how to help others in a responsible way to uncover their deepest issues and transform themselves. Then, I was allowed to go and assist in such programmes. It was not long before I had the privilege of leading these cutting-edge series of workshops myself, coaching large groups of 100 - 300 people at a time on how to deal more powerfully with the challenges of modern life and realise their goals and aspirations.

Yoga - the context for my life

As a child, I grew up watching my father regularly stand on his head for what seemed to me like hours. He was doing the Shirsasana *yoga* posture. Guided by his *guru*, the brilliant Sri Aurobindo, my father was an avid *yogi* who meditated regularly. Though Dad never taught me directly, simply watching him stand stock-still on his head and sit statuesque in deep, meditative immersions, captivated my imagination as a little girl. Around the age of twelve, I too started to attempt performing *yoga* postures. A few years later, I also began to meditate, purely guided by my intuitive inklings. On and off, I did *yoga* for twenty years but it was only when I stumbled into my first Vinyasa Flow training course did my *yoga* practise begin in earnest. This was with the extraordinary, internationally renowned *yoga* teacher, Shiva Rea. Her profound knowledge and approach to integrating the different aspects of *yoga* touched me deeply and inspired by Shiva, I took up training with her to be able to teach.

Other accomplished *yoga* masters of the Krishnamacharya lineage with whom I have studied include David Swenson, Richard Freeman, Ana Forrest, Anna Ashby, Hamish Hendry and Stewart Gilchrist. As well as Shiva Rea's Prana Flow Yoga, I also practise Mysore Style Ashtanga and other forms of dynamic yoga. I teach regularly and am committed to my daily practice.

Diving Deep

People and cultures fascinate me and I love exploring different parts of the world. My love of travel has taken me to swim with wild dolphins, exploring volcanoes, and visit temples, shrines and mystical places across the world.

I've studied several Indian and Buddhist spiritual systems and continue to delve into their richness to discover new facets of who we are. Unveiling the mysteries of the mind, spirit and what it means to be human excites me.

A keen diver, scuba diving satisfies my yearning for adventure and immersing into the unknown. The ocean can, at once, contain dangerous shipwrecks and beautiful reefs, treacherous sharks and playful dolphins.

For me, scuba diving offers a beautiful metaphor for diving into the deep ocean of the inner Self that can nourish the soul but also hold paradoxes, just like the many facets of our own beautiful being.

My years and years of soul searching have resulted in this, my first trilogy, *Karma & Diamonds*.

Karma & Diamonds

Book 1 - Moon Child

"One woman's journey from early trauma as a child in India to discovering the incredible power that lies inside us all."

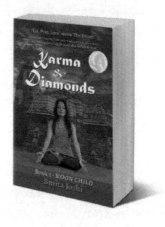

The young Smita lives with her family in Porbandar, Gandhi's coastal town in North West India. At the age of seven, a sudden shocking upheaval alters her view of life forever. This is just one of many traumatic events in her childhood. During these moments of crisis, she discovers a deep, mystical connection with the higher realms through her inner Self, which she calls her 'Inner Diamond'. She finds she has a natural ability to tap into the ancient wisdom of the Indian *gurus* purely by intuition.

When she is ten, her family moves to the UK. There, she grows into an enthusiastic adolescent but is quickly confronted with the challenge of trying to balance two very different cultures of modern-day London and a traditional Indian culture that has very specific plans for her. She struggles to find her place in the world, both physically and spiritually. Things culminate into a major crisis and she finds herself isolated.

Later, after college, there's the premature prospect of being married off quickly to a nice young man in India. She realises that this is not her destiny. She needs all her courage to try and make life work as an independent young woman. She learns the hard way and makes mistakes along the way during the start of her career, but eventually she pulls through and builds a life for herself, even managing to buy a flat at a young age.

She wonders why her life is such a constant struggle with no real prospect for inner peace and love, as she keeps on battling old traumas that have a tight grip on her, and that block her from getting close to others. The Inner Diamond shows her that she can only be free, fulfilled, and experience true love, if she can let go of the *karma* of past lives, of which she has seen glimpses through her young life. This inner wisdom tells her to leave everything behind and go on a quest to India. Trusting her inner Self because it has guided her well so far, she quits her job, rents out her flat, and leaves for India with no clue of where to go or what to do.

Karma & Diamonds

Book 2 - Web of Karma

"Will dramatic revelations about lives long past finally free her to be happy?"

Smita embarks impulsively on her India trip, purely guided by her intuition. Starting with a visit to distant Indian family, she soon finds herself on a trip to the foothills of the Himalayas with doctors, one of whom is also a well-respected spiritual *guru*. By day, they serve the under-privileged by giving them free eye operations and at night, stay in *ashrams*, where the *guru* gives daily teachings.

It is then that she discovers that what she calls her 'Inner Diamond', is curiously connected to the core teachings of ancient India, as if she had already received this age-old knowledge through other means. She walks the fire and participates in sacred ceremonies.

Back in London, she hopes she is now ready to accelerate her business career and enter into a serious romantic relationship. But then, her Diamond starts revealing to her all kinds of mysterious clues once again. She has a sudden, inexplicable urge to create peculiar paintings, which she will later discover are in fact sacred *mandalas*. She is guided to a special book in the British Library, the significance of which she will only discover later on.

She realises that these are pieces of her past lives that are starting to emerge and that compel her to explore her long lost past. The Diamond takes her to New Mexico, where she meets a remarkable woman who guides her to relive several tragic past lives. She will discover a horrible truth that has had her and her mother spellbound for centuries and she is catapulted into a special moment in history where romance, science and mysticism meet.

Now better understanding her *karma*, she realises her trip to India was not complete and she needs to go back once more, this time, for a special encounter.

Back home in London, when she thinks she's finally free of her age-old *karma*, ready to live a happy and fulfilled life, she gets devastating news that, for years, a fatal disease has been quietly festering in her abdomen. Doctors refuse to operate, as they believe it's too late.

Will all her struggle and quests have been for nothing?